It's not just that everyone can be a fraud detective, everyone should be! Fraud dents trust in organisations and undermines civil society; robs companies and public bodies of much needed funds to invest and provide services; and at worst can lead to company closure, job losses and individual ruin. And the ill-gotten gains goes into the pockets of the dishonest and the criminally minded. That is why there is an urgent need to marshal all our forces and raise a new army – an army of fraud detectives to identify and prevent fraud. You don't need to be Sherlock Holmes to detect fraud – sometimes it is hiding in plain sight, just waiting to be uncovered by someone with a sceptical eye – and this book will give you the tools to find fraud wherever it raises its ugly head. So go on, pick up that magnifying glass, throw on your metaphorical cape and deerstalker and join the hunt for fraud. You never know it might be quite a lot of fun – the game is afoot!

> – *Mike Haley*, Chair of the Joint Fraud Taskforce and
> CEO of Cifas, the UK's Fraud Prevention Service.

This book provides some practical insights of how to find Fraud and corruption before it might find you. Not looking at a problem does not mean it does not exist – as a start, have a read of this book it is an excellent read.

> – *Steven Swientozielskyj*, CEO/President
> of Business Partnering Global Ltd

How to Find Fraud and Corruption – this is a book of recipes . . . of recipes that can help organizations comprehend better how their books are being cooked; sunshine payments made, and colourful business deals signed and yet – see the bright side of it. As soon as you are empowered with knowledge and skills, any fraud stops being a vicious taboo word representing an uncomfortable and headache-causing issue, something that could never happen to your organization (and yet it did and will happen again). Empowering employees and organizations with skills and knowledge and injecting positive attitude that, yes, fraud discovery can be a gain and an opportunity to improve – this is one of the main contributions of the book, presented with playful grace and a touch of humour and with the author always there for his readers.

> – *Anna Kon*, Certified Internal Auditor
> and Fraud Examiner.

In creating a recipe book for aspiring fraud detectives Nigel has stuck two fingers up to the fraud technocrats by producing a book that is fun to read, easy to follow and crucially makes fraud relevant and meaningful. In the process he has highlighted the limitations of regulators and auditors to combat this pernicious activity, pressing the point that we all have the means and responsibility to tackle fraud in organisations, whether that is the companies we work for, governments we elect or the home in which we live. As with all good recipe collections, *How to Find Fraud and Corruption* provides the ingredients, measures and method to excel. The end result is a rich textured account of contemporary malpractice dusted with examples drawn from Nigel's vast practical experience and scenarios which encourage you to reflect on your attitudes and behaviours. All of this, when complemented with Nigel's wit and storytelling skills, ensures that uncovering the foul deeds behind cooking the books has never been so much fun.

— *Dr Matthew Higgins*, University of Leicester
School of Business.

Nigel Iyer has written a unique book on fraud and corruption. His approach is different, informative, fresh and stimulating. Going beyond the dry practices of compliance he brings the topic alive and demonstrates clearly why a concern about fraud and corruption should be a central activity of all senior managers. Drawn from his own professional experiences garnered over many years working with a variety of organisations across the world Nigel draws out in a serious, engaging and entertaining way the main lessons to be learned. He writes clearly, provides sharply focused illustrations, and keeps technical jargon to a minimum whilst maintaining the professional foundations of his approach. The book will appeal to and should be read by a wide audience, including managers who take seriously concerns about fraud and corruption in their organisations. Professional fraud detectives and academics working in the area of fraud and corruption will gain much of value from reading it. Nigel Iyer's book is likely to change the shape of professional practice in this area and must be read.

— *Peter M Jackson*, Professor of Economics and
Strategy, University of Leicester.

How to Find Fraud and Corruption

In a typical working environment in which 'fraud and corruption' is as normal as a headache or as common as a cold, everyone in the organization has a role to play in finding and deterring fraudsters. Despite universal acknowledgement that these things may be illegal but still prevalent, managers still treat them as 'someone else's problem' or 'something that happens to other businesses, not ours'. This book shows, in simple terms, how everybody can become a successful fraud detective. A series of proven and easy-to-follow recipes show how to find the tell-tale signs of fraud and corruption and work with colleagues to deal with fraud smartly, keeping the organization you work for healthy and clean.

The skills taught in this book are based on over 25 years' experience of successfully finding and dealing with fraud and corruption, all around the world. *How to Find Fraud and Corruption* offers wayfinding techniques for identifying and recognizing common frauds such as: suppliers who charge too much; sharp business partners and consultants who are taking you for a ride; and customers who take but prefer not to pay. It also shows how to spot and unravel more complex but equally serious and common frauds: hidden connections to dirty money centres (the illegitimate side of tax havens); bribes paid as a shortcut to get business; creative numbers fraud (inflation of sales figures or suppression of costs); and conflicts of interest involving individuals inside or outside the business. The final chapter is a short story (based on a real case) which illustrates a fraud detective's challenges, whether they are a reluctant whistleblower, someone who cannot turn a blind eye even if they would prefer to, or even the accused.

Accessible and practical, this book is for everyone who wants to stop fraud, including those working in accounting and finance, management, specialist functions, such as audit, compliance and security, and anyone else who aspires to be a fraud detective and stop fraud and corruption.

Nigel Iyer is a partner at the fraud advisory firm Hibis and has over 25 years' experience in detecting and preventing fraud. A computer scientist and a qualified chartered accountant, Nigel is also a recognized dramatist and has written a number of educational films and plays based on his experiences, many of which are used in teaching worldwide. He is the author of several books, including *Fraud and Corruption: Prevention and Detection*, *The Tightrope* and *A Short Guide to Fraud Risk*. Nigel lectures on fraud and corruption and is a fellow of CIMA and the University of Leicester, School of Management.

How to Find Fraud and Corruption

Recipes for the Aspiring Fraud Detective

NIGEL IYER

Featuring The Fraud Detectives – A True Case in Point

Routledge
Taylor & Francis Group

LONDON AND NEW YORK

First published 2020
by Routledge
2 Park Square, Milton Park, Abingdon, Oxon OX14 4RN

and by Routledge
605 Third Avenue, New York, NY 10017

Routledge is an imprint of the Taylor & Francis Group, an informa business

British Library Cataloguing-in-Publication Data
A catalogue record for this book is available from the British Library

Library of Congress Cataloging-in-Publication Data
A catalog record has been requested for this book

ISBN 13: 978-1-138-74245-1 (hbk)
ISBN 13: 978-1-315-18230-8 (ebk)

Typeset in Bembo, Sabon and Gill Sans
by Apex CoVantage, LLC

Veronica Morino has provided her express permission to use many of the
examples and methods in this book which were developed during her
long and fruitful working relationship with Nigel Iyer.

Contents

List of figures ix
List of tables xi
How to use this book xii
Preface xv
Acknowledgements xviii
Note on the text xx

Part I: Fraud and corruption made simple **1**

1.   What is a fraud detective and how can I become one? 3

2.   Demystifying fraud and corruption 14

3.   Turning a problem into an opportunity 26

Part II: Recipes for the aspiring fraud detective **45**

4.   Three basic examples of recipes to detect red flags 47

5.   Thinking like a thief: how to out-think the fraudster and predict where your organization is being defrauded 63

6. Seven classic recipes to discover fraud and corruption   89

7. How to follow the money and find fraud fast   151

Part III: Don't panic: there is always a way to resolve things!   **167**

8. What to do when you think you may have found fraud   169

9. Resolving fraud and corruption and restoring normality
   with minimal panic and maximum humanity   183

10. Good news for management   194

    The fraud detectives: a true case in point   201

References   241
Index   242

Figures

2.1	The Wheel of (mis)Fortune	18
4.1	Spot the red flags 1	48
4.2	Answer to spot the red flags 1	49
4.3	Spot the red flags 2	54
4.4	Answer to spot the red flags 2	55
4.5	Spot the red flags 3	57
4.6	Answer to spot the red flags 3	59
5.1	A think like a thief brainstorming session: a suggested template	81
5.2	Assessing the likelihood and impact of fraud and corruption	82
6.1	The Wheel of (mis)Fortune: focusing mainly on suppliers	92
6.2	Green Brothers' invoice with red flags	101
6.3	The Wheel of (mis)Fortune: focusing mainly on DMCs	103
6.4	The Wheel of (mis)Fortune: focusing mainly on over- and under-statement of figures	109
6.5	The Wheel of (mis)Fortune: focusing mainly on customers	118
6.6	A letter from a potential client	124
6.7	The Wheel of (mis)Fortune: focusing mainly on everybody else on the outside	125
6.8	The Wheel of (mis)-Fortune: focusing mainly on kickbacks and bribery	131

6.9 The Wheel of (mis)Fortune: focusing mainly on misuse
of the organization by employees   140
7.1 An electrical device for dummies   157
7.2 Money out/money in matrix   159
10.1 The challenge of too many rules and regulations   197

Tables

4.1   Explanation of feedback on spot the red flags 1   50
4.2   Explanation of feedback on spot the red flags 2   56
4.3   Explanation of feedback on spot the red flags 3   59
5.1   How to understand and assess the risks of fraud and
      corruption in your own organization   64
5.2   Ranking of the measures   85
6.1   Sample supplier master list   96
6.2   False figure frauds (or F³) and how to find them   112
6.3   Six methods of false bribes and how to find them   135
8.1   Important internal sources of information used in IDR   173
8.2   Typical external sources of information used in IDR   173
9.1   Possible best- and worst-case scenarios   188

How to use this book

This book is a step-by-step guide for anyone (including people working inside organizations) who wants to discover and help their organization recognize, discover and deal efficiently with fraud, corruption, or bribery. It's for all the people in organizations, everyone from top to the bottom, who would like to do something extra and useful and help contribute to keeping the organizations[1] in which they work healthy and robust.

The ten chapters take you on a journey demystifying the nature and impact of fraud and corruption, showing how to assess which are the most likely frauds which will affect your organization and providing you with many techniques to detect and resolve issues in a timely, efficient and non-disruptive manner. Included are recipes to find fraud as well as examples and illustrations of typical scenarios, documents and transactions you will come across. It's a book for aspiring fraud detectives and based on over 20 years of real-life detection, experiences and following the money.

If you are working for or with a company or any form of organization, there is one thing you can be pretty sure of. That organization is always being charged too much by a small proportion of its suppliers, paid too little by some of its customers, taken for a ride by a handful of its partners and trusted advisors, attacked by a few externals, such as malicious competitors, hackers and other criminals, and, maybe, also abused in many ways by their own management and employees. For the purposes of this book we have gathered all these harmful acts (and more), which are on an organization's radar, together under one umbrella called fraud and corruption.

It's not a pleasant experience to be an honest person who is cheated, nor is it nice to be working in or with an organization which has been ripped off or is the subject of a long-drawn-out media scandal. You feel shocked and maybe let down when a colleague or friend is involved and often feel angry when you are accused. When the news breaks, we are often shocked, helpless and confused at first and then ask the big questions: 'How come nobody managed to spot it before things got so out of hand?'

It's easy to point fingers and grumble, find people we can blame, whether they are the management team, the auditors or even the government for failing to regulate the organization. However, what is infinitely more satisfying than being a passive victim or bystander is to join the team of people who are, as part of a team, acting in some proactive and positive way.

Time has shown that the people we have looked to identify fraud, corruption and its warning signs early have very often not been auditors, regulators or so-called 'fraud experts'. The people who have spotted fraud tend to be ordinary people who care deeply about their organizations and have a sharp eye for detail. It would certainly help if more people were willing to stick their necks out like that, but it has been proven that being a whistleblower is a risky business.

What is needed first and foremost is the right atmosphere in the organization where everybody feels there is an incentive to play their part in defending the organization, without fear of reprisals. This would include feeling comfortable about pitching in spotting fraud and supporting each other as a team and knowing that it is going to be resolved in a humane and mature manner. After all, fraud and corruption, in its most basic form, being ripped off, ripping someone else off or doing something deliberately unethical for a benefit, has been around for centuries and is unlikely to go away soon.

The structure of the book

Part I leaps straight into how and why everyone can be a fraud detective with some examples to give you confidence in your own abilities, as well as outlines of some of the seven basic categories (or plots) of fraud and corruption. Then follows a whirlwind tour demystifying corruption and fraud and examining some of the challenges in how it is being dealt with today.

Part II is packed with recipes to discover fraud and corruption, starting with some very simple ones such as spotting fraud in documents, to recipes which require a little more insight such as learning to 'think like a thief', follow the money and develop simple algorithms, which reflect your own analysis and intuition. Finding fraud does not need complicated lists of ingredients, sophisticated tools or some sort of unreachable qualifications. An accomplished and generous cook takes the view that with a bit of guidance and practice, anyone can cook. Only the pompous chefs would try to exclude others – to protect their own jobs? With guidance and practice, everyone who wants to can become a fraud detective.

Part III describes what to do when you find probable fraud and corruption and explains how to find the effective and efficient resolution path where there is the minimum of disruption. Finally, there is, at the end is a 'good news' summary for open-minded management, the key message being 'one of the best ways of making money is to start to stop losing it'.

At the end of book is 'The fraud detectives: a case in point', a short 'novelette' which is based on personal experience and a true story of fraud and corruption. Through the eyes of the characters involved, the story takes you on a journey of how fraud and corruption was discovered, the emotions and reflections of those involved, how matters developed and were eventually resolved, and what the characters have learned as they reflected on their experiences.

The book focuses on 'seven basic types of fraud and corruption' which affect most organizations. Fraud detective skills, once learnt, are like any other detective skills – highly transferable. Absolutely anybody can become a fraud detective, whether you are working inside an organization, running one, or on the outside. It cannot be claimed that this book covers every possible type of fraud or attack on your organization. However, the healthy curiosity which it hopefully inspires in you and your colleagues, can help you defend against the commercial dark arts which could destroy your organization and harm you in the process.

This book is meant to be used so please feel free to read it any order you like, scribble over its pages with your own notes and experiences, even rip out pages you like (and don't like!).

Additional material, including short dramas about fraud and corruption, fraud games, and additional guidance, is available at: https://fraudacademy.hibis.com/

Note

1 Thank you to Dr Matthew Higgins, as part of his review process, for rightly pointing out that in fact all companies are in fact 'organizations'.

Preface

Dear Reader,

Thank you for picking up this book! Here's a little bit of the background which inspired me to write it.

When I was just 5 years old, my grandfather, a wise old Indian barrister who fought for truth and justice, on the side of the underprivileged, told me, 'Nigel, you can do anything you want with your life but for my sake please do something which has meaning for you.'

It has taken me almost fifty years to really understand the gravity of the last words he ever spoke to me, and what he was saying to me made me stop and think, 'Why I am writing this book?' I have immersed myself in seeking out and stopping fraud and corruption in my own small way for the best part of 25 years and I have something to write about. Some knowledge to give away. But I had already jointly written three textbooks with my mentor, Martin, had written a novel and plays and films on fraud and corruption, so why write another book?

Somewhere inside me there was this nagging feeling that I had not actually given away the best of my knowledge and experience to the people who really could benefit from it. Put simply, for over the past quarter of a century I always felt I had this uncanny knack of walking into fraud.[1] At least that is how I saw it. Or to others it could be that it was a case of 'being in the *wrong* place at the *right* time', or just that I 'went looking for problems'. One of my colleagues even went to so far as to describe me (rather harshly and incorrectly in my opinion) as the person who 'will find fraud always, even if it is not there!'

Whatever it was, for years, I felt that I had a special skill and ability, which few wanted to have. And who would blame them? As most people who have been a whistleblower in the world of fraud and corruption know, being able to spot fraud early tends not to be a skill, more a curse!

But a few years ago, something happened. Many large organizations and companies decided that it in fact was worthwhile finding fraud early, before the whistleblower, and before it was found by the media or someone else and they started asking for help. And using the recipes and algorithms we had developed, we managed to hit the target every time, with increasing accuracy over the years.

So I began to explore the reasons why some people (like me) could find fraud easily while so many others could not see it. For years I thought I had some special skills, but it dawned on me that what I thought I had invented was simply a method based on analysis, attention to detail and a healthy dose of intuitive common sense, none of which were in any way magical but were a way of combining the ingredients in the 'wrong' order which produced a seemingly magical effect of finding fraud almost every time.

So probably one of the reasons to write this book is to write down the recipes for how to find fraud and, even more importantly, to share them so that others could use them and improve them too!

To be a successful and fulfilled fraud detective, let's start with a simple list of ingredients. You will need to have:

- a clear sense of *purpose*;
- an ability to think *innovatively* and creatively;
- the *opportunity* to act (however small that window of opportunity may be);
- *belief* in yourself;
- some useful *recipes* so that you can start easily and effortlessly.

The basic ingredients are explained in Chapter 6.

So please accept this book as a contribution and something which can shed a little light on how anybody — and I mean *anybody* —can develop their own healthy curiosity and spot where the organization where they work is being cheated and do something about it.

Warm wishes,

Nigel Krishna Iyer

Note

1 The first time this happened was when, at the age of 16, I was doing a summer job at a local firm of auditors in Manchester. As the junior on the team of auditors of one of the last large clothing factories in Manchester, coming in late to work to the dusty room provided for the auditors, I knocked over a box of rags which had been left by the door. The box turned out not to be rags but hidden underneath were hundreds of wage-books, which were for the illegal night-shift. This was the first we as auditors had even heard of a night-shift, which, it turned out, had been going on for many years, far from the eyes of the tax officers or any other authorities. I cannot claim that I had any special skills for finding fraud, other than clumsiness, but I always wonder what would have happened had I not knocked over that box . . .

Acknowledgements

First, I would like to thank my maternal grandfather who inspired me when I was only 5 to try to do something useful. Next I would like to thank my mother and father for bringing me up to follow my instincts and not force me to be a chartered accountant for too long! I would like to thank my wife, Camilla, for inspiration and ideas and most of all patience over the two years I have been writing this book. Additionally, I owe my daughter Miranda, who has over the years provided me with wonderful perspectives and insights into how fraud is seen by others, and also the inspiration for Dirty Money Constellations. My son, Andreas, deserves special thanks too for reading and commenting on every chapter from the perspective of a 16-year-old fraud detective. And thanks to my cousin Anil for inspiring me with his personal experiences and helping me with writer's block when I got stuck with the story in the final chapter.

With great sadness I would like to thank my former colleague and friend, Martin Samociuk, with whom I had the honour of writing three previous books. Martin was an experienced practitioner of the best sorts, and a wonderful guide and mentor. Sadly he passed away too early from pancreatic cancer in 2013, aged just 63.

And thanks to my colleague, and co-owner of Hibis, Veronica Morino, for input and support, both with ideas and inspiration for everything in this book. If it had not been for Hibis, and the ability to try out and succeed with the recipes in this book on a host of generous and brave clients, none of this would have been possible.

I have a lot more people to thank for their help in completing this book and far too many to mention, but I should at least mention: John Wallhoff, for allowing my thoughts to fly and develop the algorithms we call 'B4'; Allan McDonagh, for, as he says, giving me the grey-haired experience for the past 25 years and lots of encouragement; Professor Øyvind Kvalnes, for his inspiration and practical advice on ethics and keeping me on the straight and narrow; my friend, Chris Waterworth, for his literary insights and also helping me shape the game 'Dirty Money'. And of course thanks to all my current and former colleagues who have been part of the Hibis journey over the last 20 years.

Thank you to my seven selected reviewers, Pekka Bask (Fiskars), Mike Hayley (CEO of CIFAS), Dr Matthew Higgins (University of Leicester School of Business), Professor Peter Jackson (founder of the University of Leicester School of Business), Anna Kon (Eesti Energia), Martin Stevens (chartered accountant), and Steven Swientozielskyj (who recently completed his term as president of the Chartered Institute of Management Accountants (CIMA) and author of *Business Partnering*) for taking time to read the draft and your generous comments as well as sometimes honest and brutal criticisms.

And finally, a very big thanks to Amy Laurens, Alex Atkinson, Susan Dunsmore, Rich Kemp and all the extended team at Routledge, as well as my former editor, Jonathan Norman, for enormous support, patience and guidance.

Note on the text

The words 'fraud' and 'corruption' tend to mean slightly different things to different people and are used and described in different ways by practitioners, specialists, lawyers, accountants, academics, the media and the general public. Sometimes one is defined as part of the other or vice versa. To simplify things in this book, I have 'glued' them together as *one* term, i.e. 'fraud and corruption' = anything deliberate and unethical, done by anybody (internal or external) which causes harm.

Part I:

FRAUD AND CORRUPTION MADE SIMPLE

Chapter 1

What is a fraud detective and how can I become one?

I am curious, then I am alive.[1]

Everyone can be a fraud detective

The word 'detective' can easily conjure up images of the amateur sleuth or 'gumshoe' in the USA, living an exciting life but also sneaking up on people or, worse still, infringing on their privacy. So let's clear up any misunderstandings up right at the start of this book.

A fraud detective is anyone with a keen eye for detail, a healthy sense of curiosity, a calm and analytical mind, a desire to speak up about fraud and corruption (so long as they are encouraged to do so) and a constructive mind-set on how to deal with it. You don't need to do anything illegal or sneaky. Just simply fill the growing vacuum left by so few people actually spotting fraud early.

To show how simple it can be to spot fraud, and how we often do it unconsciously a lot of the time, but then don't follow our instincts, let's get in touch with the fraud detective inside each and every one of us by putting ourselves in the shoes of the person in each of the following three situations. See if you spot the red flags that something may be wrong in each of the three scenarios. Do you get that 'spine-tingling' sensation that something may be wrong and, if so, are you able to stay with that feeling long enough to make an educated guess as to what it could be?

Case 1.1

You are selling the electric cycle which you bought just over a year ago. Less than an hour after your advert went online, you receive an offer that is 10 per cent above your asking price from a Mr John Jones. He would prefer to pay in cash, but you can discuss payment terms when he comes round to look at the cycle later today. When you meet John, he suggests that he pays you 80 per cent of the money now in cash, and the remaining 20 per cent next week after he has tested out the bike. You will receive the balance from his company JJ Investments Ltd, a British Virgin Island company with an address and bank account in London.

Even though it is just a bike, what does your healthy sense of curiosity tell you about John Jones and the deal he is proposing?

Case 1.2

You are having some renovation work done on your apartment. You receive a pretty hefty invoice from the builders just before Christmas, which is reasonable enough, given the work they have done, but your attention is drawn to the following charges:

Cement and plaster: €1000
Plumbing services (cost €850 + 20% admin charge)   €1020
Sundry materials and tools   €500

While the builders have been OK so far, what is it that just caused you to blink?

Case 1.3

You and your colleague are both going to a conference which is a two to three hours' drive away. You decide to lift-share as you live close to each other, with you driving. On the way back, he explains that you can both claim separate mileage allowances. And when you stop for a meal at a motorway service station, he is careful to ask for separate bills so you can both charge them on your separate expense claims.

If you agreed to this, what risks are you taking and what red flags might you leave behind?

In Case 1.1, you could say that cash is cash, and you have no idea why John Jones is sitting with so much cash. He may be offering you more than the asking price but will you ever see the remaining 20 per cent? Since he is leaving no financial trails other than the name of a company in the British Virgin Islands (which may be just a front or even not exist), how do you know if he really is John Jones? (And since you have 80 per cent of the cash, do you really care?)

Case 1.2 is much more 'down to earth'. Your brain probably was drawn to the round sum for 'cement and plaster'. Shouldn't the builders specify how much they used and charged you just for what they used? Have they just rounded things up and hoped you would not notice? And you know a plumber was there but you thought he was going to send you an invoice, not one via the builders which is marked up by 20 per cent. And what's this about sundry materials and tools? If you had not looked closely, you could be contributing lots to their Christmas Bonus.

Finally, Case 1.3 is a little more personal. You have every right to claim your own mileage since it was your car and you drove. It seems as if your colleague is also going to claim for mileage he did not incur. Of course, he is entitled to claim for the meal but will some clever fraud detective not notice that he and you ate at the same motorway service station and start to say that you were in the same car? And if someone else knows that you went together, then your colleague is technically defrauding the company. Worse still, even though it seems trivial right now, and it is trivial too, people might say that you knew about it and did not try to dissuade him or even report him. Sometimes the simplest things can get complicated and you might get tarred with the same brush one day as well.

These three examples are simple illustrations that fraud and corruption, in its widest sense, is simply part of everyday life.[2] But it also does not mean that most people, such as the builders, John Jones or your lift-sharing colleague, are particularly sinister or evil. But when we get that feeling something may be amiss, we should not just shrug it off, assume that there must be an honest explanation to everything, or put it down to paranoia. The mind often registers red flags before the eye, so when you get that funny, spine-tingling feeling, let it linger for a while, just to figure out what exactly it is that troubles you. If in the end you found that things are OK, you will not be troubled any more. Alternatively, if momentarily you embrace your own healthy curiosity and find it justified, you will probably start to understand what is going on and you will be doing yourself a favour. There are times in life when it pays to say to yourself, 'I have a bad feeling about this . . .'.[3]

But given how little fraud and corruption is detected early, the world is certainly crying out for more able fraud detectives. Fraud and corruption, in fact, is like litter – there is a lot of it around in certain places and it needs more than just a few specialists to sort it out. Imagine a future where as many people as possible are engaged in helping their organizations to detect and deal with it as early as possible.

Having a sense of purpose and knowing your target

Before starting to be a fraud detective, we should ask ourselves, 'Why am I doing this?', 'What is the purpose?'. And in this case, we also need to address the question, 'Why should I bother looking for fraud?' Surely with all the scandals which abound, the tsunami of new laws, rules and regulations imposed by governments to try to clamp down on the epidemic, fraud and corruption must soon be a thing of the past? So what is special about a book calling for everybody, from the CEO, the management team and the board, down to the assistant accountant, sales clerk and, in fact, everyone else who makes the team tick, to look for fraud and corruption?

Fraud and corruption has been around for centuries. In simple terms, it involves you or and your organization being cheated or deceived by a deliberate and unethical act done by someone else. At a very personal level, you or your organization could be:

- taken advantage of by a supplier or a seller of goods or services;
- duped into giving too much away to someone else (a customer);
- misused by an agent, consultant, middleman or similar opportunist;

- in hot water because inadvertently you became involved with dirty money (whether its cash, funds in a front company, or part of a dirty money constellation as depicted in Chapters 2, 4 and 6);
- cheated by someone who works for or with you;
- coerced into receiving or giving bribes;
- relying on false figures or information;
- or in any other way be involved in illegal, dubious or unethical activities.

Even at this simple, personal level, each of the above comes with a cost – you lose money, or you lose face, or you lose that motivation and joy of life which keep us going. Put plainly, no one likes to be cheated. These basic plots of fraud and corruption are represented in the wheel in Figure 2.1, called the Wheel of (mis)Fortune,[4] which is used as a navigator throughout this book.

Fraud and corruption, by nature, is hidden and deceptive, and usually only revealed when a scandal breaks, by which time the damage is done and the losses in monetary, reputational and cultural terms are high. It is often here where the 'blame game' starts and the costs often skyrocket even more.

And, to add insult to injury, you realize with hindsight that the tell-tale warning signs had been there all along. How could you have been so naïve not to see them before? And that is where the key lies. We can see the warning signs, or red flags, earlier, much earlier in fact – but only if we really want to.

Innovation and fresh thinking

I hope that you have come so far that you think it's a promising idea that fraud and corruption should be spotted early but that this doesn't happen much in the world today. So, we need to innovate and think afresh. We need to allow ourselves to dream what is possible and challenge the boring and safe alternatives. We can do the following:

- Learn to overcome the stigma that discovering corruption and fraud is unwelcome news and embrace every incident as a future loss which can be stopped now!
- Appreciate when people are proactive, and 'democratize' the role of spotting fraud (rather than looking for scapegoats when things go wrong).
- Support and foster cultures which recognize that early detection prevents people digging themselves into a deeper hole and sees fighting fraud all about saving careers rather than ending them.

But to do this, you should be prepared, at least to start with to join the minority. Most people don't like finding fraud early. In the film, *Minority Report* (2002), which was based on the 1956 book by Philip K. Dick, the futuristic concept of 'pre-crime' was launched. The combination of historic data banks, live feeds and precognitive abilities had led to highly successful predictive policing, spotting the crimes before they got out of control or even occurred, thereby reducing actual crime by 99.8 per cent.

This notion of pre-crime is inspiring as it can also be applied to fraud and corruption, albeit maybe in a less theatrical way. Replace the data banks in *Minority Report* with historical money flows, live data with the vast amount of up-to-date public information, use pictures and live feeds available on the internet, and instead of the magical precognitive extra-sensory perceptive abilities, you use just good old-fashioned intuition and healthy curiosity, then you are almost there.

Your personal reasons for stopping fraud and corruption could of course be many. It could be your sense of justice, or that you want to save or just reduce waste in your organization (or the world), or it could be that you just enjoy the thrill of being a fraud detective and out-smarting the bad guys. Whatever your reasons, you should know that it's possible. But be aware, while you might not be branded a whistleblower you are still likely to be in the minority . . . for a while at least.

Take the opportunity to overcome the obstacles

When a bomb explodes in a building, it is tremendously sad. It also creates more work for the rescue services and paramedics, the police launch an extensive manhunt and investigation, the media have their fill of stories, and so on. But if the bomb was detected early and rendered harmless in time, no one would die and a huge amount of cost and suffering would be avoided.

Finding fraud and corruption is also about identifying and defusing ticking time-bombs. There is, of course, a risk involved but one which can be minimized by proper training. But there is also one risk we still need to be prepared to take and that is the risk of sometimes getting it wrong. It can happen.

We need to confront and overcome three obstacles:

1 the shock factor;
2 ticking boxes blindly;
3 relying on someone else to spot it for you.

Obstacle 1 The shock factor

As far back as we can remember, stories about companies, organizations and people being defrauded, or committing fraud have caused excitement in the media. Often the public, goaded on by the press are 'outraged' or 'shocked' by what they read at the time and the search for scapegoats starts with a fury. But in the long run, we have short memories and often do not learn from history. We tend to be shocked again . . . and again! If we examine the phenomena more closely what we see is that fraud and corruption is rather common, and not that exciting after all. It's just that the media need to tell a story, and conflict sells! But fraud and corruption goes on . . . business as usual.

Obstacle 2 Ticking boxes blindly

Every time there is a major scandal, there is a call for even stricter and better rules and regulations that will stop whatever happened from happening ever again. 'Stricter and better' rules tend to boil down to the word 'more'. And more rules translate in their turn to even more work for the regulators, the lawyers, the administrators and the accountants and auditors . . . exactly the people whom we expected to find fraud early and stop it in the first place. The bureaucracy of 'compliance', which is in fact a rather new word in layman's language, has mushroomed. Whether you are opening a bank account, buying a plane ticket on the internet, or approving a new customer or supplier, we have entered the world of Obsessive Compliance Disorder (or 'OCD', as it maybe should be known). We are supposed to read mountains of new rules and the small print and then since we never really get time to read them, and most people never understand what the paperwork is for anyway, we blindly just tick the box without protesting. Everyone does so and nothing would get done otherwise.

Obstacle 3 Relying on someone else to spot it for you

Because of the constant bombardment of media headlines on corruption and fraud and increasing 'OCD', the person in the street is more aware that fraud and corruption could affect them too. The only catch is, everyone relies on those 'guardians of our economy', auditors and regulators to spot fraud and corruption before it attacks us . . . except they don't do so (or they don't want to). In the past 25 years, we increasingly have been relying on a so-called whistleblower culture. Rather than acting as a safety valve of the last resort, whistleblowing has turned into the primary channel for early warning and detection of fraud and corruption. Increasingly in organizations now, whistleblowing has its own hotline, an alert line so that some poor maligned individual can stick their neck out.

Instead of being shocked, or mindlessly ticking boxes or leaving it to someone else, it is better to be prepared and act ahead of time. But the obstacles above should not be viewed lightly. Overcoming these obstacles requires tenacity, the right tools, good recipes to find fraud and first and foremost a belief in yourself.

Self-belief

> We can only do something if we believe in our own abilities, trust our instincts and to risk making mistakes . . . and learn from them.

In the past 25 years, the most common obstacle I have met in people who should be finding fraud is the phrase 'it's not possible'. Even when we take them through the recipes and show them it is possible, they put it down to luck.

It's as if people want to hang on to the illusion that finding fraud and corruption when no suspicion previously exists is something nobody can do. Mathematicians liken this blinkered mind-set to being in a tunnel where all you can see is the walls of the tunnel and no end in sight. One of the most important aims of this book is to instil in you, the reader, a belief that anyone can discover when they or their organization are being defrauded or are engaged in corrupt practices, and do something about it.

As already mentioned, anyone can cook – they just need the right stimulation, good recipes and suggestion on how to present what they have created, as well as the freedom and opportunity to make mistakes (and learn from those mistakes). In a similar way everyone has a sixth sense, and everyone can find fraud (but they have to believe they can).[5]

Recipes and 'secret' ingredients

Much of this book is essentially a recipe book. Like any good cook book, these are recipes which have been tried out before and they work. They start simple and get a little more complicated. Some of the most popular recipes include:

- How to find which of your suppliers are milking you the most.
- Performing a 'sweep' of your organization and your transactions for signs of dirty money.

- Are you selling to someone who is suddenly not going to pay?
- Which middlemen or consultants (or lawyers) are charging you for fictitious work?
- Is someone paying or taking bribes?

The (not-so) secret ingredient in each of these recipes is that rather overused catchphrase, commonly associated with the Watergate scandal of 1972, 'Follow the money.' Money (or capital) is one of the life-bloods of any company or organization. going in, going out and flowing through the organization, and is often backed up by invoices, credit notes, payment slips, receipts and bank statements. Whereas paper trails, or verbal statements are easy to distort, financial trails are often hard-coded and very reliable. Put simply, following the money – where it comes from and where it goes – provides the biggest single clue to finding fraud.

In addition to that, there are also recipes for how to run 'think like a thief' workshops (see Chapter 5), performing desktop investigations.

In the beginning, I advise you to follow the recipe, but just like any budding gourmet chef, I encourage you to branch out and improvise.

Tenacity

The dark side is, even if we want to discover fraud, it is still quite hard to see. To make it visible requires passion and tenacity. There are examples of tenacity all around us. Take, for example, the investigative journalists who worked long hours through the night to expose the secrets of tax havens. Or the very brave non-governmental organizations which highlight the working methods and money flows of organized criminals.

I once had the pleasure of having a coffee with Andrew Jennings, the investigator who relentlessly investigated senior FIFA and International Olympic Committee members suspected of being involved with fraud and corruption. It was so clear that he did it not to sell stories but because he genuinely believed the sporting world would be better without corruption.

But tenacity also is found every day in a much more low-key form. For each high-profile example, there are literally hundreds, if not thousands, of success stories where some unsung hero has pushed through, taken a stand (or like the giraffe, stuck their necks out) and made a difference. Consider the following story in Example 1.1.

Example 1.1 Tenacity plus legwork and the power to persuade

As part of a 'find fraud before it finds you' review which we helped a client to perform, it was uncovered and proved that our client had been purchasing massive quantities of raw materials, from a front company in Cyprus, which turned out to be controlled by a group of organized criminals. Their virtually bulletproof ownership structure involved various countries: Cyprus, Austria, the British Virgin Islands, Luxemburg, the UK, Ireland, Switzerland, Estonia and Canada. It seemed like a no-brainer for management to stop buying from them, but things are never that simple. Top management's arguments for maintaining the status quo included: 'we have been dealing with them for 10 years, surely we have checked them out by now', 'they do not appear as criminals on any of the historic public databases', to the more desperate, 'it is the only raw material source which is cheap enough so that our factory turns a profit' and 'they have just recently established a website with a detailed code of ethics and whistleblower policy'.

But the youngish financial controller, who had seen the red flags and the proof with us, was not to be put off. He knew that the evidence was on his side but also did not want a head-on confrontation with the top management and board. So instead he put his case in terms of a value proposition to the chief financial officer, exemplified the real risks and costs that had already occurred and, most importantly, he kept calm. The board met, and it was ruled in the end that the company would detach itself from the relationship, sever all ties and cancel the contracts, which they did. Because of the controller's tenacity, the management were able to take a collective decision to pull out, not because they were forced to but because they recognized that it was the right thing to do. They took the view that doing so much business with known criminals was bound to hurt the company's reputation, culture and profits in the long run.

Notes

1 Inspired by 'I think, therefore I am', first expressed by René Descartes, a seventeenth-century French philosopher.
2 The words 'fraud' and 'corruption' tend to mean slightly different things to different people and are used and described in different ways by practitioners, specialists,

lawyers, accountants, academics, the media and the general public. Sometimes one is defined as part of the other or vice versa. To simplify things in this book, I have 'glued' them together as *one* term, i.e. 'fraud and corruption' is anything deliberate and unethical, done by anybody (internal or external) which causes harm.

3 'I have a bad feeling about this' is a line which became a running joke in the *Star Wars* movies.

4 The phrase "Wheel of Misfortune" was coined by experienced Fraud Detective Peter Tickner, former Director of Internal Audit for the Metropolitan Police in London, in his book "How to be a Successful Frauditor" (Wiley 2010) when describing the results of fraud risk brainstorming.

5 While reviewing the book with Mike Hayley, the phrase 'Everybody can cook' came to mind. We were sitting in Yotam Ottolenghi's restaurant in Islington, London, and it dawned on me that, however delicious the recipe, as long as it was explained with passionate self-belief and also belief in others, then it is possible that anyone, however much a novice, will be able to master the recipe (so thank you to Mr Ottolenghi for your inspiring recipe books).

Chapter 2

Demystifying fraud and corruption

This chapter addresses two fundamental questions:

1   What do we mean by fraud and corruption?
2   How can regular people working in organizations also spot fraud and corruption and why is it worth them doing so?

What is fraud and corruption?

There are plenty of definitions of fraud and corruption, some of which are longer and more convoluted than others. Often, in these definitions, meticulous attention is paid to defining the exact meaning of words like 'fraud' and 'corruption', 'bribery', etc. You could almost imagine that some of the longer, more tortuous definitions have been invented by so-called specialists so that they can lay claim to be the sole experts in this field. But that would be tantamount to accusing them of fraud (and we would not want to do that!). The definition of fraud and corruption[1] has to be simple to understand but also as wide as possible. Here is the description which we have used and is almost always universally accepted:

> Fraud and corruption are *anything* which is deliberate and unethical and done by *anybody*, inside or outside your organization, which causes harm or loss to either you and your organization, or to someone else.

'Anybody' could mean suppliers, customers, consultants, contractors, agents, middlemen, opportunists, hackers, professional criminals, petty criminals, governments, professional advisors, employees, stakeholders and management. It's a lengthy list of potential fraudster candidates. All these people can do deliberate and unethical things which are in some way beneficial to them but cause harm to you and the organization you are associated with.

By using the term 'deliberate', we are trying to exclude actions which may be unethical but were wholly and completely accidental. For example, I would not describe someone a fraudster, who accidentally walks out of a restaurant forgetting to pay, realizes a few hours later that they did not pay and returns immediately to apologize and settle the bill.

What is ethical and what is unethical are a little harder to define and this is not surprising since this is something philosophers have been disagreeing over for centuries and I do not believe are any closer to a common understanding than they were in the days of Socrates. However, in this book, the easiest way to define unethical is that you, personally would not like the action to be done to you.

By harm or loss, this would be the total cost related to: (1) loss of money or assets; (2_ anything which damages reputation; (3) erosion of the organizational culture; and (4) anything else which prevented the organization from functioning as intended or, in the worst case, even existing.

And remember, it is PEOPLE who commit fraud, not machines. For that reason, I am not a huge fan of the term 'computer fraud' (or its more fashionable replacement 'cyber fraud'). Computers, robots and 'cyber space' do not commit fraud . . . not yet anyway. This is probably for the same reason that robots still do not make a great cup of tea. People commit fraud, because they have that certain something that machines do not possess yet.

While it has been around for a long time, fraud and corruption probably went under the guise of different and much simpler names, like theft, cheating, lying, deception, blackmail, bribery, and so on. People who commit fraud would use whatever tools they had at their disposal. A few thousand years ago we can imagine that this could have included deception, charm with possibly a hammer or an axe thrown in, to assist in the theft and concealment of the neighbouring farmer's sheep,[2] just as today a fraudster might use the latest technologies, false documents, offshore dirty money centres, deception and charm and the odd threat or bit of blackmail, to whisk away millions of Euros from an unsuspecting company or bank.

It has been demonstrated[3] that humans are likely to act unethically (or fraudulently) if all of the following three factors are present:

1   We have an *opportunity*.
2   We are *motivated* (i.e. we have a reason to want to do something unethical for a benefit).
3   We can *rationalize* our actions (in other words, we can convince ourselves that we did nothing wrong and we are able to 'live with ourselves' afterwards).

Rationalization can also occur after the fact. One of the simplest examples of rationalization is that we notice we have been driving too fast, slow down but at the same time come up with multiple reasons as to why it was OK to have speeded in the circumstances. We commit the fraud because we see the opportunity and are motivated enough to want to exploit it. However, when we reflect, we maybe feel a pinch of regret or shame (sometimes referred to as 'moral dissonance'), but we try as quickly as possible to find sound explanations for actions. In other words, we are constantly rationalizing before and after the fact.

Can regular people working in organizations also spot fraud and corruption?

The short answer is a resounding 'YES! Regular people working inside organizations are OFTEN the best at finding fraud' (if they are encouraged to do so and rewarded for doing so). To provide a slightly more in-depth answer we need to examine who usually discovers fraud and corruption. When fraud or corruption is discovered, it is usually found by whistleblowers, by the media receiving a 'tip-off' from someone inside an organization, or just by accident. In the clear majority of cases it is because someone smart in an organization was awake and observant and took it upon themselves to speak up. In other words, most fraud and corruption, when it is found, is discovered by normal people, who are positively curious, rather than external auditors or regulators.

It's the same for technology.[4] Because today we have vast amounts of data and technology at our fingertips, there has been a constant quest to find the so-called 'Enigma code breaker' or 'Holy Grail' of fraud detection where machines and 'big data' take over. These systems, which are expensive to buy and run, as well as using vast amounts of data,[5] have arguably still not succeeded as well as people at detecting fraud and corruption. Steve Job's famous but somewhat ironic quote (given that he did establish Apple): 'It's not a faith in technology, it's faith in people' can help remind us that the solution to fraud and corruption, something generated by people, lies in putting faith in people back and allowing them to use the tools in a smart and effective manner.

So before launching into the three examples for you to try, we need to ask ourselves the question: Is there a lot of fraud and corruption around? While many so-called experts and armchair media-buffs would return a thumping 'yes', at the end of the day, it's up to you to make up your own mind. A lot depends on how you wish to define fraud and corruption, and what you believe is acceptable and what is not. There are no hard and fast answers despite surveys, such as the widely accepted surveys by the Institute of Internal Auditors, which puts it at around 5 per cent of the turnover of an organization, or the UK Home Office in its Fraud Surveys, which puts the cost of corruption in the UK economy at a figure often equivalent to 3–5 per cent of gross domestic product. In my experience, I have discovered that it can be a big number, or can be as low as 1 per cent or as high as 50 per cent, but this is typically in a near 'game over' situation where the company is about to collapse under the weight of the fraud being done to it, and the fraud it is doing to others.

Remembering that fraud and corruption has been around for some time, just as human beings have, it is probably unlikely that completely new methods of fraud and corruption have been invented. When we hear new words like 'phishing', cyber-crime or ransomware, these are probably variations on a tried and tested scheme, but this time just using the latest technology available.

After working on it for over 30 years, Christopher Booker published a book called *The Seven Basic Plots* in 2004.[6] In it, he claimed that every play or film that was written could be categorized under one of seven basic structures. The book was both praised and reviled but the basic idea, i.e. that there are just a few key underlying themes of categorizing, whether we are talking about *Hamlet*, *Pretty Woman* or *Star Wars*, even if you believe it is contrived, can also be used to simplify the seemingly complex world of fraud and corruption.

The Wheel of (mis)Fortune[7] in Figure 2.1 is a 'navigator' to categorize the types of commercial fraud and corruption experienced by most organizations

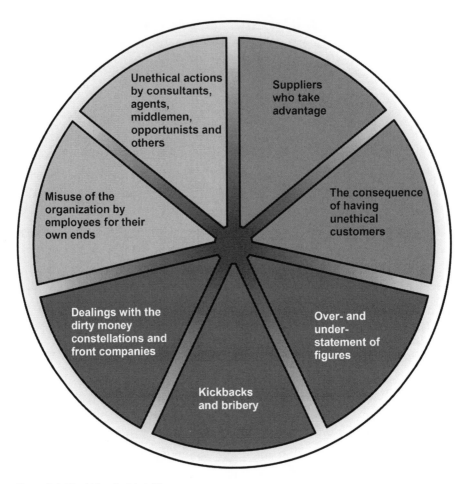

Figure 2.1 The Wheel of (mis)Fortune

and the people working in them, with an appreciation that there will always be some frauds which are in fact outside or do not totally fit into one or more of the categories.

Finding and stopping fraud early is always a positive thing. The different adaptations of the Wheel of (mis)Fortune show where red flags are *most* likely to occur for each of the seven basic types of fraud in the wheel. Normally the biggest red flag would be directly related to the fraud, but sometimes there will be other red flags showing other types of frauds, which could be 'pointing in the direction' of another, maybe even more significant type of fraud. Each segment of the wheel is described briefly below, recognizing that there is of course overlap and duplication at times:

1   *Suppliers who take advantage of you and your organization*: simply put, a supplier is any organization, person or group of persons that provides something to us, whether it is something physical, a pure service or a combination of the two. Most suppliers would, we hope, behave honestly but there will always be some who will try to get away with overcharging or providing a substandard service or goods, or those who will lie about their true nature, or those who will try to bribe an employee.

2   *The result of relationships with unethical customers*: normally for organizations operating in the outside world, the term 'customers' is a positive word. However, there will be always a small proportion of customers who may try to cheat you, either by ordering goods and services from you and not paying, stealing or exerting undue influence and pressure to make you sell to them at a loss. Pressure could also include coercing, blackmailing or bribing employees. In addition, in your enthusiasm to win customers, you could find yourself dealing with customers you may not want, i.e. unsavoury customers who have shady or criminal backgrounds, which in turn could be bad for your reputation.

3   *Misuse of the organization by employees for their own ends*: in organizations there will often be some people who feel either mistreated and undervalued or just simply are plain greedy. It is important to underline that dishonest or greedy employees are a small minority. A lot of fraud is externally initiated by suppliers, customers and other external parties (of which there are many) where employees are tempted to be involved. However, we should not exclude those people, often but not only in very senior positions who have what is known as an 'over-developed sense of entitlement'.

4   *Relationships with front companies and DMCs*: front company is a term we use to describe any form of entity which hides its true nature and/or ownership. The simplest form of front company is one where someone else is acting on behalf of the real owner and beneficiary but schemes can be complex and intricate, encompassing many different fronts (or firewalls) to prevent detection, including DMCs or 'dirty money con- stellations' (see Box 2.1) where, for example, a company could be reg- istered in one jurisdiction (such as London) but the true owner of the company is a company in, say, Guernsey or the Cayman Islands, and the bank account could be in Germany, London, Switzerland or virtually anywhere, for that matter. Placing the bank account in another country is just an extra twist added by the owners to ensure that the money trail is a little harder to follow. Front companies involving DMCs have mush- roomed in recent years and can conceal all different sorts of fraud and

corruption, including the ones described in Figure 2.1. How to keep up with and detect the use of DMCs is explored further and exemplified in Chapters 4 and 6.[8]

5   *Kickbacks and bribery*: As in the phrase 'give and take', kickbacks and bribery can go both ways. In short, what we are talking about is any form of benefit which is paid or received outside of the system to a person or group of persons, which influences their decision. The term covers a whole range of activities, including payment of hard cash, slush funds which are set up to systematically ensure that people receive personal benefits for work that they have done, facilitation payments, i.e. payments made or received to 'grease the wheels of bureaucracy', nepotism, excessive gifts and entertaining which influence a decision, and much more. This is a very wide category of fraud and corruption and often impinges on the other categories.

6   *Over- and under-statement of figures*: Typically called 'cooking the books', over- and under-statement of figures are far more wide-ranging than just manipulation of the financial statements. It can also include things, such as management and employees inflating or making up sales projection figures, supressing costs, wrongly categorizing or posting costs, manipulation of inventory figures, and other forms of misstating of costs and revenues or the withholding of information. Quite often the misstatement can take place relatively low down in the system but can have a significant impact higher up. In addition, this category would also include suppliers, customers, consultants and business partners presenting deliberately false figures.

7   *Harmful actions by consultants, middlemen, opportunists and more*: This in a way is a 'catch-all' category which includes all sorts of outsiders, such as consultants (and even ex-employees), who may have a close relationship to the organization, agents and middlemen, who could be acting on behalf of the organization, business partners, as well as rank outsiders, ranging from thieves, hackers, professional criminals and other opportunists who wish in some way to harm the organization.

These seven categories are in no way absolute categories in any form, nor are they meant to be comprehensive. For example, it may be hard at first to see where pyramid schemes, hacking, frauds involving crypto-currencies, identity theft, credit card fraud, or just falling for a 'con trick' or 'scam', etc. fit in (although often these can be mapped into the 'catch-all' category). Three examples of the types of fraud which could be said to be missing are:

What are DMCs?

A DMC or dirty money constellation, as we define it, is a place where money (or similar assets) can be hidden. But it is not just hidden out of view and inaccessible to all. The money and assets are connected to their rightful owner in a way that is usually legal, but it is virtually impossible to trace who the owner is. While hiding money from the tax authorities may be one objective of these schemes, the key is having a myriad of companies, complex ownership structures and, in the end, money which one can control, move around, use and collect, away from the prying eyes of others. Anonymity is vital, and is key to fraud, corruption and building up and using wealth in subtle ways.

In its simplest form, a DMC is a combination of a safe deposit box and legal privilege. For example, John Doe needs to hide cash and jewellery. A safe deposit firm offers the service and this firm can be based anywhere in the world. John Doe asks his lawyer (A. Smithee) to open a safe deposit box in A. Smithee's name but John Doe is the ultimate owner and beneficiary. All instructions and conversations between lawyer and client are confidential and subject to attorney-client privilege and so through this combination of confidentiality and privilege, A. Smithee cannot be subpoenaed to give evidence in court. The identity of John Doe, the beneficiary, remains private. Other arrangements which are in essence simply progressive iterations of the above include personal bank accounts in a country which permits numbered accounts (e.g. Switzerland), or nominee directors and shareholders who lend their name to the company but which through a lawyer and client privilege affords distance between owners and nominees. Complex combinations of numbered accounts, holding companies and nominee directors, provide a web of hidden ownership. Although the focus is often on former colonial territories, in reality, far from the likes of Guernsey, Panama, Bermuda and the British Virgin Islands, DMCs are almost everywhere today including (in the form of offshore LLCs) many states of the USA.

Higgins *et al.* (2018), used with permission of Routledge.

- Where the company is systematically cheating others (for example, a consultancy or service provider which regularly over-prices and cheats its customers). In this case, even if you find this out, there is nothing you can do about it, so it is not worth making yourself hideously unpopular.
- Where the whole organization itself is a scam (like a pyramid scheme asking for money and then re-using it) or where the organization plays around to cheat the entire market (one hopes that there is *some* form of watchdog which will look or someone else will use the follow the money recipes in this book to identify things).

● Theft of the *whole* company by another organizations (sometimes known as Reiderstvo – it happens in Russia when you suddenly find out you don't own the organization you have invested in and put your heart and soul into – as I know from personal experience). But often the warning signs, typically one or more of the seven types are there early in advance before you lose everything – so it is not a smash and grab, although if you ignore the warning signs, it could feel like that.

The Wheel of (mis)Fortune can also help you navigate and categorize all the different red flags of fraud and corruption which we might see, enabling us to determine what sort of beast we are looking at, remembering that often they could fit into more than one category.

Returning to the three everyday situations introduced in Chapter 1 (Cases 1.1–1.3), you could say that the proposed case of the sale of your electric cycle (Case 1.1) may involve unethical customers, dirty money centres and even opportunists. And your renovation work (Case 1.2) concerns being cheated by a supplier and possibly also consultants. And at a stretch of the imagination, the seemingly innocuous false expense claim (Case 1.3) brings together misuse of the organization by employees and also false accounting.

Fraud and corruption may be a minefield of complexities but often having a simple navigator can help us understand that red flags that are there to see when we are paying attention, and put them into some form of context.

And whichever studies or figures you want to believe (5 per cent of turnover or whatever), remembering that the true cost of fraud and corruption includes loss of money, damage to reputation or erosion of the culture of the organization, if you just add up (the first four categories): 'being cheated by supplier', 'what unethical customers can do to you', 'how unsavoury consultants, middlemen and opportunists can harm you', and the effects of having 'some employees and management with an "overdeveloped sense of entitlement"', it *will* add up.

An organization's ability to identify fraud and corruption early, in advance of them being discovered by whistleblowers, the media or by accident, is both crucial for any organization and also provides them with a competitive advantage. It often means that fraud and corruption can be stopped before it spreads or in the worst cases becomes embedded in parts of the organizational culture.

We should recognize that we as humans probably would rather not see fraud and corruption unless we really had to. In other words, sometimes, we are encouraged not to look too hard. This can be because finding fraud and corruption can be associated with painful investigations, unsuccessful court cases, bad publicity and disruption. It is therefore extremely important that the overriding goal of early detection is to prevent fraud and corruption spreading, to deal with its root causes and contribute to the health and robustness of any organization. But once we do recognize that fraud and corruption is as common as the common cold, and we stop being scared of it, we can also quickly assess the seriousness of cases, defuse potentially volatile situations and decide how to resolve them early, thereby avoiding long and painful investigations (or commercial autopsies). The earlier we can do this, the quicker we can recover the money, clean up, learn the lessons and work in a more effective way. As one of the professors I am working with and also my son told me, you learn a lot from making mistakes, but the important thing is to detect and recognize these mistakes early.[9] And also we should avoid the natural tendency of pointing fingers at the person who stuck their neck out and got it wrong. When one finger points, there are often three pointing back. Focusing on the mistake, apportioning blame and looking for scapegoats all cloud the true focus on 'what the root cause of the problem is'.

The technique of 'investigative desktop research' (internal and external) which involves looking internally and externally is highly efficient. The aim is to quickly prove 'yes or no' – to quickly recognize what could be signs of fraud and corruption and what are not. These days there is plenty of information available internally and public information externally – you just need to know how to look and to keep an open mind and not trust one single source but look for correlating information.

Finally, only in a small percentage of examples would we recommend anything tantamount to a large investigation. There are so many other and often better ways to deal with and resolve fraud and corruption. These often more effective ways usually result in quicker and better recoveries, identification and treatment of root causes, and less pain and aggravation for everybody involved, including the fraudsters. The key, which is explained in Chapter 9, is to apply the principles of restorative justice, something which is far too rarely thought of when dealing with fraud and corruption.[10]

Notes

1 A 'Joly' good piece of advice: some years ago, I was struggling to find a title for the book I was writing at the time and got some very sound and generous advice from the French anti-corruption magistrate, Eva Joly, the French-Norwegian magistrate who was at the centre of investigating numerous corruption and fraud scandals, including having a run-in with former French President Jacques Chirac (who

received a two-year suspended prison sentence). At the end of a pleasant discussion, I asked Ms Joly the question: 'Given that you have worked with some of the largest cases in Europe, can you give me some advice as to how I should define fraud, and corruption, in reality?' It was a leading question and I guess I was fishing for something, but her answer took me by surprise. She said quite simply, 'In reality, the words fraud and corruption are so interconnected that I would just keep them together.' So that is exactly what we did. Ms Joly later worked as an anticorruption activist and at of time of writing was a member of the European Parliament for the Green Party.

2 The well-preserved Babylonian Code of Hammurabi (1754 BC) covers the topic of 'fraud' in its law on trade, stating:

If a herdsman, to whose care cattle or sheep have been entrusted, be guilty of fraud and make false returns of the natural increase, or sell them for money, then shall he be convicted and pay the owner ten times the loss.

3 Based on the work of criminologist Donald Cressey, and the popularized version of his work called 'The Fraud Triangle', see Chapter 3.

4 For certain types of fraud which involve very large volumes of consistent data (such as bank or credit card information, insurance claims, tax returns, etc.), technology is of course very helpful.

5 In addition to using and matching large amounts of Big Data, these systems can quite easily be found to be in contravention of data protection and other privacy-centred legislation.

6 The summary of Christopher Booker's (2004) book which took him 34 years to write, can be found on either Wikipedia or by searching on Google for 'The Seven Basic Plots'.

7 It was one of the reviewers, Steven Swientozielskyj, who referred to it as 'The Wheel of (Mi)sfortune'. Steve also went on to say that the structure of the book should in fact revolve around this wheel. At the same time, I should point out that the wheel itself is 100 per cent empirical and has no academic value whatsoever. It is based on pure observation and, there are seven categories because I specifically wanted to have seven categories. The final category 'Harmful actions, etc.' is of course a 'catch-all' category.

8 DMCs are introduced in M. Higgins, V. Morino and N. Iyer. 'Imperialism, Dirty Money Centres and the Financial Elite', in *The Continuing Imperialism of Free Trade* (London: Routledge, 2018). At the time of writing, the 'C' stood for 'centres' but with hindsight, it should have stood for 'constellations', which is what they are today.

9 Thank you to Professor Øyvind Kvalnes for his open access book, *Fallibility at Work Rethinking Excellence and Error in Organizations*, which a systemic account of what the phenomenon of fallibility amounts to, why it matters, why it turns out to be difficult to cope with, and most importantly how we may deal with it in constructive ways. Available at: www.palgrave.com/br/book/9783319633176.

10 Thank you to my friends Lise Mitchell (formerly of the Cheshire Police and Welsh Trading Standards) and Jai Shankar Ganapathy (of the Norwegian Police Academy) for sharing their experiences with me and helping me see the power of restorative justice and applying it to fraud and corruption. Both have extensive experience of working with restoring balance in conflict situations rather than letting the problem escalate. As Jai pointed out, one of the biggest difficulties in applying restorative justice to fraud is that money is involved and people feel cheated. It seems that money is still a very powerful motivator and the desire for it or to hang on to it still leads us to behave irrationally.

Chapter 3

Turning a problem into an opportunity

Everybody talks about the weather, but nobody does anything about it.[1]

One of the easiest ways to make money is to stop losing it. This chapter examines the true costs of fraud and corruption, who is involved and why, what makes a good fraud detective and what are the incentives for being one.

What exactly is fraud and corruption, who commits it and what does it cost?

Let's begin by re-stating the all-encompassing definition from Chapter 1:

> Fraud and corruption is *anything* which is deliberate and unethical and done by *anybody*, inside or outside your organization, which causes harm or loss to either you and your organization, or to someone else.

This definition should include absolutely everything which you felt was unethical or immoral and deliberate for some form of personal gain for the perpetrators and should cover everything, ranging from organized crime to deliberate overcharging and identity theft to petty scams and thefts.

Armed with this definition, most of us would admit that there is a lot of fraud and corruption around. This could be because we hear every single day about scandals which are reported in either the media or talked about on social media, or just because we have thought it through and realized that it is human to seize the windows of opportunities which open up, even if, for some of us, it means making certain awkward choices. So, if we called fraud and corruption one of the single largest unmanaged costs in the world today, few people would disagree.

But when this is taken down to the level of individuals or single organizations, a very different picture emerges, one of 'it might be a major problem, but it does not happen to me or my organization'. For the past twenty years the same question has been put to audiences at hundreds of seminars and lectures on fraud and corruption, around the world:

> Imagine a typical organization with sales, or let's say a spending budget, if you like, of €100 million. How much money do YOU think is lost by that organization to fraud and corruption each year? By fraud and corruption, we are talking about ANY unethical and deliberate action, such as suppliers who blatantly overcharge, people who steal, falsifying figures, customers who don't pay, kickbacks, attacks on the organization by opportunists, such as hackers and scammers, and much more, i.e. anything deliberate and unethical, done by ANYBODY both inside and OUTSIDE of our organization, anything which causes LOSS. And by loss, let's imagine the TOTAL loss: lost money. In all forms, damage to reputation and erosion of the organizational culture.
>
> So, in this organization with €100 million, what would you say was the total loss from all deliberate and unethical acts, done by anybody? Is the cost less than €100,000, between €100,000 and €1 million? Is it somewhere between €1 million and €5 million, between €5 million and €7 million, or greater even than €7 million?

Over the past 20 years, the average answer almost always centres around a total loss which is somewhere between €1 million and €5 million, or when there are more cynics in the audience, even higher.

There are many surveys and exercises done across the world which try to measure the costs of fraud and corruption, all in different ways. In general, most surveys go along with the majority, the real cost of corruption and fraud *is* pretty high, maybe in the region of €1–5 million each year in our €100 million organization.

If we for one minute believe that people's intuition as well as the surveys contain some truth, then what we are saying is that the cost of fraud and corruption for an average organization is a very large number. But trying to find the organizations which make up this number is a very different matter. It's almost as if every organization is the best in class, i.e. everyone says, 'not me'.

When the same question is asked of the top people (chief executives and the like), they tend to believe that the cost of fraud and corruption is lower, maybe because they are less sceptical than the average employee. Typically, the CEO's average is closer to 1 per cent of turnover, still a very large number but a lot smaller than what typical people working in organizations tend to believe the total costs of fraud and corruption are.[2] And a random CEO from an audience, one who believes that the typical cost of fraud and corruption is around 1 per cent, usually believes this happens to others, not his or her organization.

It's understandable: Everyone *wants* their organization to be fraud-free and it's a bit embarrassing to admit that they may be the captain of a leaky ship. The paradox is that fraud and corruption is seen by most people as a real and extensive problem, everyone condemns it, but few want to see it in their own backyard. Another explanation could be that there is so much cheating, stealing and greed around us that it may be better not to see it. It's much more fun to think of ways of making money than to think about stopping losing it. If we did, for just a minute, think about how much fraud and corruption costs our organizations, and we could find the magic cure to stop it, then we would in fact be doing our organizations a huge service.

Who does it and why?

To understand why fraud and corruption happens, we need to examine human behaviour and why we as people are willing to engage in doing unethical things for a benefit. One theory, most often credited to criminologist Donald Cressey, about why people do unethical things for a benefit, appears to have stood the test of time. In short, there are three fundamental factors which enable people to engage in unethical behaviour for a benefit:

1   motivation
2   opportunity
3   rationalization.

Motivation: people do unethical things because they want something. This could be because they are desperate, or they are greedy, or they have some other need which needs to be fulfilled.

Opportunity: simply put, if you want to do something unethical, you need to have the chance to be able do it. If you have absolutely no opportunity, it does not matter how much motivation you have, you are not going to be able to do it!

In general, the people who have the greatest opportunity to do unethical things, and by greatest, I mean in monetary terms, are often people at or near the top of organizations and high up in governments. But what about motivation? Who has the greatest motivation to do fraud?

If we asked the question: 'what do people with loads and loads of money want?', a lot of people would shout out 'more money' and then it becomes clear. Big people, big fraud, small people, small frauds. And it could be that in some environments the costs of all the small frauds could in fact be larger than the total costs of all the big frauds.

But for fraud and corruption to happen, there is a third condition sometimes referred to as *rationalization*. People might have lots of opportunity, they might be very motivated too, but they know that they cannot live with themselves after the event because they know what they are doing is (morally) wrong. For fraud and corruption to happen, it is not enough to have just opportunity and motivation. We need to find a way to tell ourselves that what we have done is OK.

Try this exercise for yourself:

> Invite some senior managers to a short fraud awareness workshop. At some point, ask them all to put their hands up in the air, to indicate that they are honest, I mean, REALLY honest. Then ask them a series of questions, such as 'Have you ever inflated a personal insurance claim?', or 'Have you ever got away without paying your train or bus fare?', 'Have you ever got around copyright laws and illegally downloaded software or music?' Tell them to put their hands down the minute they feel they can answer 'yes' to a question. Don't look too hard or try to judge people but by the end of a few of these questions, there are usually not too many hands and quite a bit of sniggering.
>
> It turns out that in fact very few of us are 100 per cent honest but thankfully even fewer are 100 per cent corrupt, but the truth of the matter is that most of us fall into this category called 'it depends'. It depends on our opportunity, our personal motivation, and of course our ability to rationalize that what we are doing is OK.[3]

In other words, most of us think we are honest, but we are also able to cheat a bit. Also, we tend to cheat in proportion to what we have.

Have the conditions for fraud and corruption changed much in the last few decades?

Fraud and corruption has been around for centuries and human nature argu-ably has not changed much. We seek out opportunity, we are motivated, and we rationalize our actions. So, the question then boils down to how much has fraud and corruption really changed? There have been some big advances in technology, as well as the proliferation and availability of information, but the actual basic methods behind fraud and corruption have arguably not changed much at all. Similarly we are starting to adopt more global terminology in many spheres and it is much more likely that fraudulent practices in one part of the world will quickly be adopted in another part of the world. So, every time someone comes up with a new way of doing fraud and corruption or some new term (like 'phishing', 'ransomware'), it could be seen as just a new variation on an age-old method.

What we can see has changed is how much *information* is now available to allow people to commit fraud. For example, 30 years ago, if you wanted to set up a front company or a bank account using a DMC, you would have to know someone or respond to a 'small ad' in a journal. Today you can easily find that sort of information online, if you have already not been solicited. If you would like a second identity or passport number, or a 'degree for life experience' to use in a job application, it is the same. The basic tools of fraud and how to get hold of them today are just a few clicks away.

In addition, technology, a gift to the human race in so many ways, is also an enabler or accelerator for the would-be fraudster. It's much easier using online-payment systems, crypto-currencies and all the myriad of alternatives to move money around, to expedite transactions. Also, it is much easier to conjure up a wildly over-flattering image of yourself and your organization in cyber-space, which nobody bothers to check.

Cultures are much more integrated than ever before in some parts of the world. Many of us, including people like me who are a product of multi-culturalism, welcome multicultural societies with their richness of ideas and cross-cultural fertilization. However, the flipside of the coin is that fraudsters are often the first not to let cultural differences stand in their way and they tend to be some of the best networkers ever.

A fourth factor could be that people are greedier or more brainwashed by money and 'lifestyles of the rich and famous' than ever before, meaning the motivation to 'get rich quick at all costs' has gone up. This is debatable and something you will have to make your own mind up about, but it is worth

Example 3.1 Taking what we see at face value

In one extreme case, an organization which was selling coal and other minerals which were either stolen or illegally mined, went to great lengths to portray to the outside would that they were a legitimate company. This included a registered office in Cyprus, a very comprehensive website with a lengthy code of conduct and even a detailed whistleblower policy and help-line, and the regular funding sponsorship of international trade fairs and conferences about coal and minerals trading. At one recent conference they hired a famous television personality to host a roundtable debate, which was then filmed and broadcast at meetings where representatives from the company participated. Everything was meticulously done to portray the image that the organization was well respected and transparent, thereby concealing the criminal elements (in this case, one of Europe's most dominant organized crime groups currently involved in mining, mineral trade and transport) which controlled the company.

pondering over. Whatever you believe, it is probably not worth jumping on the next bandwaggon or buzzword connected to fraud and corruption. Something that has been around for centuries does not change radically although it will move with the times.

How well are we doing in keeping fraud and corruption down and what are the current defences like?

Given that fraud and corruption has been around for centuries, given that most people will be able to rationalize doing it, given the opportunity, and provided they have the motivation, and given that the pace of fraud and corruption is increasing and moving with the times, how well are we as a society dealing with it?

So probably the question we need to ask is that in spite of almost universal condemnation that fraud and corruption is not good, and there are new and ever-expanding rules and regulations designed to stop it, better definitions of grey areas, increased public and media attention, why is it that the amount of perceived fraud and corruption seems to be going up, not down? To answer this question, we need to examine some of the defences in place and why they could, to an extent, be counter-productive.

Let us examine five traditional defences against fraud and corruption in turn: (1) a tsunami of rules and regulations to comply with; (2) the expectations of people charged with protecting our organizations; (3) blaming the so-called 'corrupt countries'; (4) waiting for the whistleblowers; and (5) punishment as a deterrent.

Traditional defence 1: Reliance on a tsunami of rules and regulations to comply with

Rules and regulations are in themselves not a bad thing. However, too many rules can easily lead to us ignoring all of them. And when it comes to rules and

Example 3.2 Worthless signatures

Some years ago, in the days of paper documents and signatures we were looking into why contracts for the supply of steel to oil platforms had repeatedly been awarded to the same supplier, and why in every single case the estimated cost had been exceeded by between 20 and 40 per cent. The procurement department insisted that all the rules had been followed, but finally, after some persistence we were allowed to see the main document on which the latest contract award was based. What we found in the files was a document called a 'Bid Waiver' which was raised because the procurement department had reason to believe that the suppliers had organized a cartel for the supply of steel and it was better to negotiate with a single supplier, the one they believed would give the best prices and service. The bid waiver front sheet was a single piece of paper with eight signatures representing people from the procurement department all the way up to the senior management. All of them had signed the document within three days of each other.

The most senior person on the list was asked why he signed the document. He took one look at it and said, 'I have no idea. I sign so many things, but I probably signed it because I trust my colleagues have checked things out before they signed it.' The process was repeated, working down to the second last person, getting similar answers each time. When we got to the last person, who was hard to locate as he had moved jobs, he answered, 'Oh . . . that one. I remember that. Someone high up got the message out that this contract was going to be awarded to Supplier M, just like all the others, and my job was to get all the paperwork in order. I remember running around trying to collect all the signatures . . .'[4]

controls, we have more rules today than ever, so much so that compliance is a booming industry. So maybe we could argue that we have so many rules and regulations today that we are so busy following rules we don't fully understand, that we don't take time for much else,. which can leave the playing field wide open to the commercial dark forces of fraud and corruption.

It probably is time to face reality. Whether we are referring to a code of conduct on a website for a company controlled by a criminal organization, or the 70+-page code of Conduct which Enron had, or today the 200-page code of ethics of a bona-# fide organization, it is pretty unlikely that most people will ever read it, let alone follow it, but they probably have signed somewhere to say they have read it. And it's not just the volume of rules and regulations which we sign that we have supposedly read which is worrying. Also, we tend to sign documents because we are forced to, or we feel it is the best thing to do in the situation. For example, when Adolf Hitler signed Neville Chamberlain's now famous 'Peace in our time' declaration in 1939 which British Prime Minister waved as a guarantee of peacce, maybe Mr Hitler *did* read the piece of paper he was signing but signed it because (1) that's what his counterpart wanted, and (2) because it bought him more time.

Albert Camus, the Nobel Prize-winning author and philosopher, is quoted as saying, 'Integrity has no need of rules.' If Camus had been alive today, maybe he would have said that organizations do not need hundreds of new rules for

---

Example 3.3 Tick the box

Every day, people tick boxes, sign documents or agree to terms and conditions which they *never* read but do it in the name of 'compliance'. Fifty customers at the gate of a Ryanair flight were asked if, when they bought their ticket, they had actually READ the terms and conditions behind the box to tick.

☑ I solemnly swear that I have read and understand the terms and conditions.

The result? A dismal *zero*. More rules, more regulations and even more compliance are heralded as the ultimate weapon against corruption, fraud, hidden ownership in tax havens (or DMCs). Shouldn't we just laugh? Or do we just continue to tick all the right boxes and stay 'corruption-free' *on paper*?

everything because deep down people know what is the right thing to do. So why are today's organizations stuffed full or rules, policies and procedures when people barely have the chance to read them?

Senior managers who signed off on documents, as in Example 3.2, are sometimes so shocked that they ask 'Which idiot signed that?' without realizing that in fact their signature was part of the electronic approval chain. Too many controls can often mean no control at all and too many rules can lead to a pressure to comply with them without thinking.[5]

Traditional defence 2: Expectations of people charged with protecting society from fraud and corruption

When reading the annual statements of an organization and the usually clean accompanying External Auditors' report, one tends to believe that there has been no fraud this year. On the other hand, if, by fraud and corruption, we mean any type of deliberate and harmful activity done by a handful of unethical suppliers, customers, consultants and agents, criminals and, in a few cases, dishonest employees, then we just know that 'being fraud-free' is wishful thinking at best.

Maybe 50 years ago when organizations were rather less complicated, and an external audit entailed a meticulous going-over the books with a fine toothcomb, there was a much bigger chance that fraud would be found. But we should remember that today it is not even the responsibility of external auditors to discover the kind of frauds mentioned above. Some suppliers will always cheat us, customers may do unethical things, bribes can happen, and front companies will pop up in all sorts of business deals. And these avoidable costs will dutifully be reflected, truly and fairly, of course, in the financial statements.

Example 3.4 Whose job is it to find fraud?

A 'hard-talk' debate about fraud and corruption. On one side of the hall are sitting senior management and, on the other, representatives from the audit profession. The managers were asked: 'If there was fraud and corruption in your organization, would you expect the auditors to find it?' The answer was a unanimous yes. Then the auditors were asked: 'If there was fraud and corruption in an organization you were auditing, is it your duty to find it?' Not one of the external auditors raised their hands.

It's time to stop thinking others are defending the world from fraud and corruption and start doing it yourself!

Traditional defence 3: Blaming the so-called 'corrupt countries'

Maybe this is not a defence against fraud and corruption, but it typifies a defensive reaction, the sort of reaction you could give if, as a child you were accused by your parents of not tidying your room. A typical reaction is to say, 'Look at my brother's room – it's much worse', thereby deflecting attention from your own problems.

Something similar has arisen with countries who want to portray themselves as less corrupt and deflect attention away to other countries who are, in their eyes, more corrupt. This is most obviously portrayed by the organization Transparency International and their Corruption Perception Index, which, in general terms, puts the poorer, less developed countries at the bottom of the list.

If you ask a different question, 'Who contributes the most in absolute terms to world corruption?', then the figures will tell you a very different story.

> Let's imagine that the gross domestic product per capita or GDP per person of one of the *most* corrupt countries in the world (let's call this country Angeria) was $2,500 per capita, and let's say the GDP of one of the richest countries (let's call it Brexitania) was $100,000. Now imagine, as many surveys have shown, that the cost of corruption and fraud in Brexitania was 4 per cent of GDP (a relatively small figure if corruption is widely defined to include all forms of bribery, fraud, by insiders and outsiders and any other form of unethical behaviour which causes loss). This is what the surveys do.
>
> But here is the sucker punch: 4 per cent of $100.000 is $4,000 which is 60 per cent higher than the total GDP per capita of Angeria. In other words, even if the entire economy of Angeria was corrupt, fraud and corruption in Angeria would still be 60 per cent *less* than in Brexitania.
>
> It's time to stop pointing the finger at the symptoms and at the poster boys of corruption, such as the greedy dictators who hoard away money in dirty money centres. Instead we should expend our efforts in finding and targeting the underlying causes of corruption. It's only in this way that we can have any success in the good fight at all.

Pointing the finger at poorer countries may raise awareness of world corruption but it also gives us a very skewed picture of where we, as a planet, are losing most value. Pointing in the other direction allows the G7 and other wealthy countries to complacently pat themselves on the back as if the problem only lies elsewhere. Maybe it's time to stop blaming others and start looking at ourselves?

Traditional defence 4: Waiting for the whistleblowers

Example 3.5 How should we detect fraud?

At the same hard talk debate referred to above, there was a panel discussion about detecting fraud where one of the panellists was the head of internal audit of a major international bank. The host asked each participant two questions (an easy one and a hard one). To the first question, 'How do you detect fraud and corruption?', the head of internal audit of the bank proudly replied that they had a very strong whistleblower channel which was connected directly to him, and proceeded to describe the types of fraud which had been discovered. The follow-up question was, 'So what do you and your department do to try and detect fraud without asking other people to stick their necks out?'

In recent years there have been a number of high-profile cases which have come to light where people working inside organizations have spoken up about suspected malpractice, fraud and corruption but have been ignored, or in some instances, silenced or even killed. What became very evident was that, for each major fraud or corruption case which emerged, there were people who either knew the details well in advance but for some reason could not get through, or there were people who knew about it and did not feel comfortable speaking out. As a result, elaborate whistleblower channels have sprung up all over the world, sometimes called 'hotlines' or 'speaking up channels, with legislation to protect so-called 'whistleblowers' and considerably large associated campaigns to encourage people to speak up.

The merits and success of such campaigns are still being debated as are the considerable personal consequences of being a whistleblower.[6] This book is not a discussion about how whistleblowing channels should be operated and how successful they are. There should always be a channel for people to speak up confidentially and to raise concerns without facing any retribution. But is whistleblowing really the primary channel to detect fraud? Or can we do better here?

Another reason not to rely on whistleblowing as the only way to detect fraud and corruption is that, if it is overplayed, it can lead to a climate of distrust in the organization.[7] Whistleblower channels should be seen as a safety net. There are much more effective measures against fraud and corruption, ones that really work.

Traditional defence 5: Excessive punishment as a deterrent

A suggestion, which was very popular after the high-profile US fraud and corruption scandals such as Enron, WorldCom and Tycho around the turn of the century, was to increase the prison sentences for senior management who knowingly either committed fraud or allowed it to happen. While there is some merit in this proposition, we all know that one cannot continue to increase sentences as these will very soon exceed the life expectancy of a human being. Also, we need to consider if in fact fraud and corruption is a worse crime than rape, murder or genocide.

Finally, fear of detection, instead of deterring people in the first place, can have the opposite effect of encouraging people to invest in additional precautions to hide their behaviour, or if caught out, to spend more money on their defence. Many people who commit serious fraud usually have plenty of funds stashed away for an eventual defence and we all know how expensive and tortuous legal battles can be. It's probably good to note that heavy-handedness can have the opposite effect.

Three simple defences against fraud and corruption which work

Raising awareness

One of the best ways to stop fraud and corruption is to recognize that it happens a lot and to speak openly about it. People are human, we all make mistakes and can easily be tempted to bend or break the rules and sometimes it's all too easy to come down hard on the ones who are caught. We should not ignore the rules but instead apply them responsibly, recognizing that too many rules can lead to confusion.

Better defences against fraud and corruption, against the commercial dark forces, include realistic educational programmes, for everybody, i.e. education which recognizes the real extent of corruption and fraud. This creates a climate where people talk about fraud and corruption, are encouraged to own up to mistakes and failings, even when they are themselves involved, provided they are treated compassionately. and will avoid a blame culture.

Out-think the fraudsters

Rather than categorizing fraud and corruption as a risk, and then examining how strong our current defences are, look at your organization from the perspective of a potential fraudster who is trying to break through the defences. Look for all the potential loopholes and possibilities and how someone, external or internal to the organization, could exploit them to commit fraud. These recipes, called 'Thinking Like a Thief' are described in detail in Chapter 5 and enable you to see what kinds of fraud are actually taking place.

A healthy curiosity open to everybody[8]

Imagine fraud and corruption is like litter. There is lots of it around and we can choose to see it, or we can ignore it. Most of us see litter and think about picking it up and disposing it in a nearby rubbish bin. Can you imagine how unnecessarily complex things would be if spotting and disposing of litter became the protected turf of a group of 'highly trained' specialists? I like to think anybody can be a fraud detective. Thankfully today, the task of finding fraud early and dealing with it effectively does not need to be relegated to someone else, whether they are whistleblowers, regulators, auditors or the media. We are fortunate that information flows more transparently than ever before, providing a much wider group of people in organizations working together to spot the early warning signs. People in organizations are not stupid, they can spot fraud and corruption if they are given the chance to do so, especially if management realizes that no one else on the outside is doing that job for them.

Fraud detection should be open to everyone who feels they want to do it responsibly. If it is left only to the growing army of specialists, not to mention auditors, then history tells us things are going to get worse.

Finally, fraud and corruption, unlike some murders, is usually not a crime of passion. Therefore, the tell-tale signs leading up to fraud are usually there to be found, long before the major frauds happen.

Who makes a good fraud detective?

The fraud detective is any person who works inside or outside an organization who is willing and able to detect where the organization is being defrauded by its suppliers, customers, agents, consultants, competitors, other outsiders, as well as its own people. The goal of the internal fraud detective (who could be in a number of different roles) is always to identify fraud *in the interest of the organization*. From the organization's point of view, it is always better if it develops its own people to be better at finding fraud, rather than relying on, and paying, outsiders to do this. However, it is conceivable that organizations could employ consultants and external parties as fraud detectives too, but it is important that the organization controls them. My definition of a fraud detective therefore does not include journalists, hostile investigators and other third parties whose primary loyalties are not to the organization. And it goes without saying that a fraud detective should have the organization's best interest at heart at all times.

It can often happen that organizations have historically been poor at detecting where they are being defrauded until quite late in the day, and usually the fact that they have been defrauded or have engaged in corrupt and unethical business often comes to light because it is discovered by accident or is brought to light by a whistleblower or the media. It is a fact that it is very rare that fraud is detected by auditors, external or internal, regulators, supervisors or compliance or internal control experts working inside or outside the organization.

What we are saying that while these methods of detection are not obsolete or irrelevant, there is simply a huge potential today for organizations to discover where they are being defrauded for themselves. It has been inspiring to see that more companies are beginning to see the value of developing this internal skill of early fraud detection and also working as one team.

For fraud detectives to flourish, then certain conditions in the organization need to be met: (1) there is within the organization and senior management a healthy desire to find fraud and corruption early; and (2) a strong sense of teamwork, a willingness for everyone to work together in defending the organization.

Provided that there is interest at the top, then fraud detectives can be encouraged right across the business. That is to say anyone who is interested in the organization, and especially people who see how the organization works, can become fraud detectives, which is preferable to being stigmatized whistleblowers.

Once you learn the basic recipes to detect fraud through healthy curiosity, you can also apply these skills in a wide range of situations, such as:

- spotting a builder, plumber or electrician who is trying to cheat you;
- swiftly identifying a customer who is either not going to pay or has something to hide;

- staying away from what looks like a tempting investment opportunity;
- being wary of a seemingly innocuous email or false entrapments over the internet.

The rather thinly disguised attempt where the red flags (the title 'Sir', the unusual email addresses, the discrepancy between the bank address in England and a Maltese telephone number, plus the rather impertinent content of the email itself) should be plain to see. Here is an example:

From: Sir Dave Ramsden ramsden-d@boe.co.uk
Sent: 5 May 2019
To: Recipients
Subject: Business Proposition

I am Sir David Edward John Ramsden, I work at the Bank of England. I have a business proposition to share with you. If you are interested, please request more information.

Yours sincerely,
Sir Dave Ramsden, Deputy Director, Marketing and Banking
Tel: +356 79 63 1829; email: davrsd4@gmx.com

What do you do if you find fraud and corruption, but no-one wants you to find it?

If you are unfortunate enough to work in an organization where either nobody wants to look too hard or, worse still, the culture is dominated by executives with a poorer-than average sense of ethics, or greater than average sense of entitlement, then your own situation is more complicated. There are still examples of executives who use policies and governance as a smokescreen to reassure their investors and the outside world that the organization is ethical and well controlled. This might be because they simply believe it is the right thing to do or they may be indulging in unethical or criminal behaviour for their own personal gain.

You can still try to make a difference within such an organization, but it may be a little more challenging, but usually not an impossible task, particularly if you cannot get support at some level, ideally at board level.

Alternatively, if that does not sit well with you, you maybe want to think about whether or not you wish to continue to work for an organization that is happy to paper over the cracks, and move to a more dynamic and hopefully less blind and more ethical employer. If you do choose to stay in an organization with a challenging environment, then it will help if you can find support from at least one board member.

The level of support which the executives provide to wannabe fraud detectives will depend largely on their own experiences. The more fraud they have suffered, the more likely they will want to find it earlier. However, at the same time, you could find yourself alone with little support:

Example 3.6 A difficult position

With the support of the managing director and using a structured approach, it was discovered that the chief accountant had been regularly transferring amounts in the region of €3,000 from the company bank account to her own account. All the withdrawals had been backed up by falsified transactions and countersigned by the then managing director who had now moved upstairs to become Chairman of the Board. The fraud had not been detected for years and the total proven loss was in the region of €200,000. The Chief Accountant, who recently had retired, admitted it when shown the evidence, and remedial action, both to recover the loss and prevent its recurrence, was initiated by the new Managing Director.

However, as part of this review, it was also discovered that the current Chairman had also abused his position by private expenditure and was not able to distinguish between the company's money and his own. The sums embezzled were only in the region of €50,000 but what was a challenge was that the Chairman denied any wrong-doing, saying that he felt he had a right to it, he had previously been the managing director and built the company up over many years, and this was a non-issue. He did not even wish to discuss it and, worse still, he intended to carry on in the same way ('I need it to maintain my lifestyle'), and the rest of the board, who were too scared to stand up to him, supported him against the managing director.

In this case without the support of the board and owners, the managing director felt he was in between a rock and a hard place, and resigned, found a new job and put it down to experience.

Defending your organization against the commercial dark arts, and finding fraud early are generally exciting and rewarding. But you need to work in an organization which has the right sort of atmosphere. One where you feel safe to do it, you know things are going to be handled maturely and you are going to be seen as a positive contributor, not a troublemaker!

Notes

1 Usually attributed to Mark Twain. Is there anything people can do about the weather? We may not have the power to change it but we can protect ourselves against its effects, and also can transform it into something useful, as shown by the development of wind farms.

2 It should be said that this is what I have typically observed in hundreds of seminars, i.e. in the top management echelons, the general perception of the total cost of fraud is lower than what the 'regular troops' believe. However, I was not able to find any academic or other research on this topic. What, however, is very common is the belief that the problem is usually worse somewhere else.

3 You can find more questions and an online 'honesty test' on www.fraudacademy. hibis.com

4 Later on, it was discovered, as part of a police investigation, that the person high up had a long-standing relationship with the steel supplier and had received a hidden commission, paid into an offshore bank account, based on every single steel contract he had managed to steer into the hands of his favourite steel supplier.

5 As one of my esteemed reviewers, Martin Walter Stevens, rightly pointed out, it's more a question of having meaningful controls. On one hand, a machine control is less likely to fail than a human control, but as discussed in Chapter 7, human beings have a certain quirkiness, the ability to be illogical, and intuition, which is difficult to explain, which means that certain frauds will still most often be spotted by humans.

6 There are numerous examples of whistleblowers losing their career prospects, or even freedom, because they chose to speak up. There is, therefore, all the more reason for everyone to find fraud and corruption early, and not wait for the whistleblower. For a more in-depth examination of the fate of one particular whistleblower, see the final chapter in this book, 'The Fraud Detectives: A Case in Point', based on true events.

7 In 1985, I did probably one of the most stupid things I have ever done in my life. In Berlin, my friend Richard Livingstone and I bought a day-visa, crossed the then border at Checkpoint Charlie and went into East Berlin. This was fine, and legal, but then my friend and I decided to go outside of the zone we were allowed to visit and take an East German Inter-city train to the town of Potsdam. We were young and stupid at the time and simply curious, unaware that we could have been arrested as suspected spies, and then it would have been goodbye world for a long time. In

Potsdam, we noticed that the locals, not used to foreigners who stood out, avoided us like the plague. Finally, a young East German bravely came up to us, and after enquiring what we were doing there, told us we need to get back to West Berlin as quickly as possible without speaking to anyone. Later on, I realized that the whole of East Germany (or the DDR, Deutsche Demokratische Republik – home of the famous Trabant motor car) had been permeated by a culture of whistleblowing where all their concerns would be collected and actioned upon by the masters of the whistleblower channel, the Stasi. As we can see from the history of the DDR, an over-developed whistleblower culture spreads mistrust and is not sustainable in the long term.

8 In June 2018, I represented CIMA at an International Round Table in Paris where one of the topics was to discuss whether 'professional scepticism', a term used for years by external auditors, should be embraced by all accountants and finance people working in organizations. It was argued that the word scepticism was somewhat negatively charged and that for people working in organizations, the term 'healthy curiosity' would be more appropriate.

Part II:

RECIPES FOR THE ASPIRING FRAUD DETECTIVE

Chapter 4

Three basic examples of recipes to detect red flags

> There is only one thing in life worse than finding fraud – and that is NOT finding fraud![1]

Oscar Wilde may never have said the epigraph but if he had seen so much fraud and corruption around in his society and very few people finding it, he might have felt inspired to exercise his wit.

Without further ado, let's dive in and see how you can spot some of the warning signs of commercial fraud and corruption. Here are three examples of documents which you could stumble across by chance. Don't worry if the feel out of the context in which you normally work, or if initially you feel that they are outside of your comfort zone. Just relax and read the examples and see how you might respond to them.[2]

Spot the red flags I

The Britmax Corporation is trying to expand its activities into Africa and the Middle East. wny called F & C Ltd (Figure 4.1). You hear that at least two similar invoices from this company have been paid earlier and one is on the way.

F & C Ltd
71 Park Plaza
London LW1 3QE
Tel: +44 (0) 20 800 3000 (5 lines)

INVOICE FC-20XX-003
31 April 20XX

Britmax Engineering Ltd
11 Grosvenor Place
London
WE2 3WW

Marketing Support (Survey and Retainer – West Africa)

(March–June 20XX) $250,000

(Purchase order reference: MIR: PO 707382, confirmed by Sales Director Joe Northfield and project manager John Bettis)

Payments due in 14 days to:

F & C Holdings Ltd
PBK Privatbank AG
Account Number: 118027400001
IBAN: CH61086663116027400001
SWIF code: PBKBSCH22

Email: fcholding@gmail.com
(F&C Holdings Ltd is registered in the British Virgin Islands: reg. no: 467239992)

Figure 4.1 Spot the red flags 1

1 What possible indications of possible fraud and corruption, including so-called 'red flags' or questionable issues, do you see in this document which could give us possible cause for concern?
2 What do you think could lie behind this invoice?

Do not look away yet! Spend just one or two minutes gazing at the document, see where your eye lands and make a note of what you think could be interesting. The trick is to analyse the information and indications that you see and try to think of possible explanations and scenarios. Then look at the suggested answers to questions 1 and 2 in Box 4.2.

Feedback on spot the red flags I

Here is the invoice, marked up to show what you might have seen, which information could be of interest and why (Figure 4.2). This interpretation is of course subjective, but you might be interested to see how many red flags you spotted and compare what you see with my own interpretation.

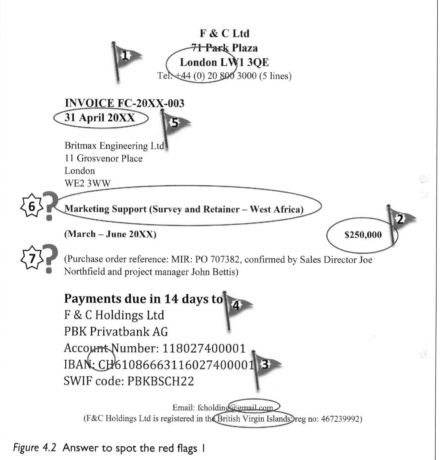

Figure 4.2 Answer to spot the red flags I

Table 4.1 is a description of the red flags, and questions raised by this document. The list, which corresponds to the numbers on the document is by no means exhaustive. The numbers in the left-hand column correspond to the markings in Figure 4.2.

Table 4.1 Explanation of feedback on spot the red flags 1

Red flag number	Feedback
1	The invoice number issued by F&C is 'FC-20XX-003'. Deconstructing this number, it could appear that:

• The 'FC' stands for the name of the company
• '20XX' is the year in which the invoice is issued or could even be the year the company, 'F&C' was inaugurated
• '003' is the number of the invoice. Since most companies tend to issue invoices in sequence, we can deduce that this is probably either the third invoice issued by F&C Ltd in the year 20XX, or the third invoice ever issued by F&C since it was founded. (However, it could also be just the third invoice F&C have issued to Britmax.)

Given that invoice was issued in April 20XX, we can infer that either this was the third invoice issued by F&C Limited in the year 20XX or only the third invoice ever issued by the company. If this is the case, then three invoices issued by a company either since its foundation, or even in four months is quite a low number and not what we would normally expect, unless the company served a particular purpose and invoiced sporadically.

| 2 | A minor but interesting indicator that the invoice is for the exact sum of $250,000 (a rather round sum) |

| 3 | The contact email address is fcholding@gmail.com. This could indicate that the company has not set up its own web-domain as yet or at least is not using it for hosting its own email. |

| 4 | The company address at the top of the invoice says 'London' (presumably in the UK). The bank account of the company is in Switzerland (which is given away by the 'CH', the international denotation for Switzerland) in the International Banking or 'IBAN' code). The note at the bottom of this invoice shows an almost similar name F&C Holdings Ltd but indicates that this company is registered in the British Virgin Islands. |

We can conclude that there are at least three distinct jurisdictions connected with this invoice. This can give cause for concern as to where the money paid by Britmax finally ends up. One could argue that there is also a fourth implied jurisdiction in that the currency of the amount (see point 2 above) is dollars (presumably US dollars).

The fact that a 'holding' company with the name 'F&C' is registered in the British Virgin Islands indicates that it is possible that the company has nominee directors and hidden ownership (but it is important that we do not jump to any conclusions at this stage)[*]

| 5 | The date 31 April doesn't exist. This could be because the person creating the invoice made an honest mistake, meaning to write 30 April. However, mistake or 'deliberate error', it does indicate that this invoice was not created by an invoicing program but was more likely to be written by hand on a spreadsheet or word processor. |

In addition, if the date of the invoice is in fact April, then some form of pre-invoicing has taken place, since the services (see point 6 below) are described as from March to June 20XX

Red flag number	Feedback
6	The description of the services 'Marketing Support (Survey and Retainer – West Africa) is distinctly ambiguous or vague. Although nothing unusual, the mention of West Africa introduces another region of the world into this invoice to add to the ones mentioned in point 4.
7	Reference is made to a purchase order number, but also emphasizes that the service has already been approved by two named persons

* See also Chapter 5 on DMCs.

Other things worthy of comment could include, the mention of '5 lines' at the top of the invoice, which could give the impression that F&C is a much larger company than it is. Another small detail is that the SWIFT code (which is an international bank code) is spelt 'SWIF', with the 'T' missing. This could be another indication of sloppiness. Finally, the variety of fonts used also indicates that the invoice could have been written by hand.

When teaching and using examples such as these, some people react either by saying 'well, that's obvious' or 'there would never be so many red flags on one document'. Both reactions are understandable, but the facts remain that these types of transactions are rather common. Also, indicators like these are rarely spotted under normal circumstances. This can be because:

● If we come across documents such as these, we tend to assume that they must be official because somebody else has checked or approved them.
● We are conditioned not to be difficult or ask probing questions as we are meant to trust other people in business.
● We simply don't have time to look at things in detail – just think how often we tick boxes or sign for something without reading the small print or looking at what is behind it.

But maybe the most important reasons these indications are rarely spotted is that when we are not specifically looking for something, as we were doing now, then it is very unlikely we will find it – especially if we have been set a different task.[3]

Ticking the boxes

Over 15 years ago, in a senior management training seminar, an invoice like F&C was put up on the screen and the participants were asked if they had been the second approver[4] of this invoice, and it had already been signed off on and approved by someone they knew and trusted, how many *minutes* (on average) would they spend before approving it? There was stunned silence, until someone suggested that seconds, not minutes were the more appropriate measure. It turned out that the average time people looked at a document such as this was 15 seconds.

More recently at a management seminar for a large international airport authority, a similar exercise was carried out with an audience of 50 managers, who all had signature authority. Technology had moved on a lot in 15 years. In this organization there were few paper invoices. Instead information was passed electronically via a workflow system where managers received electronic notification that their approval was required. They could choose to review and approve a single line summary, but if they wished, they could look at the attached documentation. The average electronic approval time had dropped to just a few seconds, and nearly all the managers present admitted that they rarely reviewed the attached documents themselves. Some even confessed that they delegated their signing authority to an assistant or colleague.

Today, when we are encouraged to sign or tick a box because 'it's the thing to do', very few people examine the underlying documents.[5] It's as if we are almost discouraged to do so. And even we gave 15 seconds to a manager to review the above F&C document, we could consider ourselves lucky if they maybe spotted one or two red flags.

Conversely, every time people are shown a document, such as in Figure 4.1, or the other two examples in this chapter, and put them under immense time pressure with a specific task to find red flags of fraud in under a minute, they manage to do so. Even more encouraging, people, when specifically told to look for signs of fraud, nearly always manage to spot three or more red flags in less than just a few seconds. In fact, it is not essential at all that you spot all of them, just enough of them to be able to say, 'I think we need to look at this a little more closely.'

How do we interpret the F&C invoice?

The first thing that should be said is that this invoice alone is not, in itself, evidence of fraud and corruption as it stands. We should never jump to conclusions. Before asking anyone about the example the best thing we can do is learn to theorize what it could be. This process of brainstorming (either alone or with a trusted colleague as to what the best- and worst-case scenarios could be) is critical because it will guide the next steps you may eventually take to understand the example further.

Below are three plausible explanations as to what the story behind F&C might be:

1   'F&C' could be the company of a small or one-person consultancy which provides a genuine service to Britmax, but where the people travel extensively and therefore are not tax resident anywhere, so are not liable for tax (or at least believes that they are not liable to pay tax for whatever reason) but wish to ring-fence their income from questions. This still does not explain the apparent vagueness of the description of the service provided.

2   It appears to be a deliberate attempt to conceal the nature of the service provided, the details of what the money paid to 'F&C' was spent on. The use of at least three jurisdictions, including the British Virgin Islands, could indicate that the invoice could be some form of commission payment or even be partly related to bribery to win business.

3   It could be proof of embezzlement by an employee or closely related party to Britmax, using consultancy and vague marketing services as a cover story.

In the real example upon which this is based, the true answer was interesting. Around 15 per cent of the fees paid to F&C were genuine expenses, 15 per cent were real bribes and the remaining 70 per cent were pure embezzlement by senior employees, who felt that the company would never pursue them because the fact that the company had knowingly paid bribes acted as a kind of 'insurance policy' in their favour.

Currently, at this stage, we do not know what this invoice represents but what we can say is that, like every other document, there is a story behind it and this invoice appears to be indicative of an interesting story which is worth tracing. How we explore this story further and how it can be resolved are the subject of Chapters 6 and 7. How such documents, including the subjects of Examples 4.2 and 4.3 can be found is covered in Chapter 5.

For now, and when trying the next two examples, remember the importance of attention to detail and taking time to think 'What could this be?'

Spot the red flags 2

Examine the email which has been sent by Eve, a sales assistant working for the Miralux Corporation's Northern European Sales Team to Maria, who works in Miralux's accounts department (Figure 4.3). The invoice was found scanned attached to a credit note dated 3 January 20XX where €1.3 million was credited to the Swedish customer EAB Systems AB. Miralux's Northern European Sales team is headquartered in Hamburg, Germany, but Eve works in the UK office in Basingstoke. Miralux's financial year end is always 31 December.

Waugh, Eve Lynne

From: Eve.Lynn.Waugh@miralux.com
Sent: 03 January 20XX 11:28
To: Maria.Neumier@miralux.com
Subject: Clearing against advance invoices (EAB Systems AB)

Dear Maria

I have received a credit note from the Northern European sales team. They have given strict Instructions that this credit note should be posted to the EAB Systems AB Customer Account (number R 470043) in this financial year and booked against invoice number 1638467 to EAB Systems for the same amount of €1.3 million date dated 16th December. A replacement sales invoice will be issued in February and should also be booked in this financial year. I am acting on instructions from Max, the head of NE Sales. If you have any questions, please let me know as it is easier to explain.

Best regards

Eve ☺

Eve Waugh
Sales Assistant
Miralux Northern European Sales Team

Figure 4.3 Spot the red flags 2

1   Even though you know very little about the context of this email or what the company 'Miralux' is, by reading what is actually written and what is written between the lines, what do think *could* be going on?

2   What is said that could be of cause for concern and what possible worst- and best-case scenarios could you imagine?

As in Box 4.1, spend around 60–90 seconds looking carefully, jot down your notes as to what you think could lie behind it, and then look at the suggested answers to questions 1 and 2 in Box 4.4.

Feedback on spot the red flags 2

One of the first things to do is read the email in the context of the little background you already know about Miralux and the credit note issued to EAB Systems AB. Since EAB Systems AB is a Swedish customer, if the sales are made from either Miralux in the UK or Germany (which is the

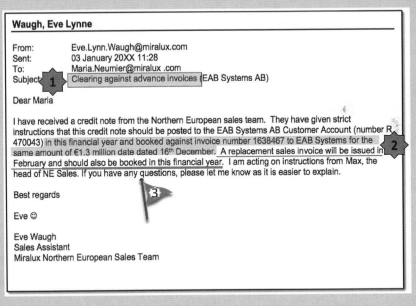

Waugh, Eve Lynne

From: Eve.Lynn.Waugh@miralux.com
Sent: 03 January 20XX 11:28
To: Maria.Neumier@miralux .com
Subject   1   Clearing against advance invoices (EAB Systems AB)

Dear Maria

I have received a credit note from the Northern European sales team. They have given strict instructions that this credit note should be posted to the EAB Systems AB Customer Account (number R 470043) in this financial year and booked against invoice number 1638467 to EAB Systems for the same amount of €1.3 million date dated 16th December. A replacement sales invoice will be issued in February and should also be booked in this financial year. I am acting on instructions from Max, the head of NE Sales. If you have any questions, please let me know as it is easier to explain.

Best regards

Eve ☺

Eve Waugh
Sales Assistant
Miralux Northern European Sales Team

Figure 4.4 Answer to spot the red flags 2

most likely scenario), then they would count as international sales. There are a number of clues in the email which indicate that amounts have been accounted for in the previous financial year, but since the actual sale has not been made yet, they were reversed early in the new financial year and were going to be booked in February when the actual sale took place. Being a cross-border sale, maybe the Swedish customer EAB were not even aware that this was going on? Let's examine the 'evidence' which points in this direction (Figure 4.4).

Table 4.2 explains the red flags.

Table 4.2 Explanation of feedback on spot the red flags 2

Red flag number	Feedback
1	The text 'clearing against advance' invoices could be interpreted as 'we are deleting an invoice which was issued early'
2	The highlighted text clearly infers that that may have happened
3	This is almost the 'give-away' line where Eve tells Maria that they will be issuing a new invoice

Once again, there is no hard evidence of fraud or malpractice, but there is clearly an interesting story which needs to be further explored. In the actual example on which this case is based, there was a very simple explanation. Miralux had already issued a profits warning but towards the very end of the financial year, it was realized the company had been too optimistic. Sales teams were urgently encouraged to invoice everything they could, and, in this case, 'Max' probably overstepped the mark in his eagerness to help his company meet their sales targets by invoicing a sale which might have been agreed in principle but was only going to happen in the next financial year.

The real and recent example upon which this is based was not discovered by the external auditors. Today's external auditor approach is based on sampling, materiality (of which this transaction alone was far below any materiality limit pertaining to Miralux) and a disclaimer according to auditing standard ISA-240, whereby the senior management of Miralux in practice 'agree' with the external auditors that the risk of accounting fraud is low.

Even if the salesmen were on commission and needed to reach a target for the year, to get paid a bonus, which could easily have been the case, they could have rationalized their actions by saying 'I am worth it', or 'it's only

Spot the red flags 3

The following credit note comes across your desk (Figure 4.5). You are aware that some of Miralux's factories which produce aluminium sheeting, have a contract with

Credit Note

CRN-2-20XX-AB-9876

01.04.20XX

Quarterly commission to be paid based on primary metal sales to
Lazer-Berman S.A., Milan.

Calculation of 5% Commission Payable based on all deliveries over €50,0000			
Delivery date	Port of Delivery	Sales Value €	Commission payable €
05.01.20XX	Ventspills	245,056.00	12,252.80
06.01.20XX	Civitavechia	145,624.00	7,281.20
26.01.20XX	Napoli	136,293.00	6,746.15
29.01.20XX	Bar (Montenegro)	398,345.00	19,917.25
07.02.20XX	Civtavechia	150,023.00	7,501.15
28.02.20XX	Ventspills	48.000.00	0
10.03.20XX	Ventspills	129,012.00	6,450.60
20.03.20XX	Bar	294,941.00	1,4747.05
Total Commission Payable			74,996.20

Commission payable to:
LB Marton Holdings LLC
7632 W. Azure Dr
Ste 140
Las Vegas, NV 89130
USA

(see Customer Master File for LB Marton Holdings LLC Bank Account and payment details)

Miralux Corporation Ltd
46/7 Knight Street, London WC1 4GG, UK
Tel +44 (0) 20 347 9822
VAT Reg No. GB 443 0727 68
Registered in England and Wales No. 1742 743

Figure 4.5 Spot the red flags 3

an Italian tin can manufacturer, and deliver rolled aluminium to their highly automated processing plants in Italy, Montenegro and Latvia. You are told that this customer is called Lazer Berman, based in Milan, Italy.

Study the document for a couple of minutes. What can you deduce could be happening and what sort of relationship do you think Miralux has with Lazer Berman?

moving a sale which is going to happen anyway from next year into this year, it's not as if I am cheating anybody' or 'everybody else does it, so why not me?'

What is interesting from Eve's email is how she makes it clear that she is simply 'acting on instructions from Max' and invites Maria to get in touch if she is curious. Finally, the fact that Eve has attached the mail to the credit note to ensure it remains part of the accounting documentation of Miralux could be to ensure that she will not get blamed in the unlikely event that this 'accounting fraud' is discovered. Or it could be that Eve in her heart wanted this to be discovered but knew that if she made too much noise, her job could have been on the line.

While the red flags themselves may seem trivial in nature, the whole basis of the transaction could be questioned. For example, this document leaves us wondering, when we make sales to a company in one country, why are discounts which are applied to high volume sales paid to another company, in another country? Is this a scheme by Lazer Berman to avoid tax in some way, or is it some form of bribe? Does it involve employees of Miralux?

The real-life example on which this example is based, centred on a long-established deal with a customer which had been in place for over 10 years. The commercial relationship was highly profitable for Miralux and, as a result, the production sourcing director at Lazer Berman had set up a shell company in Nevada which he owned and into which the 5 per cent rebates were paid. This arrangement had become routine and accepted. When it was discovered through the sort of structured analysis described later in Chapter 5, the head of risk management and business ethics had a discussion with the head of Miralux's Aluminium Sheeting Production. They both agreed that they were helping an employee of Lazer Berman accumulate wealth privately in his own company in the USA, but while the head of the production division saw it as a commercial arrangement which he could tolerate, the head of risk saw it as a possible bribe to an employee of a customer, something which conflicted with Miralux's own code of ethics.

Feedback on spot the red flags 3

This credit note is worth examining for some time (Figure 4.6). In a sense, its very existence should be questioned. Table 4.3 presents the explanation for the red flags.

Credit Note

CRN-2-20XX-AB-9876

01.04.20XX

Quarterly commission to be paid based on primary metal sales to
Lazer-Berman S.A., Milan.

Calculation of 5% Commission Payable based on all deliveries over €50,0000			
Delivery date	Port of Delivery	Sales Value €	Comission payable €
05.01.20XX	Ventspills	245,056.00	12,252.80
06.01.20XX	Civitavechia	145,624.00	7,281.20
26.01.20XX	Napoli	136,293.00	6,746.15
29.01.20XX	Bar (Montenegro)	398,345.00	19,917.25
07.02.20XX	Civtavechia	150,023.00	7,501.15
28.02.20XX	Ventspills	48,000.00	0
10.03.20XX	Ventspills	129,012.00	6,450.60
20.03.20XX	Bar	294,941.00	1,4747.05
Total Commission Payable			74,996.20

Commission payable to:
LB Marton Holdings LLC
7632 W. Azure Dr
Ste 140
Las Vegas, NV 89130
USA

(see Customer Master File for LB Marton Holdings LLC Bank Account
and payment details)

Miralux Corporation Ltd
46/7 Knight Street, London WC1 4GG, UK
Tel +44 (0) 20 347 9822
VAT Reg No. GB 443 0727 68
Registered in England and Wales No. 1742 743

Figure 4.6 Answer to spot the red flags 3

Table 4.3 Explanation of feedback on spot the red flags 3

Red flag number	Feedback
I	The first thing which should strike you is that there is a 5 per cent commission payable on sales to Lazer Berman, which appear to be based in Milan, Italy, yet the commission seem to be paid to a company called LB Marton Holdings LLC in Nevada, USA. Also, if this were an Italian company, we would expect the type of company to be 'S.p.A', rather than 'S.A.'

(Continued)

Table 4.3 (Continued)

Red flag number	Feedback
2	A further clue can be found in the fact that commissions are paid on all deliveries which have a value of over €50,000 (see point 3). If the commissions were just simple discounts, then normally we would expect them to be paid back to the same company, but in this case, they are going somewhere completely different. This in itself raises a few eyebrows.
3	The delivery with a value of €48.000 does not generate a commission. While we might say 'so what?', this in itself indicates that some form of 'system' is in place to ensure that only the commissions which are truly deserved are paid out.
4	There are no details of which bank account these commissions should be paid into, other than a reference to the fact that the bank account is on file.

What do these three examples tell us?

From experience, most people who spend a couple of minutes looking at each document in a situation where they are aware that they *should* be looking for something related to possible fraud and corruption, will tend to notice some of the red flags (or things they feel they would want to question). Most people spot a few warning signs in just seconds. In other words, you do not need to be a genius to spot fraud and corruption – you just need to know it exists and have a desire to find it.

F&C Holding (Box 4.1) appears to involve a DMC, it could be

- fictitious overcharging by a supplier or consultant;
- the payment of a kickback related to a sale to an unethical customer;
- the insertion of a fake cost designed to artificially lower profits for whatever reason;
- pure embezzlement by an over-zealous and entitled employee or manager.

In other words, the red flags related to F&C Holding could indicate any of the categories, some of them or even *all* of them.

Conversely, the email from Eve to Maria (Box 4.2) points more clearly in the direction of someone artificially trying to show increased sales, although we should not forget that there could also be an element of 'over-entitled' or greedy employees wanting their sales commissions, and possibly even bribery if a customer is involved in some way.

Finally, the credit note issued to Lazar Berman (Box 4.3) looks very much like a well- established system of kickbacks paid to a person or group of persons working for a major customer. However, we could also envisage that there could be employees in our own organization involved and benefiting by tapping into some of the illicit money flows centring around the front company LB Marton LLC.

The main challenge is that, normally, when we come across documents like this, we are not in any way looking for anything out of the ordinary. The accounting and audit professions have tried to define a balanced approach to reviewing information called 'professional scepticism' but so far it is the subject of a lot of debate, given the multiple scandals and issues where auditors and others were blamed for not detecting fraud and corruption early enough.

If we are looking for signs of fraud and corruption in a large enough selection of transactions and documents, then we are likely to find it, because there is enough of it around to find. However, if we are not looking or we do not believe it is there, then we are very unlikely to find anything at all.

The three examples above are examples only. This book is a recipe book on how to detect commercial fraud and corruption, something that has been taking place for hundreds of years, and we are not specifically addressing personal frauds, such as scams and identity theft. Similarly, I have avoided trying to focus on one particular industry such as banking, retail, construction, etc. but instead tried to ensure that the examples used are applicable to all industry types. And, finally, we are not focusing on the latest buzzwords, whether they be 'crypto-currencies', 'phishing' or 'blockchain', for the simple reason that these are just recent developments which will be replaced by others, while the fundamentals of fraud and corruption remain the same. Whatever the kind of fraud, the principles of 'healthy curiosity' 'attention to detail' and 'follow the money' tend to apply. Some basic rules of thumb are:

- Whenever you see or receive a document, pay attention to details and inconsistencies. Tiny things that are wrong or out of place could be tell-tale signs of an attempt to deceive or of some form of on-going fraud.
- Try not to be fooled by the use of important-looking words and phrases. They may well have been inserted to provide a sense of authenticity.
- Always maintain a healthy and balanced sense of curiosity. Try to brainstorm alternative scenarios for both best- and worst-case scenarios.

- Learn to trust your intuition. Fraud and corruption is not as rare as you might want to believe. When you look at a document, such as the three examples, or a seemingly innocuous email, if there is something there, it is likely that your brain will immediately register something, but it might take you a little time to process and identify what could be the problem.
- Avoid jumping to conclusions or feeling that you need to act immediately. Often you have much more time to think than you realize.

You receive an unsolicited email with a header which says that 'your PayPal account requires urgent authentication'. Before you jump to click on the mail, first consider: (1) Why am I receiving this mail?; (2) Why is the sender's email account not sent from a PayPal domain?; and (3) maybe, 'I don't have a PayPal account!' In a world where we tend to rush, just slowing down and thinking for a few minutes could save your computer being infected by a virus, ransomware or some other malicious attempt to compromise you.

Notes

1 Oscar Wilde, in his novel *The Picture of Dorian Gray*, wrote: 'There is only one thing in the world worse than being talked about, and that is not being talked about', see www.goodreads.com/quotes/5560-there-is-only-one-thing-in-the-world-worse-than

2 These three examples are based on real cases but have been suitably anonymised and created for demonstration purposes only. All place names appear without prejudice and names of persons or companies are entirely coincidental. Since these examples are timeless, years appear in the format 20XX.

3 In his (2015) book, *Moral Reasoning at Work*, Professor Øyvind Kvalnes describes 'the Monkey Business Illusion' and how we do not spot what we do not expect to be there (such as a gorilla appearing momentarily in a basketball game). Because our given task is to count passes of one team, most of us do not spot the gorilla.

4 It has been customary practice that an invoice like this would require two approvers to ensure that one person alone cannot take the decision alone. Having more than one person required to complete a task in business is a key concept within internal control intended to prevent fraud and error. It is commonly referred to as 'segregation of duties', 'separation of duties' or 'the four eyes principle'.

5 Imagine how long it would take, and how many people would get irritated if, when you hired a car at an airport, your read all the small print every time you had to put your initials or signature on the car-hire form.

Chapter 5

Thinking like a thief

How to out-think the fraudster and predict
where your organization is being defrauded

> I may be on the side of the angels, but don't for a second think that I am one
> of them.
>
> (Sherlock Holmes to James Moriarty, BBC Television Series, 2012)

Seeing the ghosts of past, present and future
fraud and corruption[1]

The aim of this chapter is to provide you with a menu, consisting of three
important recipes in the form of an appetiser, a main course and a dessert,
which will enable you to assemble one of the most realistic 'pictures' of the
types of fraud and corruption which can afflict your organization in the future,
and, most probably in some cases, have been, or are, already taking place but
have not yet been discovered.

It is, of course, possible, using today's technology, which enables virtual
meetings which are almost as real as face-to-face encounters, voting buttons
and shared documents, to perform the whole process in a way that nobody has
to physically meet any business associate. It is also technically possible today for
a group of good friends to sit down to a virtual dinner together, share the same
meal and have a good dinner conversation. But most of us would agree that
there is still something special about the experience of meeting real people in

real life. Either way, I would recommend that when doing the exercises in this chapter, for the first few times, at least, people should to be in the same physical space, and paper, pens, flipcharts, whiteboards and body language should take precedence over technology.

Typically, the menu in Table 5.1 (excluding the synthesis) would take about three or four hours to accomplish.

These recipes are extremely useful and have been used by leading fraud detectives for over 30 years. They are based on using knowledge we already have, brainstorming with an inverted mind-set so that we can mirror that of the potential fraudsters and criminals, and a clear-thinking 'blank-piece-of-paper' approach, free from preconceptions and denial.

The name of this approach, 'think like a thief', was coined in the 1970s by Michael J. Comer and Martin Samociuk (two highly experienced and maverick practitioners, whom I was fortunate enough to have as my teachers), who saw that corporate fraud was rife but not being discovered. Applying the 'lateral thinking' ideas propagated by Edward de Bono, the two experienced fraud investigators and maverick authors of books on fraud and corruption, developed the seeds of an exciting new methodology which gave people working in organizations the chance to put themselves in the shoes of the opposition, to really see how they would attack. This method was new to fraud and corruption, given that the standard methods (which are still dominant today) are still

Table 5.1 How to understand and assess the risks of fraud and corruption in your own organization

	The à la carte menu
The appetiser (Recipe 1)	Warming up the audience to be able to recognize that fraud and corruption is taking place
The main course (Recipe 2)	Using the 'think like a thief' method to reveal the invisible fraud and corruption which is already happening (or could very easily happen)
The dessert trolley (Recipe 3)	How to develop a realistic and living profile of the most significant methods of fraud and corruption which affect you and your organization.
The aftermath	Not a recipe as such, but more instructions on how to use the output from everything to create a first-draft *unique* fraud and corruption profile of your organization. Often this session is done in a small group after the main guests (i.e. most of the participants) have departed.

very much checklist-based. However, the idea is not new at all. Trying to out-think the enemy is an ancient concept and is relevant in many arenas, ranging from warfare to modern-day football.

Some people ask, when they are told to think like criminals, whether the method itself is dangerous and wonder if they will become criminals. This is a natural question to ask but experience shows that it is rare.

Example 5.1 The trigger

Many years ago, Martin Samociuk gave a 'think like a thief' workshop to a group of Scandinavian auditors and IT security specialists where they were encouraged to identify loopholes in the system which could be exploited by fraudsters and hackers. The organizer of the workshop, a young and enthusiastic computer auditor, was very pleased with the response and results.

Years later when involved in investigating for a Scandinavian bank, a simple fraud took place where the same organizer of the seminar, now working as an IT auditor working for the bank, had gained access to client accounts and transferred several small sums of money to his personal account (also with the same bank). It was one of the simplest frauds to investigate and prove and the person involved confessed almost immediately.

What had happened between the seminar and his act of theft from the bank, was that the young IT auditor had been involved with a young lady, whose relatives were mixed up in low-level organized crime. She was also, unfortunately and previously unknown to the IT auditor, a drug user. At some point in the relationship, her brother had 'leaned on' the IT auditor to find a way to procure ever increasing sums of money for her to buy drugs. It seems that 'blind love' was the motivator, and the seminar he attended a decade previously had very little to do with it whatsoever, other than making him think once before acting.

Most fraudsters are leaps and bounds ahead anyway, so think like a thief (or 'TLAT') just allows honest people in organizations to catch up a little.

Before diving straight into the recipes, it is useful to examine why this method works so well and some of the reasons why it has not been used enough in the past.

Why don't we see fraud and corruption normally?

In truth, there is and should be no shame in being cheated or duped. It happens to most of us regularly, often without us realizing. In today's fast-moving world, being cheated or scammed does not mean you are stupid or have something to be ashamed about. It happens to the best of us. Also, there are few paragons of virtue around. Those people whom we hold in high esteem for doing admirable deeds one day, the next can do fraudulent acts often without being 100 per cent sure that what they were doing was fraud.

And there are few pathological fraudsters and corporate psychopaths, although they do exist. Most people who commit fraud are really 'fraudsters for life'. As discussed previously, almost everybody could potentially be a fraudster. And at the risk of sounding a little flippant, one of the catch phrases of Michael J. Comer was 'shit happens and so does fraud'.[2] Or as we put it a little less bluntly, 'fraud and corruption happens'. There will always be some outsiders, such as suppliers, customers, agents, consultants and opportunities who are deliberately trying to do something unethical for their own personal benefit, and maybe they are helped by insiders. Or if we are a bit unlucky, insiders do it on their own.

On the contrary, when we read about fraud and corruption in the newspapers, we feel shock horror, whether it is the latest news about a former FIFA president, billions of dollars syphoned off by an oligarch or president or the latest collapse of a major corporation or small country (such as the financial collapse of Iceland in 2008).[3] Deep down, we probably all know that a lot of this goes on, a lot of the time and what we read about is just the tip of an iceberg which may or may not be uncovered. But we are, I hope, all realistic enough to realize that if we don't see the rest of the iceberg, it has not just magically disappeared.

The paradox, that we know fraud and corruption is normal, but like to think of it as exceptional impairs our ability to recognize it. The key lies in the use of the word 'risk'. Call fraud and corruption a 'risk' and there is that wonderful get-out clause which allows you to say it 'may' or 'may not' happen. I have a colleague who would argue that it must be called a risk even though he knows it happens all the time. But my colleague would also say that 'death' is a risk, even though all of us (even the Dalai Lama) would say that death is inevitable.

Most annual reports and financial statements of large organizations and corporations now include a section with the title 'Risk' or 'Risk Management'. Like external audit reports, the 'risk section' tends to be quite long and written in small print and is probably one of the least-read portions. But it ticks all the right boxes and covers all the right topics related to risks that the organization could face. It feels as if someone has written a section of the annual report which just has to be there.

What is almost always glaringly obvious as missing is a section which details all the different methods of fraud and corruption which are probably taking place. Is the risk report meaningful? The answer is probably yes, but not in the context of fraud and corruption.

Example 5.2 Fraud: severely hyped but rarely found

A government-owned scientific research centre did its own research and commissioned research as well as assessing applications and award-ing grants. The organization had in total a research budget of around £500,000 and literally hundreds of on-going projects. In the 178-page annual report, the word fraud was mentioned 17 times in total. In all but one case, the context was to say how seriously the organization took fraud and how it recognized fraud or how important it was to report fraud. The report went on to say that risk analysis was continuously being done to assess the risk of fraud. Towards the end of the report, buried in a note, was the statement: 'In the financial year 2017, two frauds were dis-covered, the associate loss of which was less than £1000 in total.'

This example is quite typical of almost every organization which is required to describe risk or fraud risk in its annual reports. Fraud and corruption is rarely mentioned and, if it is, it is usually in the form of a disclaimer: 'to the best of our knowledge we do not believe that there have been any significant instances of fraud', etc., or as an obscure footnote.

Because of this inherent desire not to see fraud for what it is, there is a tendency to not want to see it, or to avoid mentioning it, because of its neg-ative connotations. So, although we know there is a lot of it around and most probably affects us too, putting it back on the agenda is no easy task. And given today's serious under-reporting of the risk, it is unlikely that many people are going to be pleased if suddenly the risk reports lurches from 'we don't think there is a major risk of fraud and corruption' to 'it is normal, and the impact is x per cent of our expenditure budget or revenue'.

Putting fraud and corruption back on the agenda

Once we can recognize the challenges, it is easier to bring the fraud and corruption words back in. The clue is to recognize that fraud and corruption is happening under our noses and, at the same time, see the challenges and obstacles that prevent us from seeing it. Here are some rules to help you do so:

- *Be realistic rather than naïve:* This is nicely summed up the Sherlock Holmes quote in the epigraph, which can be interpreted as: 'We understand how fraudsters think and how they act, in order to be able to predict what frauds are already happening to our organization, without actually becoming a fraudster.' At first, this might sound like a tall order, but as Professor Dan Arielly recognizes in his famous talk, 'The honest truth about dishonesty',[4] most honest people are able to cheat at times and find ways to discount (or rationalize or normalize) this, so they don't see it as cheating. So, all we need to do is tap into those reserves of energy that we all have. By recognizing the potential fraudster within us all, we are also taking steps to bring it under control, i.e. taking precautions that we will not become a fraudster ourselves.
- *Think laterally:* The second, and related, rule is to think outside of your own comfort zone, also known as thinking outside of the box or thinking laterally. Don't be constrained by what can't be done, but think what can be done[5] ('carpe diem' in Latin or seize the day). The TLAT method allows you to tap into that creative side which we all have, use our fantasy and not feel boxed in by either predefined beliefs or our circumstances.

Example 5.3 Fraud awareness

A fraud awareness workshop was held for a group of people working in the Finance Department in the head office of a multinational corporation. The participants were each asked to think, if they were dishonest and had an urgent need of cash, how they could defraud their own organization, but wanted to avoid being caught. Many of the participants found the task quite easy and came up with the seeds of rather simple and powerful methods. But one lady said she felt she was 'too honest' to even be able to think this way. When asked what her actual job was, she replied that she was responsible for executing payments, many of them in the region of tens of millions of dollars.

At the risk of sounding simplistic, I would like to kick off this chapter by stating the obvious. You won't understand how fraudsters think by being appealing to your fundamental belief that you are always 100 per cent honest. Somehow you must allow yourself to walk in the shoes of your enemy. Also we need to ask ourselves the question: what is the difference between the unthinkable and the unknowable?

Allow yourself to think the 'unthinkable', even if it means pushing yourself to imagine scenarios you would rather avoid

It is just human nature that we do not like to imagine the worst case because it is something we cannot bear to think about. To make it a bit easier to think the unthinkable, we can ask ourselves questions such as:

1   Would a well-paid, well-respected CEO commit fraud and corruption if they could find a way to do it and not get caught?
2   Would an external business partner or supplier like to make more money from their clients if they could, even if it meant the client paying a little bit more than they had to?
3   Would a respected doctor who already had a comfortable life, but feels he or she does not get the respect he or she deserves in society, start to put some of his or her most hypochondriac or unnecessarily depressed patients out of their misery (by humanely killing them), provided he or she did not get caught?

Most of us could answer yes to the first two questions. Certainly, not all but many people, at the top of their game, feel that they are worth it and often worth a bit more. Some of these people are willing to do whatever it takes to get more money even if this means doing something unethical. And for question 2, everybody 'in business' would say it's about maximizing your returns – it's just if you maximize them too much, especially in the short term, you can end up doing something unethical.

And, as discussed in Chapter 2, we can accept that almost everybody who does something which either before or after they see is unethical, will attempt to rationalize their actions. The excuses are: 'I was worth it'; 'this is business, not fraud; the price is whatever people can pay'.

But what about the answer to the third question? Along with judges, doctors occupy a place high up in society. In my own personal experience, my father was a consultant in the National Health Service, and prior to that worked in India, he was always talking about fraud in the health services: whether it was (in India) professors taking bribes for admissions (the reason he chose to leave India), or later on doctors and dentists who would either use public resources for private treatment, accept too much sponsorship from pharmaceutical companies or medical equipment suppliers and thereby were influenced, or just simply cheat on expenses. Doctors are, after all, human. But this is fraud and humans can commit fraud. But a doctor who deliberately kills his or her patients (in spite of taking the Hippocratic Oath) sounds more like a monster. One of the most powerful and concise, albeit macabre, examples is the case of Dr Harold Shipman (see Example 5.4),[6] as it illustrates both our unwillingness to think the unthinkable and (if we are not willing to think the unthinkable), our inability to notice the warning red flags. Just like most customers, suppliers, agents, consultants and employees are decent, basically honest people, the same can be said for doctors too. But there will always be potential rotten apples and we should not be naïve.

In the same way, one of the greatest obstacles to detecting fraud is that most relatively honest people find it difficult to believe that a colleague, manager or third party is dishonest – that is the nature of people. In a normal, safe and nurturing working environment, people do not want to believe that something terrible is happening – whether it is fraud or some other shocking event.

Example 5.4 A case of the unthinkable

No book on fraud and corruption would be complete without a horror story. The following true tale illustrates just how serious the consequences can be when red flags are overlooked.

In July 2002, an inquiry in England concluded that a doctor called Harold Shipman had murdered at least 215 of his elderly patients during routine home visits, by injecting them with lethal doses of drugs. He had carried out these activities over several years and, to the outside world, he appeared to be a nice, family man, and a respected doctor. The reality was that he was a killer. Today, the question continues to be asked why no one reacted to the tell-tale signs, including abnormally high death rates on his call-outs or exceptionally high order rates for certain drugs which were eventually used to murder his patients. The reason Dr Shipman managed to get away with it for so long was because the caring, honest people around him could never have imagined or believed that something so terrible was going on. As a result, nobody looked for the red flags.

Why was Shipman not discovered until he had killed hundreds of his patients? It was a classic case of blocking out the unthinkable and not accepting the truth that was staring us in the face. Shipman was a lone doctor seeing multiple patients who were often elderly and maybe a little fed up or suffering from something. He had lots of drugs which in certain quantities would be lethal. He had the perfect opportunity.

As for motivation, it was not money this time. Shipman had a comfortable enough life. However, he could simply have been bored, or felt that he was not respected enough. Whatever we speculate, he certainly had the motivation and as many experts who have analysed the case note, his overarching motivation was that he wanted to 'play God'. If we search the darkest deepest regions of our souls, who can say they would not also like the chance to play God from time to time (it's like the stranger on the bus, who says 'If I was in charge, I would . . .').

And as for Shipman's rationalization, he could have come up with a number of reasons including, 'they were not happy with their lives, so he helped them end it, humanely' or 'he was putting them out of their misery' or, stretching it a bit, he was saving the National Health Service money, in avoiding long and expensive treatment in the future. However ludicrous you may think his rationalizations were, the point is that he believed them.

The facts are that, whatever his motivation and reasons, a well-loved doctor killed over 200 of his patients, people who went to see him because they trusted him (and should have too). What happened was that collectively the system of recognition and detection failed. And this is what happens again and again with fraud and corruption. We often don't see it until it is too late. But if we can find a way to see it, to predict it, then we can learn to spot it. The key is to learn from Shipman and think the unthinkable.

To turn the tables on fraud and corruption, we need to be pre-emptive using two powerful techniques:

1   Stimulate people working in organizations to start to view their own organizations from the vantage point of a potential fraudster (using the menu in this chapter).
2   Follow the money and find fraud and corruption early (part of which is covered in Chapter 4 and will be explored further in Chapters 6 and 7).

It is often said that an outsider can see the organization more clearly. However knowledgeable internal people, who can free themselves from any biases, will see even more.

Recipe I The 'appetiser': preparing to be able to think like a thief and see fraud and corruption

I have called this recipe 'the appetiser' because you should think of it as a way of warming up a group of people in an organization to recognize that fraud and corruption happens and, despite even the most stringent controls and security measures, people who are motivated will always find a way. Think of Recipe 1 as a warm-up exercise which precedes the main event where people start to brainstorm which frauds are the most likely ones to happen in their organization. I would recommend that the typical time needed for this recipe is in the region of 15–45 minutes, depending on how much the participants wish to engage in the preparation.

Ingredients and tools

Before starting, you will need:

●   *A group of reasonably motivated people who work in the organization.* This can be a cross-section of people from one department, from across the whole organization, or also people working with one or two key processes in the organization. The key to the selection is that the people who are attending should feel that they 'know' the organization enough to be able to recognize (with some coaching) how it could be exploited. Where possible, ensure that diversity in gender, age and cultural identity is represented in the small cross-section. The people who know the organization best are the people who work there! The size of the group could vary from as few as eight to as many as 40, although the higher the number, the more time will be necessary.

- *An invitation to participate* tells the people that they are joining a fraud and corruption awareness session which is going to be different and where their participation is invaluable.
- *An airy room with a large whiteboard or flipchart.* The room should be set up with tables for four or five persons or cabaret-style, as is it is often described. Try to avoid people having laptop computers plugged in or phones on the desk, as it just creates unnecessary clutter and distractions. Ask them to turn their phones or pagers off.
- *Coloured pens* to draw on the whiteboard or flipchart.

One note of caution before starting: senior management should support the brainstorming session but not try to dominate it. Management can participate actively, but in small numbers, and at the same time they should encourage their staff to think critically and want them to see the iceberg below the tip. From the outset, they should foster the mind-set. 'We want to find fraud early and we want to be ahead of the game'. That would be the sort of message that management need to genuinely send.

Method

Open the brainstorming by telling the participants why they are there and what you are going to take them through. Tell them this is not a session about finding fraudsters among the staff, but today they are going to identify how external fraudsters can exploit and attack the organization. Depending on the room layout, make sure people are sitting close enough to be able to work in twos or threes. Let the audience know that quite soon we are going to run a 'think like a thief' session. And if some of the audience look a bit startled or worried, then reassure them that they will receive expert guidance and they are not going to become criminals.

Before launching into the TLAT exercise, you should spend 10–15 minutes warming the audience up or getting the audience into the zone. The aim is to dispel any illusions that fraud and corruption is not real and is not something almost everybody is involved in. This should be done using a short awareness session:

1   Define fraud and corruption for the purposes of this workshop as 'anything deliberate and unethical, done by anybody, inside or outside, which causes loss'. Define loss, for example, as the sum of 'loss of revenue and profits + damage to reputation and brand + erosion of the organizational cul-ture'.[7] You can ask for a show of hands by asking the question, 'Using this

definition, who here might have seen something which looks like fraud and corruption?'

2 Ask the audience what they believe is the total cost of fraud and corruption (repeating that you mean 'everything deliberate and unethical done by both insiders and outsiders'), giving them the model of an organization with sales of €1,000,000. Remind the audience that, by cost, you mean *all* costs, which include loss of money or value, damage to reputation and erosion of the organizational culture. Just give them the choices below and ask them to make their best intuitive guess at the total cost which can be quantified (writing up the categories on the whiteboard):

€0–€100,000
€100,000– €1 million
€1 million–€5 million
€5 million–€7 million
€7 million+[8]

3 Give the audience about 60 seconds to respond and then ask for a show of hands trying to go through this as quickly as possible but still ensuring that everyone does have an opinion and then write up the answers. The results almost always show from an intuitive exercise like this that people believe that the average costs of fraud and corruption is around 1–5 per cent of sales. If you like, feel free to make comparisons with relevant and current surveys and statistics which are constantly being updated but put the value in a similar ballpark.

4 Then ask the question: 'Who commits fraud and corruption?', starting with the factors as to why fraud and corruption can take place. Explain that there are three fundamental factors underpinning why fraud and corruption happens.[9] Tell them: 'You would never be able to do fraud if you had no opportunity. And you would never be able to do something deliberate and dishonest if you had no reason to and you absolutely were not motivated. And finally, you would only do something bad if you were able (maybe only after the fact) to justify to yourself at least your actions.' This third factor is known as 'rationalization' and was covered in more detail in Chapter 3.

5 Deal with opportunity first. Keeping in mind the true cost of fraud and corruption, which you have established, ask the question, 'Who has the greatest opportunity in money terms and per incident to commit fraud? Is it, in general, people near the top of an organization or is it people near

the bottom?' (Almost always, you will get the answer that it is people near the top but there should be some hands which believe it is people near the bottom.)

6   Then say that we are going to deal with motivation next. Ask the question, 'What do people with loads of money want most?' The most common answer is in fact 'more money'. Then you can comment, 'Big people, big frauds, smaller people, smaller frauds.'

7   The last part is asking the question, 'Who then are the criminals?' What we are trying to establish here is that most people in the room have the opportunity, have some greater or lesser degrees of motivation, and are typically able to rationalize their actions when they need to. However, this is quite a difficult and sensitive part of the warm-up process and needs to be practised in advance before trying it out on a live audience.

In order to emphasize that anybody, with the right opportunity, motivation and rationalization can commit fraud and corruption, do the following exercise. Ask everyone in the room to put their hands up and keep them raised. If they answer 'yes' to even one of the questions, then they should put their hands down. These are typical questions, although you can vary the nature and number of questions depending on the audience:

●   Who has at some time in their life written an amount which they believe is just a little too high on a personal insurance claim?

●   Have you ever, and please be as honest as you can, not declared all your income, even small amounts, for tax purposes?

●   Have you paid someone to do work for you, like a builder, electrician, cleaner or plumber, where you paid them in cash and you did it because it was simpler without an official invoice being submitted?

●   At some time in the last ten years have you avoided paying a bus or train fare?

●   Have you driven more than 20 km over the speed limit, noticed your own speedometer and then not 'done the right thing' and reported yourself to the nearest police station for dangerous driving?

Turn your back on your audience when asking the questions. Feel free to vary the questions. You can find additional questions in the format of an online game called 'How far can we bend the rules?' at www.fraudacademy.hibis.com. This exercise usually creates laughter in the audience as most people have lowered their hands after five questions. However, it is important to practise this, and at no time be judgemental, as it is most likely that you too fit into the category, 'I am also a fraudster'. The purpose of this exercise is so that you can finally say 'now we are ready to think like thieves' because we can now see that being a fraudster is just human nature.

Helpful hints and tips

Preparation and the warm-up exercises above require practice and you will improve your presentation and facilitation style with experience. Remember you are not holding a lecture as such. Keep your presentation and style always light, not flippant, but add some humour at times. Participants need to feel involved but also relaxed from the start. If you can get them interacting and talking very soon, then they will be much more generous with their ideas when they have to brainstorm and think like a thief in recipe 2.

Recipe 2 The main course: using the TLAT approach to make the invisible visible and recognize fraud and corruption

This recipe is the essence of thinking like a thief. It requires more time and sensitive handling of the participants. They now should be in a frame of mind where they recognize that fraud can happen and probably does happen in most organizations, they realize that the total cost of fraud and corruption is 'a substantial chunk of change' and they recognize that nearly everyone can be a fraudster. These are perfect conditions to stimulate them to start thinking like a thief.

Typically, around 45 minutes should be allocated to this stage, allowing you to develop a fairly diverse and relevant list of methods of fraud. However, the exercise can be longer, but it is very likely that in this case you keep it focused and write down all the methods.

Ingredients and tools

The tools and ingredients are essentially the same as for Recipe 1. In addition, each participant should have some sheets of paper and a pen. One person should be nominated (by the group) as a scribe, who can write down all the methods which are generated in freeform text. (Alternatively, and this works well in sessions with larger numbers of participants, have an assistant who will mainly focus on writing down the methods.)

Method

1   Tell your participants that you will be giving them an exercise which we call the 'five-minute fraud manager'. Write up on your whiteboard the following:

You can BE anybody you like outside or inside of your organization. Then, think of a fraud where you need to be able to get at least €10,000 from your organization, and not get caught. Ideally pretend you are an outsider who does it alone (although you could be an insider but ideally not you!). Look for the loopholes in the system, i.e. the opportunity. Be motivated and driven and think of a method where you will not be caught!

2   To be sure that everyone is following, repeat the instructions and explain that this exercise is about your own gut feeling, pushing the limits and putting yourself in the shoes of someone who is determined to commit fraud and corruption. Explain also that the best results come when you think of being someone who is highly motivated and has a big (in terms of money) opportunity. In the best situations, people are asked to make notes of their method so that they will remember it.

3   Ask the participants to think in complete silence for 2 minutes and then ask them to write down some bullets describing who they are and what they would do.

4   Then ask the participants to pick a partner in the room and tell their method to them (and vice versa). But give clear instructions that the person who is listening is only allowed to constructively criticize the method. It would be tempting to say something like 'this method would not work because . . .' because people like to trust in the defences rather than admitting how easy it is to be exploited. So, it's important to encourage the participants, for this exercise, to help each other improve or 'sharpen' their methods rather like a whetstone is used to sharpen a knife. It's fine to identify obstacles as to why a method might fail but then it's important to try to identify how to overcome or circumvent these obstacles.

5   The aim of the brainstorming and feedback sessions is to generate as many methods as possible. Encourage each pair to refine their methods and then jot them down in the refined form.

Presenting what you find

After around 20 minutes of this brainstorming, ask for feedback from the audience. Depending on time, ask each pair to present their two methods and then listen carefully. Ask them to present in, say, 30 seconds in the format 'I would be Mr X who is . . . and I would do this . . .'. It's important to listen to *all* methods without judgement. People should not say 'my method is the same as the person earlier' but should be encouraged to describe their method, focusing on the small differences and nuances. And it is important to write down all the methods. This recipe should be an 'ideas generator', allowing people to think creatively about how the organization can be defrauded. An experienced facilitator can often generate 30–40 methods in a one-hour session.

Helpful hints and tips

The TLAT workshop, as this is called, is a very powerful technique to help change the mind-set of a group from one of 'denial' or 'I don't believe we have fraud in my country or my organization' to one of openness to that fact that it probably is very likely. However, like Pandora's box, the results need to be contained. Below are some tips and advice based on the experience of running these sessions hundreds of times:

1   Do not be judgemental and try to foster a spirit where no one in the room is either overly critical of anyone else, inside or outside the room, or judgemental. The idea is to 'enjoy' thinking like a thief.

2   The value does not need to be €10,000. It can also be more (or less) but try to pick a number which is not trivial.

3   Sometimes people when they think about a method, want to tell you instead, in the third person about something that already happened, which others in the room know about. You want to avoid this. You should try to remind the person that you have asked them to put themselves in the shoes of someone on the outside or inside who will commit fraud and then describe it using the 'I' pronoun. For example, 'I would be a supplier and I would invoice for services and add a 20 per cent mark-up which would not be noticed, because I would be the supplier on Project X which has such a high budget that the project manager, Mr Y is not looking at the costs in detail but just signing off based on reasonableness.'

4   If someone says, 'Will I become a criminal?' or tries to say that this method is dangerous, you can easily counteract this by saying that the real criminals are several steps ahead and all we are doing here is catching up.

5   Try, when listening to people's methods, to help them 'build' the method. Your role is that of a facilitator where you want to get the best (or in

this case the 'worst'!) out of people. So, if someone has a method which is 'half-baked', try to help them develop it by asking questions, or even allowing another participant to help them develop it. You can always say that 'Fraud was not invented in a day. What you are looking for are the seeds of an idea.'

6   Quite often there are people in the audience who wish to talk about possible frauds that they have seen but never reported and, when talking about their method, use the feedback session to point fingers at parties or people. This should be avoided. Say you are looking for methods and stories without reference to specific parties and people at this stage. However, do say that you can talk with them later. It is important that you do genuinely set aside time for this if needed.

Sometimes people get stuck and say they are unable to think of a method. It is usually obvious which people don't wish to speak. I have found that they typically fall into three categories:

1   People who simply feel they are too honest to be able to commit fraud. In this case, you need to first commend them for their honesty, and then ask them the question: 'If you had access to huge sums of money but were too honest to misuse them, what would others have to do to you to coerce you into doing something dishonest?'[10]

2   Senior management who feel that, for one reason or another, that fraud does not happen in *their* organization. Maybe it's because they have had so few incidents, maybe it's because they have had clean external audit reports for years and believe that external auditors find fraud, or maybe it's because the system of compliance, risk management, audits and policies has made them believe that fraud cannot happen, or maybe they are just idiots. Who knows? One way is to give them the 'dishonest chair scenario' described in Example 5.5.

3   People who are already involved in something and who are feeling uncomfortable. This is quite a difficult category to handle and needs to be done very sensitively. See Example 5.6.

Holding a TLAT workshop requires some experience and it needs to be handled sensitively because situations as in Example 5.6 can easily arise. In other cases, people who have wanted to speak up but for one reason or another have not done so, can tend to talk about real events. In all cases, the situations need to be managed in a calm and collected way.

Example 5.5 If there was a dishonest person in your chair?

In one TLAT session for a senior management team of a large IT company, the nine managers sat around a table smiling confidently. The methods that they came back with were almost the same. They felt that they had very good controls and procedures but felt that some of their employees, who were travelling a lot, could cheat on their expenses. There was no talk about senior managers working in collusion with suppliers, individual client account managers overbilling their customer for services that they did not really require, or similar major fraud. At this point it became apparent that this senior management team believed that the company had no fraud, or very little, because they saw themselves as 'good' people.

Each one was then asked the question, 'If there was a dishonest person in your chair, what could he or she do?'. Going around the table it was as if the floodgates had opened and method after the method simply poured out.

Example 5.6 Hard-pressed to think of anything, or . . . ?

At one session, with around 25 people from a local authority participating, one gentleman did not engage with a partner, when asked to think like a thief. When it came to the feedback session, with arms folded, he said he could not think of anything. A little curious, I asked him what his job was, and he said he was responsible for purchasing PCs and other IT equipment for the whole of the organization (an organization where over 10,000 people worked). However, I felt even though it seemed strange that he could not think of a method, it felt more appropriate to politely accept that he did not want to contribute at this stage and move on to the next person but I made a mental note that it could be interesting to speak to him on a one-to-one basis later.

This was not necessary because, at the end of the workshop, the gentleman approached me to say he felt very uncomfortable as he himself was the joint owner of a company which sold computer equipment, which was run by his brother, and he knew that this company had been a sub-supplier to one of the local authorities' major suppliers of PCs. In other words, during the seminar it had dawned on him that he was probably involved in some sort of fraud or conflict of interest and had simply not realized it until now.

These workshops are a very powerful way to both recognize fraud and corruption, discover where it is likely to happen, and crystallize the methods into a fraud and corruption profile (as per the final recipe in this chapter). However, it needs proper preparation and some experience to do it well.

Recipe 3 The dessert trolley: how to start developing a realistic profile of where fraud and corruption is happening

The aim of this recipe is to produce a first draft of a fraud and corruption profile for your organization. By a fraud and corruption profile, what we mean is a sort of dynamic map of all the methods, which are ranked according to a combination of how likely each method is and what the impact of each method is. This recipe builds on the work done in Recipes 1 and 2 and takes into consideration the methods generated at the end of method 2. What we do here is to generate more methods in a systematic way, most likely those which are the most relevant to this particular organization. The typical time needed to generate and document the methods as well as do an initial ranking would be around 1½–2½ hours where most of the time the participants would be working in groups. After this, the synthesis and evaluation, which are done in a smaller group, can take a few hours.

Ingredients and tools

The same participants from the workshop in Recipes 1 and 2 above, but now working in groups of approximately four around a table. Pens and paper and put a simple form on each table showing Figures 5.1 and 5.2. Figure 5.2 can be photocopied as many times as necessary. The form is deliberately simple. Each group should also have the hand-written notes of different methods that they generated in Recipe 2.

Fraud and corruption risk brainstorming using the TLAT methodology

What do we value in our organization?   Who are the potential fraudsters?

_____   _____
_____   _____
_____   _____

etc.   etc.

Figure 5.1 Capturing the results from a think like a thief brainstorming session: a suggested template

Method of fraud and corruption	Likelihood		Impact		
	Vulnerability	Frequency	Profits/Value	Reputation	Culture

Figure 5.2 Assessing the likelihood and impact of fraud and corruption: a suggested template

Method

Explain to the participants that now for 45 minutes or so they are going to repeat Recipe 2 but in a structured way to generate as many realistic methods of fraud and corruption as possible. What you would like them to do is:

1   Nominate one person as the group's scribe, preferably someone with legible handwriting.
2   Think of all the things that they feel are of value in their organization (or if they prefer they can think of 'assets' in the widest sense). This could include everything from 'money' to 'a nice organizational culture'. Try to come up with at least 10 completely different types of value in just 5 minutes of brainstorming. Write this list on Figure 5.1.
3   Then spend 5 minutes thinking of all the different groups of people (from professional criminals to dishonest management!), the 'opponents', who could defraud or harm your organization in an unethical way (for their benefit). Once again, use just 5 minutes on this and try to come up with a list of around 8–10 different opponents. Then brainstorm as many methods as possible where people can do something unethical which causes harm to something of value in your organization. Write them down on Figure 5.1.
4   Try to generate at least 10 methods in 30 minutes and write a few lines about each method in the left-hand side of Figure 5.2.
5   Once you have generated at least 10 different methods, then write H (for 'High'), M (for 'Medium') and L (for 'Low') in any of the boxes on the right

next to a method in Figure 5.2. The heading should be self-explanatory, but you may want to point out that the reason that Likelihood is divided into 'Vulnerability' and 'Frequency' is that 'Vulnerability' measures your feeling as to how possible it is to commit this method, whereas 'Frequency' measures your feeling as to how often you think it happens.

6   Before starting, remind participants that they should not get stuck in lengthy discussions. The atmosphere should be one of 'anything goes' and 'nothing is a stupid idea'. And ensure that the groups write things down.

Serving suggestion

At the end of 45 minutes, participants should have done enough. Say, pens down, ask if it is OK to collect the forms and give the participants a well-deserved break. Read the forms and select (ensuring that each group is recognized) some 'highlights' such as some particularly interesting types of value and 'opponents', as well as some particularly interesting methods. Feed this back to the participants, thank them very much for their time and ask them for some feedback and comment on the workshop.

If it is appropriate, do also explain to the participants that they will be getting more feedback in different ways, but for now their creative energy and output are going to be reviewed and synthesized.

Useful tips

One typical question from this sort of session is 'what happens next?' You can answer this by saying that now you (and a small group) will review the results and see if any really obvious methods which are important have been missed. Usually because our organization is rather unique (as all organizations are), then it is likely that 90–95 per cent of the most important methods have already been captured in this workshop. Synthesizing the results of the raw brainstorming into a fraud and corruption profile of the organization with the most serious frauds at the top, is something which is done afterwards. Under the right circumstances, I believe that this profile can be shared with the participants of such a brainstorming session but one also has to consider confidentiality.

Sometimes in the brainstorming, participants get stuck or hung up on particular issues. Keep reminding them that this is a free-thinking brainstorming, and that they should not get obsessed with details and technicalities. Often the simplest methods work best.

Afterwards: synthesizing the results of the structured brainstorming into a unique first draft fraud and corruption profile

Let's assume that you have run a successful and interesting workshop using Recipes 1, 2 and 3 in that order. The participants have generated lots of ideas, especially during the second and third courses and provided you with a lot of very useful input to help you prepare 'a first cut', or first picture of the major methods of fraud and corruption which will affect their organization. While you can be sure that not every significant method will have been covered or even addressed as yet, what you should be pleased with is that the methods generated are those which are really applicable to that organization, and are recognized by people working inside as things which could really happen. In other words, what you will be developing will be a living document which is unique to their organization.

Immediately after the participants have departed, ensure that you have collected all the output, including any views on fraud and corruption which came out of the 'appetiser' session, methods of fraud and corruption which came out of the TLAT exercise in the second course, and the completed forms which were distributed in the group exercise, which was course number 3. At this stage it is not crucial who said what, just that it was said and was recorded. Make your own short reflective notes and then, ideally, take a break, which could be a few hours or even a few days. This break is very important as it gives the mind time to think and reflect on all the information you have absorbed during the workshop. When you do return to the material, in order to synthesize it, be aware that your goal is to create a single, balanced and harmonized fraud and corruption profile of the organization.

The five steps you need to go through (either alone or in a small group of two or three persons) are as follows:

1   Review all the methods which have been described (at any stage in the workshop) and try to distil from them between 20 and 40 unique methods which are still very much related to your organization or the organization which you are helping to do a fraud and corruption risk assessment on, but make sure that they do not implicate individuals or named departments as far as possible.

2   Based on the material you have collected (including also the methods), create two distinct lists, in order of importance if you prefer, spelling out what is of most value to the organization and who are the parties and people which could commit fraud against the organization.

3   Sit back and review the methods in the context of the lists of what is of value and who can be the potential opponents. Think of *your* organization. Then ask yourself the question: 'What are the most obvious things that are missed?' There will almost always be one or two things which have been probably addressed in passing but not described explicitly. Feel free to write these methods down and. if appropriate, add them to the list of methods.

4   Using the participants' own rankings of 'Likelihood' and 'Impact', try to come up with something which represents an informed gut feeling for each method. Table 5.2 is just a guide. The most important thing you need to do is be consistent in your thinking and application of the categories High, Medium and Low (as the participants were asked to do in Recipe 3).

Table 5.2 Ranking of the measures

Measure	What the measure means	Ranking (High' (5), 'Medium' (3) and 'Low' (1)
Likelihood	Vulnerability	How possible is the method?
	Frequency	How often do you think it is going to happen?
Impact	Value (or profits)	In relation to the organization, how bad would it be if the method happened once? What would be the impact on profits or value?
	Reputation	In relation to the organization, if the method succeeded just once, what would the reputational impact be like?
	Organizational culture	If the method happened just once, what would the impact be on the organizational culture (including, for example, trust among employees and colleagues)?

5   Once you have allocated 'H', 'M' and 'L' to each of your methods, you are then in a position to do a basic ranking. The purpose of the ranking is to identify those methods which are highly significant, i.e. they are real and could have a very high impact, or they are real but have a low impact but happen all the time, or some combination of the two. A simple but effective way to do this is to use a formula where you allocate the numbers 5 to 'High', 3 to 'Medium' and 1 to 'Low' which corresponds to the

likelihood and impact factors, thereby creating a Fraud Risk Factor for each method as follows:

The Fraud Risk Factor = (Vulnerability + Frequency) multiplied by (Value + Reputation + Culture)

6   Then re-order your table of methods in *descending* order of Fraud Risk Factor.

In this very simple but effective way you have started to create a realistic and actual profile of the fraud and corruption which is affecting the organization today or is most likely to affect it soon. You will have created a first draft which will be subject to a lot of debate and refinement as well as being challenged. However, you can always use the argument that the methods were developed and recognized by people inside the organization and have not been conjured out of thin air or applied theoretically.

Once the Fraud and Corruption Profile has been accepted as a snapshot of the major fraud and corruption threats facing the organization, then it can be used to focus on the most important fraud and corruption methods in awareness training and swift and effective action can be taken to close loopholes.

Example 5.7 Closing the gap immediately

In one session with a major treasury department of a financial institution, one of the top methods identified showed that the back-up payments solution, should there be a system failure, was highly vulnerable to attack because nobody had identified that anyone, including outsiders, could send payment instructions if they had just a little extra knowledge from the inside. Once the method was recognized in the workshop, the CEO insisted that immediate action was taken to remove the gaping loophole.

Your Fraud and Corruption Profile is a unique and living document which will need to be continuously updated and improved. The overriding principle should be to keep it simple. But you should not care or even enter into a discussion as to whether a particular fraud risk has a factor of 42.13 or 43.62. The key is whether a method has been recognized at all. Dissemination of the Fraud and Corruption Profile is something which needs to be discussed internally.

On the one hand, it should be an open document as it helps employees provide feedback on which methods are occurring, and also which methods may have been omitted. On the other hand, the ranking itself can lead to the organization being held liable for recognizing the risks but not taking sufficient action to mitigate them.

Finally, be aware that people will see the whole fraud and corruption profiling exercise as 'a fun day out' and part of a training course. If that happens, then there is always the challenge that people will go back to their organization after being on a training course to try to implement what they have learned but may be disappointed. To avoid having to prepare participants for this disappointment:

- Ensure that the senior management team are involved and participate in the workshops.
- Present the result in an authoritative manner and include in the workshops real examples from the organization, or make sure that they are identified and documented during the workshop, and followed through afterwards.

In this way, people will appreciate the validity of the exercise.

Notes

1 Fraud is entrenched. As Professor Peter Jackson, one of my esteemed reviewers and mentors in the academic world remarked, Jacob Marley, who was Ebenezer Scrooge's deceased business partner in Charles Dickens' novel, *A Christmas Carol*, adopted practices which ensured that he would not be defrauded but made other people's lives a total misery! Marley was so greedy that in the novel he appears as a tormented ghost who succeeds in changing the life of his former partner Scrooge, by offering him a path to redemption.

2 Quoted with the permission of Michael J. Comer, practitioner and author of several practical books about fraud and how to investigate it.

3 In a seminar about the financial crash of Iceland in 2008, Professor Vilhaljmur Arnasson, who was commissioned by the Icelandic government to write a report into the human reasons for the crash, commented that while there may have only been a few instigators, there were comparatively many people who saw the signals but chose, for one reason or another, to do nothing. I remember distinctly the catch phrase from this illuminating session being 'the worst people are the good people who do nothing'.

4 See Dan Arielly's 'The honest truth about dishonesty' on www.youtube.com/watch?v=XBmJay_qdNc&t=39s

5 When I was 9 years old, I was selected (most probably at random) with other kids to appear on one of presenter Gordon Burn's first editions of the TV programme *Granada Reports*, with Edward de Bono, the man who coined the phrase 'lateral thinking', which is also known as 'structured creativity'. I remember very little of that evening other than that I was terrible at it and managed to break a lot of eggs in one of the exercises, so much so that it was shown as one of the 'embarrassing moments on TV' on New Year's Eve that year. But what did stick was de Bono talking about lateral thinking and thinking outside of the box and how it's important to think creatively and generate ideas. I am reminded of that evening each time we run TLAT workshops, thinking of how narrow-minded I was as a child (and probably still can be today).

6 For Harold Shipman, see the article in *The Independent*, 26 April 2018. Available at: www.independent.co.uk/news/uk/crime/harold-shipman-doctor-death-serial-killer-gp-mass-murderer-hyde-manchester-itv-documentary-a8323176.html

7 If profits is not a commonly used terms in the organization, one could instead use a similarly appropriate measure such as increased costs, loss of pure financial value, etc.

8 The currency, amounts, and ranges used here are purely arbitrary. But it helps to use numbers which recognizably translate into percentages.

9 As per Donald Cressey's three factors, 'opportunity, motivation and rationalization' as described in Chapter 2.

10 In one particular case, the honest lady who could not think of any methods was working in the 'cash payment' department with millions of dollars per week passing though her function. After just a few seconds, she responded to the question of how someone could get her to behave dishonestly: 'If someone had kidnapped my two beautiful children and there was no other way to get them back other than transfer the money, then I could do it with no hesitation, but I would still be afraid of being caught.'

Chapter 6

Seven classic recipes to discover fraud and corruption

It is the brain, the little grey cells on which one must rely. One must seek the truth within – not without.

(Hercule Poirot, in the ITV series, *Poirot*)

Introduction to the seven recipes

A seasoned chef tends to rely primarily on their experience, creativity and intuition, using recipes for inspiration and guidance. A first-time cook, with aspirations, may at first stick closer to the recipe, but will expand their horizons and develop their own personal brand of variations on a theme, as their experience grows. Either way, a recipe is important as it provides a tried and tested framework.

I find comparing culinary recipes to recipes to find fraud is quite an appropriate analogy. A recipe can be broken down into the following five steps: (1) what inspired the recipe and what makes it special; (2) which ingredients do we need?; (3) how do we do it? (i.e. the method itself); (4) serving suggestions (i.e., how do we present what we have produced?); and (5) useful tips.

Preparing a delicious meal is not just about having the latest equipment, very exclusive ingredients or following a recipe like a robot. A good cook can make a decent meal in most circumstances, without too many fancy tools or ingredients at their disposal. It's also about having passion, thinking on your feet and using your own ingenuity and creativity. Of course, a well-written and instructive recipe book provides confidence, inspiration, guidance and, not least, some basic rules of thumb. The same can be said for the fraud detective. You don't need lots of fancy tools and complicated instructions to find fraud. If Agatha Christie had been alive today, her enigmatic Mr Poirot might have interjected at this point, 'If we told people the brain was an "app", people might start to use it again.'

This chapter describes seven recipes which can be used to find commercial fraud and corruption, how they are structured, what they do for you, some examples and some tips on what to avoid.

How to use these recipes

Finding examples of where an organization is being defrauded or being involved in something undesirable or unethical sounds like a daunting prospect. But it can be broken down into a series of steps. Finding the red flags of possible fraud and corruption, understanding and interpreting them to recognize those which are critical, and then deciding how to resolve them pragmatically and effectively should not be confused with the business of complex fraud investigations. Traditional, or 'old school', as I would describe them, fraud investigations tend to be complex, long-drawn-out affairs and involve teams, if not armies of specialists, lawyers and accountants, which, if you are not careful, tend to multiply. They result in legal battles and often divert vast amounts of precious time and money from much more important activities. The 'Find Fraud Before it Finds You' or 'B4' method,[1] on which this chapter and the book are based is an attempt to define a new, more effective way of looking at fraud and corruption in the workplace.

The most rewarding experiences after teaching these recipes in fraud detective courses are not the immediate feedback from the participants. Most people enjoy being detectives in the classroom. Because putting the skills into practice is much harder, the most rewarding response is when someone tries a recipe and succeeds. There are numerous examples of this like the story in Example 6.1.

Combined with structured brainstorming, discussed in Chapter 5, these simple recipes should be seen as the building blocks to find the seven basic plots of fraud. More advanced ways of finding fraud are introduced in Chapter 7.

Example 6.1 Putting knowledge into practice

After completing a fraud detective training workshop, participants from the Finance Department of a European Parliament immediately used simple but effective recipes to identify consultants who were abusing their position and circumventing procedures to influence purchases of services from companies related to them. Due to, among other things, mistakes made in the tendering processes and the number of jurisdictions involved, any form of legal action against the consultants would probably have been long-winded and would have cost possibly more than what could have been recovered through the courts. However, the Head of Finance adopted the more practical and, in this case, sensible approach of recovering the money first and then issuing a warning to the persons involved (who got the message, and a strong reprimand).

It's good to know what you are looking for but always keep an open mind to what you may find

In Part 1, fraud and corruption was divided, somewhat artificially, of course, into seven recognizable categories covering abuse of the organization by suppliers, customers, consultants and middlemen, and employees, as well as instances of bribery, false reporting and, of course, dirty money. The idea was to demonstrate that while fraud and corruption could, on one hand, be described as complex (making it hard to deal with for normal people), it can also be categorized into simple recognizable 'types' or 'plots'. These are not definitive and are just one way of representing fraud and corruption. However, the main point to be made is that it is better to simplify rather than over-complicate.

In Chapter 2, it was also emphasized that the categories would quite often overlap, for example, an instance where a supplier was able to overcharge quite grossly could also involve the coercion or bribery of an employee, or the supplier lying as to who they really are, and possibly having a connection to a front company. Similarly, a customer who demanded and received rebates far above what was allowed, which were paid into an account which was not their primary account, could also be involved in taking bribes, accumulating money in a front company or a bank account connected to a DMC. In addition, an example such as this could also involve the salesmen recording the sales figures as sales, but somehow hoodwinking the accountants by posting the rebates to a separate cost account, thus ensuring that sales were inflated, and if their salary was based partly on profits and sales. This would also ensure that they received a higher commission than they deserved. So, while the primary target of a recipe may be one fraud, it is possible and quite likely that other related types of fraud will be discovered by the same recipe.

The secret of using recipes such as the ones below is to use the simple categorization of seven basic plots of fraud and corruption as a navigator to analyse what you find, as represented in Figure 6.1, and keep an open mind as to what you may find. The basic Wheel of (mis)Fortune is repeated throughout this chapter with red flags placed in different sectors to emphasize which area of fraud to concentrate on.

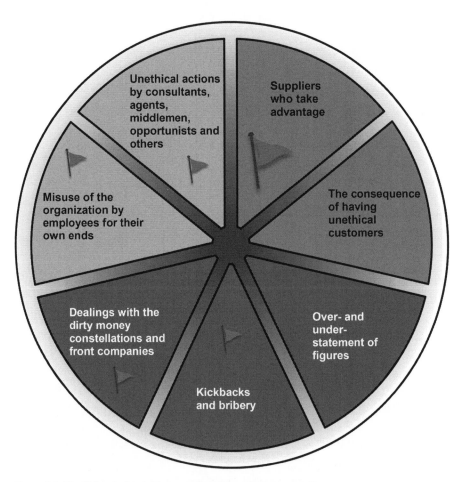

Figure 6.1 The Wheel of (mis)Fortune: focusing mainly on suppliers

Example 6.2 Attention to detail

A multinational company had established a subsidiary in the Ukraine for sales of its chemicals and agricultural products. These were shipped in from the western European manufacturing plants and sold. For a short while the business appeared profitable but then the bad debts began to mount, sales revenues did not materialize, and costs were rising. The head office decided after two years to cut their losses, after consulting with their local legal advisor, Mr B, a Russian, based close to the border with the Ukraine. After the process of liquidation was almost complete, a former finance manager of the company pointed out that in fact the company had been very profitable, but that the assets of the company and its customers had been 'legally' transferred to a new shell company, where Mr B and the former local managing directors were owners. After a short investigation, it was found that this was exactly what had happened. The subsidiary which the multinational company thought they owned had been, to all intents and purposes, stolen from them, was trading under a similar name, and all the multinational owners were left with was an empty shell.

Instances such as this (referred to as Reiderstvo or 'asset grabbing'[2]) appear to be quite common in certain parts of the world. One could say that these are quite difficult both to discover and to do something about as the people behind these schemes are usually very professional. However, in this example, if the invoices from Mr B had been scrutinized more closely over the three years he had been submitting them, it would have been noticed that he was invoicing alternately through a Liechtenstein and Luxemburg company and using a variety of different bank accounts in London and Frankfurt. Just this alone, if it had been recognized as a red flag, could have given rise to additional scrutiny.

Simple tests done thoroughly can often uncover a much more complex and intricate scheme than first meets the eye. In Example 6.2, had the red flags related to Mr B's invoices been spotted earlier, this could have led to some more discreet enquiries as to who he was, and what sort of organizations he was involved in. Instead because it was assumed that he must be a bona fide individual, nobody questioned his actions and authority until it was too late.

The seven recipes are in a sense quite pure and simple, as essentially all of them are a variant on the fraud detective's mantra, 'follow the money'. They

Example 6.3 Don´t jump the gun

It seemed like the internal team had found the perfect fraud. A temporary Chief Financial Officer, who was on hire for two years as a consultant, was found to be invoicing through two companies at the same time for the same work. One of the companies was in Sweden and the other was in Spain, in parallel for the same expensive services. Worse still, the Spanish company was in liquidation, so it was very unclear where the money was going. The team approached the managing director showing the two, scrappy-looking invoices. The managing director's first reaction was 'Which idiot signed off on these?', to which the team had to reply, 'You did.' He did not take this comment well, and, while not being involved in any fraud directly, was less eager to investigate the temporary CFO, as he might lose face.

don't require extensive studies of behaviour, body language or human psychology, nor do we need huge data sets and expensive external databases.

Recipe 1 is longer than the other six recipes. Part of the reason for this is that it covers money flows out of an organization which often are one of the most obvious targets for fraudsters. There is also a lot of cross-over between the types of fraud described in each of the recipes. The final reason is that, as has been stated before, fraud detection skills, once learnt, are highly transferable to all types of fraud and corruption, and also the other six recipes. It makes sense to study Recipe 1 in detail first before reading any of the others.

General advice on following through

Each recipe has specific tips and suggestions as to how to follow through on what you find. However, it is worthwhile providing some general pointers before we start:

- These recipes are well tried and tested and are designed to avoid false positives[3] as much as possible, but don't jump to rash conclusions when you see something.
- Similarly, even if you are right and can prove everything, do not rush in (only fools rush in). You could be stepping on a landmine.
- Avoid jumping to conclusions. Keep an open mind as to what things may eventually turn out to be.

- Consider each example from a 'best-case/worst-case' perspective (as described in Chapter 9).
- Don't rush to interview potential suspects every time you find something 'interesting'. You could be spending a lot of time, disrupting the organization constantly. Interviewing is an art.

Recipe 1 Spotting suppliers that take you and your organization for a ride

One of the most common ways, although maybe not the most expensive, of losing money is to be cheated by a supplier. A somewhat limited and erroneous name for this is 'purchasing fraud'.[4] There are many types of suppliers, ranging from suppliers of goods and materials, an entire range of services including financial services and consultancy, licences and property. Whatever type of supplier they are, the one inescapable fact is that most of the time they are generally keen to sell as much as possible, and usually the people who work there are under some pressure to sell. Selling is not a sin, but *overselling*, overcharging, not delivering what is promised, bribing an insider to get a contract, are all things we would prefer not to happen because usually we end up paying too much for something which is not worth it. Not all suppliers will behave in this way, in fact, if we are a well-managed organization, only a few troublesome suppliers will be greedy because they realize that if they are caught, then this could affect their future sales and possible even their existence. The idea behind this recipe is to highlight those suppliers who should be examined more closely.

You can be cheated by a supplier in a multitude of ways, from simple to complex, including being hoodwinked or overcharged or by receiving substandard goods and services, right through to complex schemes involving collusion with employees and/or coercion and bribery.

This recipe attempts to shine a light on some of the most common examples where a small proportion of suppliers are behaving unethically and, in some manner, or another cheating you and your organization. You should not be fooled by this recipe's apparent simplicity. Simple methods often work best. The results, time and time again, have proven to be very telling.

Ingredients and tools

Before starting out, you should have access to the following:

- Information about suppliers (usually held on something called the 'supplier master file') which contains their names, information as to where they are located, which country, the telephone number and email address, and when (the date) the supplier was first registered as a supplier.

● Information showing transactions with suppliers (such as invoices and credit notes from the supplier), ideally in an electronic form showing, *as a minimum,* for each supplier the following information: the date the invoice was raised, the amount of an invoice, the supplier's own invoice or reference number. Typically, you should try to obtain enough transactional data covering at least the past 12–18 months.

Method

Advance preparation

Start by putting your transactional data and limited master data into an Excel spreadsheet as shown in Table 6.1. The data that you have access to will vary a little, depending on your situation or circumstances. However, the rule is not to have too many fields and also to try to extract the data you need from the accounting system using a commonly used report or file generator which is usually built into the accounting system itself. Further tips on how to extract data are discussed in Chapter 5.

Once you have the data in a suitably analysable form, you are then able to start sorting the data to look for patterns which will allow you to highlight and pick out the rotten apples, identifying those suppliers who are displaying signs of greed. While there are several tests you can do, here are the three very basic steps which, if performed consistently, can be quite effective.

Table 6.1 Sample supplier master list

Supplier name	Currency	Amount	Date	Invoice Number*	Address	Email
Supplier X	GBP	51,725	27.09.XX	123	3 Acacia Avenue, Colchester, England	info@supplierx. co.uk
Supplier Y	USD	−125,345	03.10:XX	X.789	Milton House, Park View, Washington, DC, USA	
Supplier Z	EUR	100,000	09.11.XX	20XX.983	Bahnhofstrasse 17, Frankfurt, Germany	Frank2567@ gmail.com

Note: This is the invoice number provided by the supplier

Step 1 Looking for signs of supplier dependency

Begin by looking for suppliers who could be quite dependent on your organization for their survival. One of the typical fields which can indicate this is the supplier's own invoice number, a piece of information which is unique to a supplier. If the invoice numbers over a period of a few months for Supplier X in Table 6.1, are, for example running in the sequence 123, 124, 129, 130, 132, then you could deduce that given that there are few gaps, that this supplier is to some extent quite reliant on your organization and not working for anybody else. This can be done by simply sorting the data according to the supplier name plus the Invoice Number and using colours to highlight the most interesting patterns you observe.

Step 2 Rooting out possible supplier 'complacency'

Continue by identifying those suppliers where the invoice amounts from particular suppliers are quite regularly 'large and round'. If this happens many times for a particular supplier, there is a good chance that the services or goods that this invoice is representing will be specified vaguely in some way, and not given in detail.

How we define a large and round amount will vary depending on the currency of the invoice, of course, but typically, at least in the currencies shown in Table 6.1, three trailing zeros is an indicator.[5] If the data are sorted by supplier name and invoice date, it will be easy to pick out and highlight significant round amounts by eye by scrolling through the data. If there are too many transactions to scroll through, then you could consider using the following formula (written in Excel or a similar or more advanced tool to select the round amounts).

It is a round amount if: the integer value (INT) of the amount divided by 1000, multiplied again by 1000 equals the original amount.

For example, 51,725 divided by 1000 equals 51.725. The integer value of 51.725 is 51 (because all the numbers after the decimal place are ignored). This value, i.e. 51, multiplied by 1000 equals 51,000, which is NOT equal to 51.725. So, by definition, 51,725 is not a round amount. However, if we applied this same formula to the number 100,000, it would prove that the integer value of 100,000/1000, multiplied again by 1000, was in fact 100,000 (i.e. demonstrating that 100,000 is, in fact, a round sum).

Step 3 Indications of inconsistency or abnormality

Sort the data by supplier name and then invoice date. Then scan the data (you can do this either by eye or by writing a small routine) to identify suppliers and patterns where there were striking and unusual inconsistences related to the dates. For example, you should be looking for instances where there are many invoices from the same supplier on the same day. This could indicate that this supplier is rather happy to send you lots of invoices (easy to manage for them but more difficult for you to control). You could highlight patterns where, for the same supplier, invoice numbers are out of sequence, for example, invoice number 123 on 04.07.XX and invoice number 111 on 26.09.XX. Other things to look out for could also be if there appears to be more than one invoice number series for the same supplier.

After performing steps 1, 2, and 3, you should then sift out those suppliers (for example, the 'top 20') which are of high value (if you like, you can do this right at the start too) and where you feel that at least one or more of the criteria in steps 1, 2 and 3 have been met. Sometimes multiple indicators can be a stronger indicator, but this is not always the case.

The three steps above should be all you need to put your finger on where a lot of potential supplier-related fraud can be found. Be aware that at this point there will be some exceptions, also known as 'false positives', which will eventually turn out to be fine. This is a natural consequence and you should not be concerned but do not discard them yet from your selection.

If you like, at this stage, you can perform a few additional small steps to refine your selection such as:

- Looking to see if billings from suppliers in your top 20 list appear to be increasing or decreasing over time, and how they are increasing. For example, a pattern of exponential growth in their billings, something which often can be unhealthy (for you), could indicate that the supplier is taking control.
- Checking if the supplier has suddenly just been taken in (or registered) as a new supplier which has just popped up on your organization's radar and has immediately started billing you with gusto.
- Examining if there are occasional credit notes from the supplier. Often when a supplier pays money back, it is seen as a good thing and can be a volume discount but it could also indicate that there was some problem. Most typically, credit notes which are round sums can indicate that there was a dispute which was smoothed over, in the supplier's favour.

Once you have reduced your selection down to only the most interesting ones, the next step would be to perform some basic 'litmus' tests:

1   Google them to find out who they are (i.e. what footprint do they have on the internet?, does the supplier have a registered sales figure?, what sort

of premises do they seem to be registered at?, is what does the supplier says about themselves inconsistent with what they are doing for you?, etc.).

2   Review some sample documentation, such as invoices or credit notes for the supplier you have selected. Decide whether these strengthen or weaken your suspicions.

Finally summarize all the inconsistencies for all the suppliers you now are suspicious about. And remember, finding fraud, unlike baking, is not a precise science. Allow yourself a little 'gut feeling'. As you become increasingly experienced and proficient at doing this, you will also become more confident in trusting your instincts.

Classify the suppliers which are both significant and have the most inconsistencies and start to ask yourself (or brainstorm with yourself[6] or a colleague) the big question. What are the best- and worst-case scenarios? Do not jump to any conclusions but give yourself space and time to reflect on what you found might be. Once you are sure that something could be wrong, then start to examine the worst examples in a little more detail but looking at more source documentation, such as invoices and credit notes, look at the invoicing patterns in more detail and do a little more careful internet research.

How to present what you find ('serving suggestion')

You should always be careful in how you present what you find. It is still the case today that management are not used to having possible fraud and corruption served up on a plate. Typically, fraud and corruption is discovered by a whistleblower, disgruntled persons, tip-offs, by accident or because of a storm in the media. One of the original 'gurus' of fraud investigators, in the 1970s, Mike Comer wrote in his book, *Corporate Fraud*,[7] 'People will believe things more easily if it is whispered through a crack in the door.' What I believe Mike was trying to say was that if you, a normal person in a company, do what no one is expecting and find fraud in a calm and collected manner, using structured analysis, the irony is that people are not going to believe you easily. Therefore, lay all claims to brilliance aside and serve up the valuable fruits of your labours in a factual but modest and not judgemental style. This will help ensure that you at least receive a warmer reception.

Finding fraud is relatively easy, proving it to others who do not want to see it can be a long haul. Therefore, as with all of the 'serving suggestions' for these recipes, you should present the facts plainly and logically and let them speak for themselves. This is one sort of recipe where garnish is unnecessary. There are two types of 'serving suggestions' in general which can be used to convey what you have found, where storytelling is fundamental, see Examples 6.4 and 6.5.

Example 6.4 Sticking to the facts

A supplier, called Exhi Events Ltd, had been providing services for events and exhibitions for many years. Each year the amount that they billed seemed to increase considerably. Previously nobody had noticed anything untoward. However, when the invoice patterns were analysed, it was as if our organization had received around three-quarters of the supplier's invoices, based on the invoice number series. Looking at the last published turnover from this supplier on the internet for free, it confirmed that our organization accounted for around 60–70 per cent of this company's turnover in many of the prior years and 98 per cent of its turnover five years ago. Around one-third of the invoices were for relatively round sums and examination of some of these round numbers indicated vague and unspecified services, such as 'For services rendered', 'Additional costs as per verbal agreement', and 'Marketing services as agreed': all of which strongly indicate overcharges or possible fictitious services.

Example 6.5 Highlighting the red flags

In the years 2015 and 2016, major repairs and maintenance work, including renovations, were carried out. The contractor who was supposed to be doing the work was a company called Green Brothers Ltd and had invoiced us for over half a million pounds in 2016. Green Brothers had started to invoice cautiously in 2015 but the amounts appear to have taken off later that same year and into 2016. It also appears that the company was only registered with the official UK companies register in March 2015, after it had already started to invoice as a limited company. Additionally, there were a few round sum credit notes in late 2016 for sums such as £10,000 and £35,000 which, when examined, were described as 'refund based on negotiation' (or similar). Further examination using open sources revealed that the company Green Brothers was registered in early 2015 in the UK. All of the directors had addresses in Latvia except the company secretary, which was a company called 'Instant Incorporations Ltd'. A quick look at the company's premises using Google, indicated that 25 Naunton Terrace, Cheltenham, which is the registered address of Green Brothers Ltd and the address on many of the invoices, was a private house in a typically residential area. Initial indications, including the sample invoice in Figure 6.2 (showing the additional red flags observed on the document itself) indicate that this company is not a fully-fledged building company but could be acting as a front for another company or group of people who were actually doing the work.

INVOICE: GB 15
INVOICE DATE: 15.12.2015
PAYMENT TERMS: 30 days net

See reference: verbal agreement

Green Brothers Ltd

Renovation specialists

Myorganisation Ltd
Farage House
Pole Star House
Constellation Avenue
Cambridge CB2 23X
United Kingdom

Urgent repairs as agreed with plant manager Rob Kearns

Date	Description of service	Qty	Price
01.11.2015	Analysis and assessment of damages	1	25 000,00
06.11.2015	Purchase of equipment according to specifications	1	39 549,00
12.12.2015	Plaster	1	70 000,00
	Material (9 673 963 @ 0,016 EUR, plus 20% administrative charge, import duties, etc.)	3	156 348,00
	Summa (GBP):		311 197,00
	VAT 20%:		62 239.40
	Grand Total (GBP):		**373 436.40**

As Rohelised Vennad (OOO)	Tel: +371 20 554 734	Account nr:60-16-13 32926819
25 Naunton Terrace	E-mail: nikolay.suurlinn@online.lv	Bank: NowBank Inc.
Cheltenham GL53 7BD, UK	Reg.nr.: 341987676	IBAN: GB29 NWBK 6016 1331 9268 19

Figure 6.2 Green Brothers' invoice with red flags

Example 6.6 Exhi Events Ltd (postscript)

Once the facts were presented to the Chief Financial Officer or CFO, it was recognized that this supplier had somehow managed to avoid any form of supervision for years. All fingers pointed to someone in the department who could be working in collusion with them, but no obvious link was found. What was discovered was that some years ago, the person who founded Exhi Events was 'promised' a golden contract if he left where he was working and set up on his own. The one who made this promise had long since retired. The CFO was faced with two options to resolve the matter. The first was a long-drawn-out investigation where the chance of finding out who, what and why was possible but difficult. The chance of recovering any money was even less. The CFO took a mature decision not to 'throw good money after bad' and finally (something which the purchasing department applauded as they had felt 'shut out for years') put this contract out to public tender. The results spoke for themselves: (1) Exhi Events did not win on merit and since they were dependent on our organization, they went bankrupt soon afterwards; (2) two people in the department, who subsequently were discovered to have accepted some free trips paid for by Exhi Events, protested loudly at the decision of the CFO and the purchasing department to re-tender the contract, and resigned in 'protest' because Exhi Events did not win the tender; and (3) the actual external costs of running the events which Exhi had been running were reduced by around 50 per cent.

Additional tips

- Try to understate what you find. It usually produces a calmer and more mature response from management.
- If you are asked for an opinion, present alternative possible scenarios such as 'it may not be as bad as it seems, but it looks as if they may be taking us for a ride. Worst case, someone inside could be involved but we have not seen any evidence of that yet.' In the case of Green Brothers Ltd above, you could say 'Possibilities include hidden mark-ups, illegal labour, etc. but these are yet to be explored.'
- Underline that you have not done an investigation yet and a full-blown and expensive investigation may not be necessary to resolve this. Explain

that there is no need to panic! You have performed a structured analysis to find likely fraud and corruption early (rather than wait for whistleblowers).

- Remind management that, as a rule of thumb, long and complex investigations (the sort they may have experienced in the past) should be avoided. Instead management should favour more effective and pragmatic solutions which stop the immediate losses (see Chapter 7).

- And remember (as mentioned earlier), after years of external auditing and, in general, people not finding fraud and corruption before it is too late, people might have given up thinking that it is possible.

Finally, should you wish to illustrate things you could also use a relationship diagram, but be wary of over-complicating matters.

Recipe 2 Finding where you could be dealing with organizations which have something to hide and are involved in dirty money

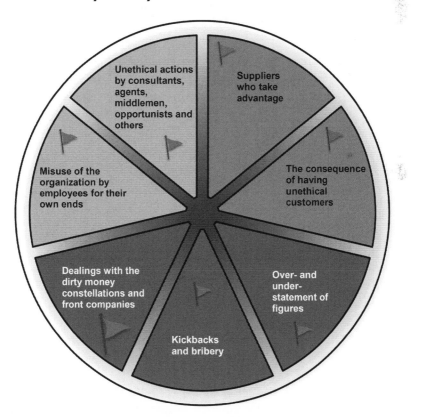

Figure 6.3 The Wheel of (mis)Fortune: focusing mainly on DMCs

Let us start with a question: which one of the following jurisdictions or destinations could be part of a dirty money constellation (DMC)?

☐ London
☐ the Cayman Islands
☐ St Kitts and Nevis
☐ Estonia
☐ the USA
☐ Russia
☐ Cyprus
☐ Guernsey
☐ Vanuatu

Today, potentially all of them could be, but this does not mean to say any of these jurisdictions can be called centres of fraud either. For example, while the Cayman Islands, the British Virgin Islands or the Isle of Man have been called tax havens to prevent disclosure of ownerships, to hide dirty money and evade tax, possibly due to leaks and subsequent regulations, the system of firewalls has developed considerably to involve several countries and cross-ownerships. For example, today the UK and the USA have joined the DMC world, by allowing companies to register subsidiaries and branches, or in the case of the USA, offshore LLC corporations. Of course, to give the additional protection, the expense of setting up a DMC is not often much dearer than it used to be, but it does seem that while the landscape is continuously evolving, so is the demand for such impenetrable shells.

In Chapter 4, Example 4.1 (F&C Ltd) was a company registered in London on the UK companies register but with owners being shell companies in Cyprus and the British Virgin Island, directors who were members of a law firm based in Switzerland, a managing director based in Moscow, a company secretary which was a 'fit-for-purpose' company somewhere in the UK and a bank account in Estonia, and this is par for the course. Seemingly complex international structures like this are not so difficult to set up today, due to the huge expansion in online filing and verification systems which have developed in most countries. But the main purpose of many of these structures is to be able to hide. Front companies and so-called dirty money have developed over centuries and arguably never more rapidly than in the past two decades. For the purposes of this recipe, we will define a DMC or DMC-related organization in simple terms as:

> An organization which, for one reason or another, is structured so that it is not easy to see who the true owners or beneficiaries are, and in which people are party to the money flows associated with that organization.

DMC or dirty money constellation or dirty money centre loosely describes jurisdictions or combinations of jurisdictions which provide the benefits for a would-be criminal or fraudster of hidden or disguised ownership of companies, bank accounts and other assets. Some of the more unethical uses of a DMC include, but are not limited to:

- use of company-controlled 'slush funds' and the payments of bribes to and from offshore companies (bribes are often politely referred to as 'marketing commissions');
- payment of secret salary and bonuses to top managers;
- kickbacks paid to management on the acquisition or disposal of a subsidiary;
- fraudulent invoicing and overcharging by suppliers;
- transfer, embezzlement and other movement of assets or cash by the owners of a company;
- hiding conflicting ownership interests in suppliers, customers and business partners;
- bribes that are not 'real' bribes but are the cover story for embezzlement using the need for a bribe as an excuse (in our experience, this happens far more often than is reported but companies are too embarrassed to disclose the embezzlement/misappropriation component, because of course they have sanctioned the bribe itself);
- avoidance of trade sanctions;
- funding other illicit activities;
- and, of course, illegitimate or illegal tax evasion.

Because the landscape is constantly changing, often to keep a few steps ahead of legislation, it is not so easy to issue a blacklist of jurisdictions which are involved in DMCs. Even pointing the finger can lead to either being accused of slander or even, in some cases, diplomatic incidents.

But from a commercial and fraud detective point of view, it is enough to recognize that these DMCs do exist and if we are dealing with an organization in any form which appears to have something to hide, then we need to be extremely careful. Dealing with companies where you have little idea who or what is behind them, where the money comes from and where it goes, is a dangerous business.

In this set of mini-recipes we have provided some basic methods for identifying organizations where your suppliers, consultants, agents, representatives, customers could have something to hide.

Ingredients and tools

Before starting out, you should have access to the following:

- supplier, customer and business partner master data;
- spurious payments data;
- your own organization's bank information with payments and receipts;
- a list of the different most commonly used country codes which can be found on www.nationsonline.org or a similar site.

Method: the first DMC 'sweep'

Think of what you are doing in looking for front companies as very similar to sweeping a room for bugs (either the entomological type or the listening device type). Here are six of the typical signs you would be looking for:

1   Flag up, using the address information you have on file, any organization with which you have had financial dealings in any jurisdiction which is traditionally well known for hosting front companies. This could include, for example, Guernsey, Jersey, the Cayman Islands, St Kitts and Nevis, but the remember that the current list could be over 100 different destinations. The key factor is not the destination itself but whether it is natural for your organization to have any normal form of commercial dealings with organizations in these jurisdictions.

2   Building on point 1, look for any business dealings with organizations which you would not expect to have. The examples are many and one needs to apply common sense but could include, for example:

   a   Your organization operates mainly in Europe, but you appear to be buying consultancy from a Singapore company, this could indicate a front company.

   b   For sales to Europe, the Middle East and Africa, one of the major customers is an LLC based in New York, which appears, at least from initial online research, to be located in a small office suite.

3   Look out for the use of multiple jurisdictions on payment and receipt documents (Example 6.7). For example, a company which was operating according to its documentation in Germany but had a bank account in London, an email address which was a generic domain based in Turkey and a telephone number which was Belgium, is the typical scenario which should trigger interest.

4   Identify mismatches in company type and jurisdiction. For example, it is unusual to have a company of type 'SA' based in the UK, or a company called 'Ltd' based in France, and so on.

5   Hunt down companies which are at 'care of' addresses. This can be quite simple because the abbreviation 'c/o' is included in the address details. However, it can get a little more complex where organizations are operating from an accommodation address, such as a law firm, an incorporation agent or some other form of address typically used for multiple companies. Often something in the address itself can be a giveaway.

6   Identify to which bank accounts bonuses to employees are paid, fees to consultants and non-executive directors (Example 6.8). Normally these should be paid into the country where the person resides. However, if the country of the bank account differs, it gives you grounds to look a little deeper.

While the above tests are just a start, it is often very eye-opening what can be discovered by a DMC sweep, especially in larger organizations. Typically, once a potential DMC is discovered, some basic desktop investigation needs to be performed, although often confirming that a front company is indeed involved is not that complex.

Example 6.7 Money from nowhere

Sales invoices where the deliveries of vehicles to Columbia were invoiced to a company in the Cayman Islands. Money received often came from a bank account pertaining to this Cayman Islands company in London and on occasions from an account in Switzerland. Internal enquiries into the nature of the customer revealed that these were very profitable sales transactions but to an organization in Columbia whose main source of income was derived from a range of criminal activities.

Example 6.8 Salaries to someplace else

It was discovered through a DMC sweep that certain members of the senior management were not on normal payroll contacts but some or all of their salaries were paid to companies which they had set up in jurisdictions (such as the Isle of Man, Belgium, etc.) where they did not reside or work. Later on, it was found out that many of them were also involved in other types of fraud.

Example 6.9 Hiding the true identity

Purchases of website development services were from a London-based company, which issued monthly invoices in the sequence 001, 002, 003. The company had very recently been registered in London, after the date the contract was awarded. Examination of the company address showed that it was a company secretarial services company, where local online telephone directories listed over one hundred companies sharing the same address. Two of the directors were lawyers working in Spain, and the ultimate holding company was in Cyprus. The managing director of this holding company turned out to be the son of the employee who awarded the website development contract in the first place.

Example 6.10 Bribes disguised as salary

A consultant living in the USA, invoiced through a company in the United Arab Emirates for large round number consultancy services in the region of $30,000, $100,000, etc. Initially it appeared as if the consultant was being paid exorbitant sums of money and deliberately avoiding US tax. A little more analysis showed that the same consultant also had a parallel company in the USA which was invoicing for work done on an hourly basis, plus travelling expenses, for relatively smaller sums of money. The large sums were being invoiced in the consultant's name but were in reality bribes paid which were 'fenced' by the consultant.

Many other examples are given in the rest of this book, but it can be said that a DMC sweep can be one of the quickest ways to discover fraud fast. I would go so far as to say that DMCs in their widest sense are often one of the single largest red flags of fraud and corruption.

How to present the results ('serving suggestion')

It is always important not to jump to any conclusions and, in the case of potential DMCs, the story behind can be quite unexpected at times. There-fore, it is very important to proceed cautiously and always present the facts to management as they are. Pictures of documents (for example, with multiple jurisdictions) can be useful, as are relationship diagrams.

Recipe 3 Finding false figure frauds

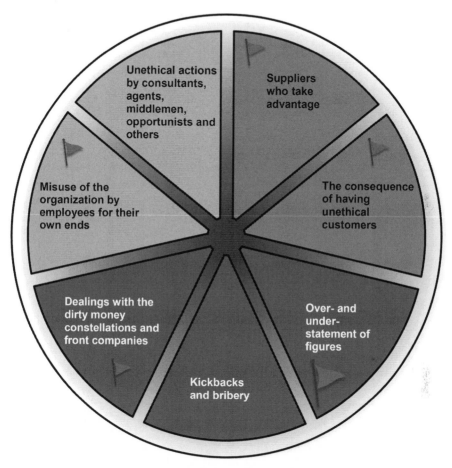

Figure 6.4 The Wheel of (mis)Fortune: focusing mainly on over- and under-statement of figures

'Falsifying figures', to use a general expression, embraces a whole host of different things. For example, it can be massive and highly sophisticated like the Equity Funding Corporation of the USA, where the senior management, including the chief actuary, in the early 1970s used their computer system to create, maintain and re-insure fictitious insurance policies . . . for fictitious people. Or equally massive and relatively recently the Enron Corporation, where the management, assisted by their legal and financial advisors, set up front companies to which they made fictitious sales ... once again to increase profits. Alternatively, falsifying figures can be as mundane as moving sales from one year to another, misreporting actual costs against budgets or padding of expense reports.

The term 'false figures' therefore covers a whole myriad of actions, most of which the perpetrators will justify by rationalizing that they were done for a good reason. Years ago, when I was a trainee external auditor, I was sent on an audit senior training course where we watched a BBC film called *The Billion Dollar Bubble*, based on the Equity Funding Corporation of America, where the Chief Executive, Stanley Goldblum, played brilliantly by the actor Sam Wanamaker, was totally convinced that creating fictitious policies was not only not wrong, but actually was a decision he had to take to save the corporation for the employees, the shareholders and also 'the people of America'. Big or small, altering figures for a good reason is one area where rationalization is prolific, if not rampant. Soon after the course, I found myself in charge of the audit of a large brewery and national chain of pubs and hotels, one of the prestigious clients of the Manchester office of the major audit firm I was working for.

During the final week of the audit, my team and I were not able to confirm roughly £250,000 when trying to match what cash was owed by the pubs that were managed by the brewery and the mother company. I worked late at night to find the cash, and despite the chief accountant being unavailable due to lumbago, I managed to conclude that in fact this money did not exist and a write-off was required. When I told the manager in charge this, he was at first horrified because the company had already announced its pre-tax profits for the year to its shareholders, but soon calmed down once he found the solution, which was to make an adjustment called a 'deferred tax provision' which would both account for the money in a way, and also not irritate the client. As a 24-year-old newly qualified chartered accountant with just three years' experience, I protested vehemently and was treated to lunch at a Chinese restaurant by the manager who told me that he admired my tenacity but very kindly said that I also had to learn to accept reality as I had a good chance of making partner in the firm.[8] Often people do not fully appreciate that moving figures around could be seen as fraud, or at least, wrong and they tend to talk about it quite openly.

When I interviewed the owner of Exhi Events Ltd who had engineered and benefited from a mutually dependent relationship, etc. (see this chapter's Recipe 1), I popped the question as to why all the budgets for large exhibition and event contracts were always spot on. The answer he gave me was one time I found it hard to keep a straight face and I still remember his words pretty much verbatim:

> Nigel, what you have got to understand is that the internal department which we serve is under a lot of pressure. Nobody knows what the cost of an sales event will be as they are planned and executed, over six to nine months usually, and things can change all the time. So what we do is use a system called 'living budgeting'. The event costs what it costs, then we add up all the invoices, produce a budget which of course we are forced to backdate. It's a bit more work of course, but by making sure that the actual costs incurred equal the budget for each project, then everyone is happy.

Big or small, discovering fraudulent figures does not require sophisticated detective skills but just a realistic and open mind and a healthy sense of curiosity. As Nick Leeson, the trader who is believed to have single-handedly brought down Barings Bank, said, when I was teaching fraud detection at a conference where he was giving the keynote speech: 'I think the only reason Barings Management in London did not want to see that the trading profits I was reporting in Singapore were fake, was their desire to make so much money.'

Ingredients and tools

Because falsifying figures is like a large mezza or tapas table for accounting frauds, a large myriad of different things, it is hard to write one specific recipe but we will share a number of real but fairly simple examples and the various methods used to uncover them in the method section below. Before starting out, you should have access to the following:

- A recognition that fraud and corruption happens (this goes without saying).
- An appreciation that people often will, for any number of reasons 'polish the apple', i.e. make the truth look as good as it possibly can look, even if at the end of the day they have departed so far from the truth that the 'apple is no longer an apple'.
- Access to basic accounting data, which will vary depending on which type of accounting fraud you are trying to detect, but will often involve some transactions, some summary data, management accounts, budgets, 'trial balances'.

- Someone to ask who is an accountant and someone who will give you straight answers. (Remember many people would willingly talk to you about how the figures were constructed because, unlike serious fraud, they think of this rather more as bending the rules rather than breaking them.)
- And, of course, a VERY open mind.

Don't be like an external auditor who claims they are 'professionally sceptical' but don't find much, think of yourself as having a healthy and professional sense of curiosity, i.e. a nose for 'something being wrong' and the presence of mind to do a reality check.

Method

There is such a large variety of different types of false figure frauds that no single recipe could do it justice. Table 6.2 is a small selection of nine recipes (rather like a tapas menu) showing an example and the techniques which you can use to find it. The general rule, which applies to most false figure frauds and manipulation is to 'think the unthinkable' and recognize that people will be as creative as it takes.

How to present the results ('serving suggestion')

Presenting the results of false figure fraud is never easy because you could be seen as the bringer of bad news, a 'business killer' or alternatively could be seen as someone who is going up against and challenging the better judgement of people who are senior and potentially very valuable to the organization.

Table 6.2 False figure frauds (or F³) and how to find them

Typical manifestation(s) of F³	*How to detect and interpret F³*
I Falsified expenses While also associated with 'employees with an over-developed since of entitlement', forged expenses, especially if widespread or re-charged to customers, can be an indicator of a 'falsification culture' as well as excessive costs. Consider the following rudimentary example: a senior divisional manager flew from Athens to London for a meeting. His travel expenses for taxi receipt showed the cost of his minicab from London Heathrow to Paddington station as £235.00.	A simple online search of taxi rides from London shows the cost of a taxi ride is less than £50 if ordered in advance and less than £80 on a metered taxi, even in very heavy traffic. So, £235.00 is simply out of proportion. The detection technique for 'falsified expenses' is to simply look for anything too high which does not seem reasonable. Experience shows that people who falsify documents also tend to manipulate other figures.

Typical manifestation(s) of F^3	How to detect and interpret F^3

2 Touching up aberrations is also a form or falsifying figures

A large office building, which won an environmental award, was fitted with movement sensors to ensure that lights in all office and communal areas went off when no-one was in the building. Unfortunately, after some maintenance work was done on the program which controlled the sensors, the engineers forgot to turn the sensors on, so for the whole of the month of April, and before this was noticed, energy costs related to the building were exorbitant. To avoid showing an embarrassing 'spike' in monthly environmental reporting, the management smoothed the figures, allocating the overuse in April across the other, low-energy months.

We should first recognize that falsifying figures is not just restricted to financial figures. Anything which also affects reputation or image is subject to falsification, as is the organization's reputation as an environmental champion. An appreciation and recognition that people will often cover up for mistakes are half the battle. Since the sensors normally would be working, then it would be hard to detect the correction although one way could be to schedule out electricity bills. The lesson learnt from this example is that when it comes to environmental reports, corporate responsibility reports and even advertising, a certain level of curiosity must be maintained.

3 Special account or transaction codes

In the case of certain customers, when shortages occurred, or discounts were to be paid, these credits, in the customer's favour, were posted to a special ledger account, which would be paid out, in cash to the customer's representatives, either when they visited the seller's premises, or when required. In order to easily identify these special customer accounts, the accounting department always placed the number '99' as a prefix before the customer account number.

Look for unusual internal account numbers or transaction codes such as 9999, 888888, 666 XXXX555 as these are often made up for a purpose.

Finished goods from the factory which were considered 'seconds' and were sold separately were given an inventory number which started with 'XX'. Normally the quantity of seconds was very minor, and the goods were clearly marked as 'seconds' and sold separately. However, in this case, one salesman had identified the opportunity (with the help of someone working in the factory) to denote first grade product as seconds and sell the product to a special channel he had.

Identify account numbers and transaction codes which have very little, or vague descriptions attached to them.

(Continued)

Table 6.2 (Continued)

Typical manifestation(s) of F³	How to detect and interpret F³
4 Accounts for decision-making	
In one instance management accounts were produced to show an over-flattering picture of an investment, in order to attract more investment partners	Sometimes a simple 'reality' check or common-sense analysis is all that is needed to identify wildly speculative results.
Budgets for the next year showed an almost unimaginable increase in profits	While historic financial statement can be also inaccurate, they are often a sound yardstick against which to compare recent figures and proposals. Just remember to ask yourself the question 'do things make sense?'
5 Sales commissions	Identify 'side-systems' which are used to calculate payments such as commissions and bonuses. Be wary that these systems, since they are not specifically accounting systems, may not be checked with or reconciled to the original data over time. Look for commissions and bonuses which are 'too good to be true'.
In a company which sold vehicles, old vehicles were often taken in part exchange from customers who wanted to renew their vehicle or fleet. The company then reconditioned their vehicles and re-sold them. Salesmen were paid a commission based on the calculated profits on sales of used vehicles. The commissions were calculated in a separate system. An elaborate system of schemes grew up whereby costs were posted to old deals.	
6 False costs	False costs can be identified because they are large number transactions with little substantiation or any form of delivery behind them, or by the nature of the text supporting the costs (in this case, they used the term 'deferred costs' which itself was a giveaway), or that, in this case the costs were paid to a company whose purpose was not in line with the activities being undertaken.
A regional marketing director, believing that the new owners of her company were going to drastically cut the marketing budget in the coming year, decided to put through a whole range of expenses now which would only be eventually used in the following year. To do this she had invoices sent by a supplier owned by her then boyfriend, who then held the funds for use the next year. Interestingly after the fraud was discovered, it was proven that the marketing director, or her boyfriend did not benefit personally at all, but acted totally in the interests of the company and actually used all of the money on genuine transactions.	
7 False names	The creation of falsified customers, suppliers, contractors, etc. will tend to leave footprints. For example, in the case of my cousin, he was not creative enough in inventing customer names, many of which were identical first name or similar last names.
This particular example involves my own cousin, who possibly could win the award for 'most incompetent fraudster ever'.	

Typical manifestation(s) of F^3	How to detect and interpret F^3

After getting a new job at a bank selling credit cards, in a desperate attempt to please his employers, my cousin produced multiple customer applications for credit cards, paying in the small sign-on fee himself, and then creating the customer application to a bunch of addresses of his friends and relatives. In order to finance the fee, he 'borrowed' the money from his aging father's bank account for which he had signature power. When the case went to trial, the courts found him guilty but also found that that on balance (because he had not received his bonuses as yet), the bank actually owed him so much money that the courts ordered his employer to reimburse his father's account.

The same techniques can be applied to false loan applications for example, where names and or addresses are too similar or the same.

It is possible to 'invent people' but you need to be a real professional to keep the legends consistent.

8   The unexplained adjustment

In a power company, the financial controller noticed that for five years the company had under-billed a group of customers small costs for grid charges that should have been added to each bill. He realized that there was no way that customers would accept these charges today and probably rightly assumed that if the company tried to retroactively force these charges on customers, it would lead to a mass walk-out in a highly competitive market.

However, fearing for his job, the controller decided around summertime to create a highly complex accounting entry (called a journal entry) of 72 lines, which mostly moved money back and forth and had no effect but concealed one particular set of accounting entries which showed the loss (which was in fact €7.2 million), but booked it against profits for the whole year in a way which looked reasonable. Interestingly the external auditors did not notice the manipulation which was substantial because this year was a particularly good year for profits and they compared results to previous years rather than looking at the details or documents themselves.

Large unexplained transactions are usually possible to spot because they are complex but at the same time lack description and are difficult to understand. They could exhibit a 'broad-brush' nature, or even the sort of sweeping arrogance which is in fact quite easy to spot.

However, the overriding message to a fraud detective if you wish to find these sorts of fraudulent adjustments is to LOOK at transactions and what lies behind them. Sometimes the absence of information and documentation (which is a recurring theme) is the biggest giveaway.

And sometimes the simple 'this does not make sense' approach is all that it takes.

(Continued)

Table 6.2 (Continued)

Typical manifestation(s) of F^3	How to detect and interpret F^3
9 Stock manipulations A very large alumina plant had owners who lived in another country. Every three months a major maintenance project was completed as part of a programme to keep the plant fully running. Before each project, budget figures were submitted for the costs (which were basically parts, tools and labour) and after the project was finished, the final, actual, costs were sent in. What actually was happening, was that until the maintenance project was started, the local management had no idea what the real costs would be but because they were being measured on performance against their estimates, what they did was build up a stockpile of spare parts and tools from each project by over-estimating in the first place and, then, when these parts where not used, transferring them to a special warehouse which they built, behind a row of trees, and kept these goods at zero value, ready for a 'rainy day' project where they encountered massive and unexpected costs.	In the particular case of the warehouse and 'rainy-day inventories', there were a large number of red flags including: • All projects for maintenance and repairs came in within 3 per cent of budget (which when you think about it, is rather impossible) • The warehouse itself was not actually recorded as an asset in the accounts (the costs of constructing it were absorbed as part of one of the early maintenance projects) • The stock of parts and tools was recorded at zero value, but in fact was rather valuable and sooner or later a whole theft system grew up around this stock.

Example 6.11 The hidden warehouse

In the stock-manipulation example 9 in Table 6.2, I made the mistake of presenting the example at a management meeting where the finance director was there. To try to inject some humour into the already tense atmosphere I made the joke that the stock control system in the ghost warehouse was in fact much more reliable than the main warehouse, where the system had only worked intermittently for the past year. The finance director angrily challenged me saying, 'I have not even heard of this other warehouse', to which I stupidly retorted, 'When have you last been around your own complex, then?' (Such responses, I have learnt from personal experience, are not productive.)

The most important thing to remember when presenting possible falsified figure frauds is to present the facts but do it in a way that people can choose to believe if they like that the so-called manipulation was accidental. This allows everyone to have a more open mind and stick to examining the facts instead of jumping to conclusions as to who is to blame and how they may have personally benefited.

Useful tips

- Recognize that rationalization and the 'I did it for the company' argument play a huge part.
- Always, always be polite! Don't blame others for not finding, but instead commend others for challenging and taking things up (like Maria and Eva in Chapter 4).
- And remember that people will always be creative, whether they are designing false documents, coming up with false names or even trying to cover up false expenses, and will feel justified in doing it as in Example 6.12.

Example 6.12 When is a hotel not a hotel?

A loyal employee was sent on a regular basis to work on a contract in Paris, from Athens where he lived. This meant that he had to be in Paris on average every other week. After two weeks of staying at the Golden Tulip Hotel, the employee met a local girl who lived close to where he was working, and she suggested that he came and lived with her when he was in Paris. This he did, but for private reasons did not want to disclose to anyone in the company his relationship with the girl. So as a result, using an earlier electronic receipt, the employee regularly falsified around 50 bills from the Golden Tulip Hotel on his own computer, ensuring that the bills matched exactly with the lowest going rates at the hotel, meals, and the dates of his work in Paris. And of course, he felt fully justified in doing this because the company would be being paying his expenses anyway, some of which he used on entertaining his girlfriend as gratitude for housing him. The only thing he FORGOT to change was the room number, which remained as Room 415 on every single hotel bill. (A quick call to the hotel and the booking manager confirmed that at the Golden Tulip Hotel one would have to reserve the room in advance for the whole year if you wanted to have the same room each time you booked to stay there.)

Recipe 4 Catching customers who could be taking advantage of you and your organization

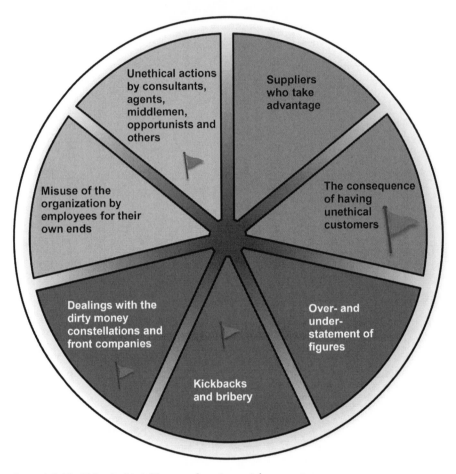

Figure 6.5 The Wheel of (mis)Fortune: focusing mainly on customers

Normally customers are seen as a good thing, whether they are people who buy directly, indirectly or users. The majority of customers are good and good for our organizations. But also, there are those who in some way may be taking us for a ride. For example, they may have no intention of paying at some point. There may be hidden agreements with people in the organization for the customer, or someone at the customer's end could be receiving a sum of money as an inducement to buy (commonly referred to as a bribe). The customer could be receiving our products very cheaply (too cheaply) and selling them on for a super-profit. And remember, there could be possible links and relationships to insiders, but this should not normally be your first port of call.

Questioning suppliers who may be causing harm is usually acceptable. However, for many people, questioning the behaviour of customers can be seen as a 'business killer' so it is important to tread carefully. But remember your organization will not benefit from a rotten customer in the long run. This is a basic recipe designed to flush out potentially rotten customers

Ingredients and tools

Before starting out, you should have access to the following:

- the customer's names and when they were registered;
- where the customer is located (address, country);
- the value of sales invoices issued to this customer in a period (for example, the past 18 months);
- the number of sales invoices issued (in the same period);
- the value of sales credit notes and adjustments which reduce total sales (for the same equivalent period);
- the number of sales credit notes and adjustments (in the same period);
- when the customer first became a customer (often this is the registration date in the customer master file);
- hard or electronic copies of sales invoices and credit notes if needed.

Method

Customer-related fraud can be a whole number of things and can get quite complex involving inter-relationships between customers and connections with suppliers. The recipes in this section are designed to pick the large and 'low-hanging fruits'.

Start by identifying customers which display some or all of the following characteristics (focusing on the larger ones in terms of sales volumes or large credit notes first):

- Where the level of credit notes (or rebates) are extraordinarily high in comparison to other customers. Look at the frequency of the rebates and, where possible, identify if there are any unusual or obvious patterns. For example, a high volume of rebates could imply that a particular customer has a 'special relationship' with someone in your organization and is receiving far too favourable treatment.

- Customers where their account is almost always in credit, in other words, it is *you* who are owing the customer money (not the other way around which would be more to be expected). A permanent account in credit, if this is the only account for a customer, can indicate that the customer is in fact not a customer at all but a supplier.[9] If there are many accounts for a single customer but one of them is always in credit, this can also mean that the customer has a special account where discounts and rebates are collected. While this can be OK, the circumstances surrounding it should be examined a bit more closely.
- Customers who purchase large quantities too cheaply. To do this, divide the total amount billed by the number of sales invoices issued. If you get a relatively low value, this could indicate that the customer is getting things too cheap or almost for free.
- Customers who appear to be a form of front company, such as a company based in a DMC (see Chapter 4), especially in the sort of jurisdiction where maybe we do not have any sales.

These four 'tests' are enough to highlight customers where their nature and your relationship to them are worthy of further examination. If you wish to go a little further, you could, for example, look for customers who buy a lot from you, but often in small amounts and buy lots of different things, but where the average price is always low (compared to a large customer who is always buying lots of the same thing from you). What this can indicate is a trader or middleman company who is buying your product simply for resale in the market, often undercutting your own sales. All the above are clues to flush out customers whom you should be looking at a little more closely.

Once you have done some initial analysis as described above, the next step is to pick the top 10 or 20 customers, focusing on the biggest ones (by value, volume or both). You may also wish to have a quick look on the internet to see what sort of footprint a customer has, what do they do, what kind of organization they are, when they were registered, does what they say about themselves make sense?, etc.

Searching for the footprint of customer-related fraud can be extended to look at invoicing patterns (similar to supplier fraud). This can be quite complex at first and we recommend sticking to the basics as described above. However, after some time you can start to look for patterns which indicate, for example, that a customer is buying more and more, but soon is going to disappear and leave you with large debts unpaid (as Example 6.13 from the leasing industry illustrates).

Example 6.13 A lease to nowhere

A large leasing company was aggressively growing its customer portfolio of finance and operating leases, usually secured on a particular asset. A1 Machine Partners seemed to have been the perfect leasing customer. Their business model was simple; they purchased heavy equipment needed in the agricultural sector; tractors, harvesters, planting and seeding equipment, hay baling equipment and so on, all financed with long-term leases. Small farmers, who only needed certain equipment for one or two weeks at a time, would rent what they needed from A1 Machine Partners. A1 Machine Partners didn't use the machines themselves, or even maintain them. This was all handled by the equipment manufacturer's service organization. So, the organization was very small, in fact, only the owner and his son. Every month A1 bought more and more equipment. The business model seemed very successful, and they made their financing payments right on time. Company financial statements also showed a profit. In just one and a half years the number of machines leased grew from 0 to 49, with a total value of more than 4 million Euros. The company clearly had international connections; in fact, sometimes A1 Machine Partners made financing payments from offshore accounts. Then one day, after A1 missed a lease repayment for the first time, the finance manager called the customer and was surprised that the phone number for A1 no longer worked. The company had simply vanished, and 3.6 million Euros of bad debts had to be written off.

With hindsight, this fraud could have been detected had the following indicators been looked for:

- The dramatic increase in lease requests was 'too good to be true' and not commensurate with such a small company (even though the company gave assurances that it was always renting out its equipment).
- Lease repayments which arrived from other companies and accounts (and not A1) indicated that already the company making the payments was moving its money into a DMC-like structure.
- A more in-depth look at A1's 'footprint' on the country's official company register showed that the company had only submitted accounts for one year (i.e., it was newly registered) rather than having a five-year history which had been submitted by A1 when applying for the lease finance.

How to present what you have found ('serving suggestion')

Classify the customers where there are significant red flags and, in the context of your organization, brainstorm what could be taking place and why. Do not jump to any conclusions at this stage but try to summarize and present each example in the form of a story where first the facts are presented, followed by possible hypothesis as shown in Examples 6.14–6.17. When presenting, it can be useful to include some limited sample documentation.

Example 6.14 The credit note from nowhere

The credit note shown in Figure 4.5 is a good example of what can be found by applying this recipe. For example, we would have found that the 'customer' L.B. Marton almost always had a credit balance (in other words, it always owed us money) and we would have noticed that the company was registered in Nevada, USA, possibly a place where we had no sales.

Example 6.15 When a customer is a supplier

A customer account which was shown to be in permanent credit turned out to be in fact a supplier account. One supplier, realizing that the procedure to become a customer was much simpler than that of becoming an authorized supplier, simply ensured that it was on the books as a customer, and thereby authorized to trade, and then proceeded to act as a de facto supplier.

Example 6.16 Money in scrap

Large numbers of invoices were issued to customer X, but each invoice was of very low value. The first question to ask was 'who the customer is' and the second question was 'why the low values?'. By looking at a few of the sales invoices it was clear that the customer was buying scrap materials and parts, but what was interesting was that, for these types of materials, the 'waste percentage' was around 14 per cent, a lot more than the average typical waste percentage of 2 per cent. On further examination it was discovered that first grade materials and parts were being classified as waste and being deliberately sold at ridiculously low values to one particular customer who then made a huge profit.

Example 6.17 Selling to the middleman

One of the largest and seemingly most profitable customers of finished goods turned out to be a small company which purchased goods and sold them on in the market at profits of over 25 per cent, but still cheaper than we were selling the products on the market. It turned out that one particular salesman had connections in the factory to downgrade perfect grade products to second grade, sold these to his favourite customer who then reinstated the goods as first grade and sold them to existing customers in the market, undercutting the sales of other salesmen. The middleman company did not in fact do anything, and in most cases the goods were shipped out directly to the end customer. The fraud was picked up because analysis of transactions revealed far too many low value transactions to customers, where we covered high transport costs which were not re-charged. Further examination uncovered the manipulation of the quality from firsts to seconds, and the fact that the customer was simply a front, controlled by the salesman himself.

Useful tips

- In relation to detecting customer-related fraud, we should repeat that it is always important to tread cautiously because sales are often seen as the 'holy cow' of business. Customers are seen as income-generating and not to be messed with.
- It is also possible to discover that our organization is overbilling its own customers, which is also fraud, but something salespeople prefer not to discuss!

Finally, where customers are located and what sort of business they are involved in, usually are often met with the response 'That's none of our business.'

C-JUGGERNAUT LTED

Leading offshore logistics in Green Energy production!
(a NOR-SEAS partner company)
Enderby Boatyard, Unit 3, 6 Langham Lane
Colchester, Essex CO2 4HJ
Tel: +44 752 356 0000

Strictly Confidential

Big Scandi Bank ASA
attention Morten Skoggard
Stranden 24
Aker Brygge
0021 Oslo
Norway

21st March 2018

Dear Morten,

Further to our telephone conversation today, IO am providing you with a file which contains information about our company, background to its founders (myself and NorSea included) as well as our relationship with your client NorSea ASA, past and projected performance figures, and details of our proposed fleet of vessels which are specifically targeted at the growing offshore renewable energy sector.

I also enclose signed MOU's which gives us exclusive rights to transport the equipment of one of the leading German manufacturers in the sector, thus guaranteeing you a steady stream income in the years to come. Please do not hesitate to contact me if you have any further questions.

Yours sincerely

Jørgen A. Andersen

Registered office 1st Floor, 72 New Bond Street London WIS 1RR
Directors: Stuart Andrew Little, Jørgen Amt Andersen, Lars Miller
Emails Jorgen.Cjuggernaught@Onetel.co.uk. Info@CJuggernaught@OneteLco.uk
CIS UTR 683/1436782789, VAT RegNo: 987654321
(Holding company CJUG BVI Ltd reg no: 467239992)

Figure 6.6 **A letter from a potential client**

Example 6.18 When spotting the red flags is not always everyone´s cup of tea

In one ethics training seminar for a major bank, I was asked to take up the issue of potential customers who were applying for finance. Of the 200 persons at the seminar they all agreed that there were numerous red flags on the customer letter (Figure 6.6), including the one that the customer was effectively a British Virgin Islands company with a London front company and it would be suitably rejected for lack of transparency.

Just two years later, the same bank itself was the subject of a national enquiry following an exposure in the press for dealing with exactly these types of customers. Many of the employees involved were exactly the same employees who had attended the training seminar. Finding customer-related fraud in a training seminar is, however, rather different from a situation where the pressure to sell tends to dominate.

Recipe 5 Spotting unusual behaviour of consultants, middlemen, agents, and other opportunists

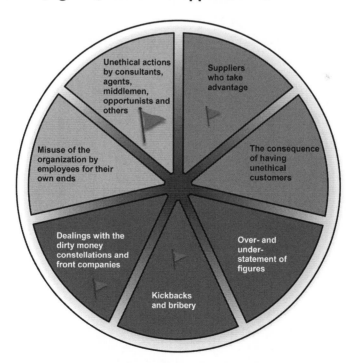

Figure 6.7 The Wheel of (mis)Fortune: focusing mainly on everybody else on the outside

This recipe is a catch–all category which tries to answer the question, 'who else could defraud our organization?' Who are they? What can they do and how can we weed out the bad ones from the good? Examples of people, who, for the sake of this recipe we will call 'trusted outsiders', include:

- individual consultants whom we consider more as 'quasi-employees' rather than suppliers;
- agents who perform work on our organization's behalf but are not formally employed by our organization;
- 'middlemen': people or small companies through which simply we buy or sell and who make a profit doing so.

The one category which is very hard to trace are rank outsiders, such as hackers, thieves or even competitors who wish to in some way to harm our organization for their own advantage. They may not be connected to our organization in any way, but they could use social engineering techniques and nurture contacts with either employees or, more likely, trusted outsiders to glean information which they can use against us.

The main distinction between this recipe and Recipe 1 (finding the suppliers who take advantage of our organization), is that here we are focusing on either *individuals* who have some connection with our organization or 'rank outsiders', who could also be a group of individuals. Once again, clues can be found by following the money (which is often the easiest and most unobtrusive way). Here are a couple of examples.

Example 6.19 Mr coffee and cake

It was noticed that the spending budget for Corporate Communications had been going up and there was some talk about external companies coming in and 'taking over' the jobs that internal teams had been doing in the past. The holder of the post of Director of Corporate Communications, Andy Stevens, was not a permanent employee but was a so-called 'management for hire'. He had been in the post for 18 months while the organization was still trying to fill the post. Mr Stevens did not live in Gothenburg where the head office was situated but travelled from his home near London to either the head office or other destinations where his services were required by the company. Andy Stevens submitted an invoice once a month, in accordance with his agreement, for fees, which was in the region of £15,000 per month, plus travel and other incidental expenses. What was interesting when analysing the invoices he had submitted over the past year were some small, but interesting red flags. Mr Stevens' invoice number sequence had some gaps: was he also working for someone else? Also, on almost every single invoice submitted, in addition to the fees, costs of flights, parking, hotels, where applicable, there were small itemized charges for 'coffee and cake' at airports for sums in the region of £2.50–£6.

The constant 'coffee and cake' became a subject of discussion. Was it just that Andy had a sweet tooth? Why did he itemize it separately on each invoice? And even if he did have coffee and cake each time, why did he bother to even ask the airport restaurant for a receipt and re-charge the expense, when he was paid so much anyway? Was it because he could, or was it just a little display of arrogance that he could? In the end, a simple examination of Mr Andrew Stevens in the UK showed that, among other things, he had been the director of a company called Quodos Branding Ltd (and was, according to the latest accounts, still a major shareholder). Quodos, which specialized in brand management and communications, had recently been appointed as a major supplier to Corporate Communications, and one of the most instrumental people in securing this apparently arm's length deal with the supplier was . . . guess who?[10]

Example 6.20 The lobbyist

To be able to open doors in the Asian market, Britmax Engineering[11] used a self-styled lobbyist or agent called B.J. Mehta. Mr Mehta was paid the comparatively small sum of $3,000 per month as a retainer to work exclusively for Britmax, which he did. In his contract it said that he would also receive a 3 per cent commission for all sales leads he had provided which were converted into real contracts for Britmax. The contract was vague and did not say what the 3 per cent was based on or where the money was to be paid. But by finding and following the payments, it was discovered that the 3 per cent was based on the higher of the first quoted sales price and the eventual price following negotiations. And the money was to be paid from Britmax's HQ accounts to any company and account, anywhere in the world which was nominated by Mr Mehta (which was discovered subsequently to include some DMC and front companies).

A note of caution before starting. One should not be over-sceptical or paranoid about outsiders. Only a small minority of all consultants, middlemen, agents, etc. behave unethically or have hidden agendas. They key is to find them and weed them out. This can be done by following the money and by thinking how, if they were dishonest, they could commit fraud or bring the name of your organization into disrepute. In other words, put yourself in their shoes, and try to 'think like a thief' (as has been described in Chapter 5).

Ingredients and tools

Before starting out, you should have access to the following:

- a list of consultants and temporary staff (who are not paid though the payroll) showing who they, and what organizations, if any, they represent;
- an official list (if it exists) of agents who are used for selling, lobbying, sourcing and any other sort of related activity;
- internal information about the organization, which is not confidential or sensitive, such as published internal organizational charts, information on the intranet, lists of email accounts of internal, organizational emails (provided the correct permissions are in place);
- a transaction file of supplier invoices and customer credit notes pertaining to consultants, agents, etc., with access to physical invoices and supporting documentation, where it exists;
- access to open-source research (via the internet) and, where possible, direct access to local company registers in the countries where business is being done as well as where the consultants are located.

Method

Here are seven of the simpler, and often most effective, methods ways to single out potential consultants, agents, middlemen and the like, whose 'sense of entitlement' could be a little overdeveloped or who are putting your own organization's reputation in harm's way. Each method is in the form of a question we should be asking ourselves. Often the simple questions are the best ones.

1   *Who has a position in the organization, has had it for a long time (because they are on organizational charts, online catalogues, etc.)* but is NOT on the normal payroll? There could be sound reasons as to why a particular person has that position and has held that position in the organization for a long time,

but apply your 'healthy curiosity' and ask 'why are they not keen to be an employee?' and if there is no logical reasons, start to ask some of the question numbers 2–7.

2   While it is often normal for any organization to engage trusted outsiders, *are we clear about their motives and agendas and are they in line with what we would like them to do for our organization?* For example, through open source research we can discover if they are operating businesses on the outside and they could be using their position, influence and contacts inside our organization to help furnish their own agenda.

3   Examine some of the more expensive 'trusted outsider's' own invoices (and the supporting documentation, such as their timesheets and itemized expenses). *Can we spot tell-tale signs of arrogance, nonchalance, other interests or just sloppiness?* Examples could include:

   a   vague of rather meaningless descriptions such as 'service', 'work done as agreed', etc.;

   b   an unnecessarily high number of hours which do not seem to make sense (for example, in one case, more than 25 hours in a day);[12]

   c   lavish or unnecessary expenditure;

   d   inadequate documentation to explain why we are paying a consultant or person (for example, where there is no supplier invoice but instead an 'instruction to pay' or some other form of internal documentation or email correspondence).

4   What other connections (ascertained from open source research, careful analysis of social media, etc.,[13] does the consultant, middleman or agent have? Who else are they working for or working with? (Sometimes this type of analysis can demonstrate that in fact the consultant is part of or at the centre of a web of companies and organizations which are surrounding your own organization, which previously you were completely unaware of.)

5   *How and where are the consultants, middlemen and agents paid?* (Once again using basic 'follow the money' techniques.) If they are being paid in odd destinations (DMCs, for example) or in places where they are not working or residing, or even to a company which prima facie does not have any connection with them, then you need to ask the simple question 'why?' and follow through.

6   *Can we identify (through simple data-matching and open source research) hitherto hidden connections which link together customers, suppliers and trusted insiders which appear to be playing a role as 'middleman'?* Based on what we find, can we identify other agendas?

7   *How likely is it that somewhere in our organization there are tasks which need to be done which, for one reason or another (for example, 'cost' or legislation), we are engaging outsiders to do for us because we do not wish to have our own employees doing it?* Examples could include:

    a   circumventing local employment legislation by engaging people on temporary contracts which are repeatedly renewed;

    b   paying below the minimum wage (maybe in a country where it is possible to circumvent laws);

    c   using consultants, agents, etc. a 'cut-out' for bribery;

    d   paying our own employees working abroad an additional 'tax-free' salary as a consultant (usually through a DMC-related company) as a way of avoiding paying higher salaries and higher taxes in the country where they are temporarily stationed.

These seven questions are like 'shaking a tree', allowing the loose fruit to fall so that they can be examined and interpreted in more detail.

How to present what you find ('serving suggestion')

Presentation should always be objective, impartial and based on evidence. Often these examples are not so complex to understand and are relatively easy to present in the form of a short summary, perhaps, if needed, accompanied by a diagram. However, it is important to present all information in an objective manner without jumping to conclusions. While it should not be a factor in the end in determining whether fraud has been committed or if the trusted outsider has breached the trust, it is also worth bearing in mind (and making management aware of) the following:

- all the useful things the trusted outsider has been doing for management (who may be concerned about 'killing the golden goose');
- the middleman/consultant/agent could be doing 'dirty work' people inside don't want to do;
- what sort of leverage could the trusted outsider have, enabling them to blackmail the organization?

Recognizing that there are many ways to interpret evidence, it is also important to be clear about how the evidence has been interpreted.

Useful tips

It is always important to remember we are talking about 'people' not companies or organizations which can be made to seem faceless. So be wary of defensive reactions both from the consultant (agent, middleman, etc.) themselves and from the people inside who know them well and have come to rely upon them. And remember to respect all privacy laws. Just because these 'trusted outsiders' are not formally employed, it does not mean that they do not have the same rights as any employee.

Recipe 6 Pinpointing the payment of bribes and false bribes

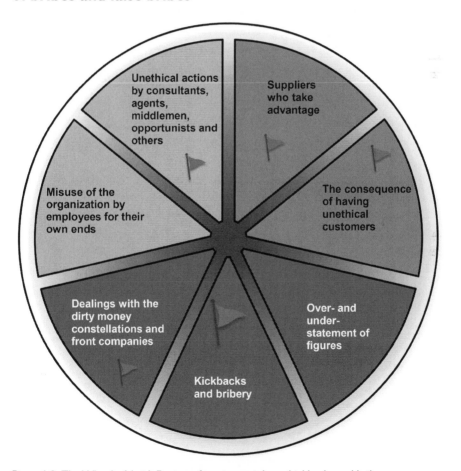

Figure 6.8 The Wheel of (mis)-Fortune: focusing mainly on kickbacks and bribery

'Bribery' is itself an ambiguous and nebulous term. For example, the word 'bribery' refers to an act where it is not even specified whether this refers to the giving of bribes, the receiving of bribes or both. Also sometimes bribery is used interchangeably with the even broader term 'corruption'. This recipe just focuses on how to discover:

- where your organization is paying bribes, either to try to win business or influence (something which is extremely common but usually well disguised);
- where 'fake bribes', a smart way of someone stealing from the organization using bribery as an excuse, are being paid.

In both cases, the clue to finding them lies, more so than ever, in 'following the money' something which is explored in Chapter 7.

Bribery to build a business is, arguably, one of the most rationalized behaviours I have come across. Some would say that most bribery is in fact not bribery at all, it is being done legally and is just a sort of lubrication payment and is a cost of doing business. And, provided it is done legally enough and nobody is caught, it in facts adds to the bottom line and value of the organization, so it is a benefit to the organization, not a cost. Quoting one of the characters in the Fraud Detectives story at the end of the book: 'How do you think they built the pyramids, the Taj Mahal or even America without a bit of bribery to oil the machinery of progress?' And in Chapter 3 we looked at the excuse, which is often given that, in some parts of the world it is impossible to get anything done without a bit of bribery (the so-called 'blaming the corrupt countries' defence).

'Fake or false bribes' are much more common than one would think. A lot of so-called bribery serves little or no purpose at all, something we could call 'unnecessary or useless' bribes. Either it is just a pure waste of money, or, as we have discovered on many occasions, part or the entire sum goes back into the pockets of the people who are involved in paying the bribes. In this case the thieves are using the bribe as a cover story for their theft.

Because fake bribes (or almost fake bribes) tend to look like real bribes, it is often difficult to distinguish between the two, until they have been more thoroughly investigated, so for the purposes of these short recipes, they will be treated together.

We will not in this recipe deal with identifying bribes which are received by persons in the organization so that they will provide work or grant favours to suppliers, customers, agents, consultants, and the like. Because the money flows are outside of the system and outside of your organization, and are

Example 6.21 Direct marketing, dirty money or both?

It was common practice at the time in a Swedish multinational company that agents were used to help develop the company in so-called 'new markets' (such as parts of Asia and the Former Soviet Union, South America, etc.). Some of these agents were front companies in so-called DMCs with bank accounts in countries like Switzerland and Austria at the time. That way an effective 'cut-out' was in place to ensure that it would be very difficult to trace the source of the money, and the costs of these 'facilitation payments', as they were considered, were handled by a department at head office called 'Direct Marketing' (or DM).[14] When the system was finally exposed for what it was, i.e., a widespread system for the payment of 'necessary bribes' and the money flows were traced, it was found that a very small and select group of senior managers, including the head of international sales and the chief financial officer of Austria, had paid around 30 per cent of the money to the persons who were supposed to receive the bribes, and kept the rest for themselves (minus, of course, fees to lawyers and external accountants whom they had to pay to help set up the front companies). When confronted with this, they explained their rationale for doing it. They were taking a huge personal risk on behalf of the company and this was their compensation for doing so. They also were sure that the company would not pursue them for theft because the company would be implicating itself at the same time (in other words they felt that they had a gold-plated insurance policy).

often well protected by privacy laws, it is much quicker and more effective to look for the systems, and then start exploring the root causes. Sometimes, for example, an examination of a supplier's books and records can show money paid to officers of our organization but this is becoming more and more uncommon simply because people have wised up and are becoming much cleverer at hiding their trails.

Ingredients and tools

One of the most important steps to prepare, before even examining the money flows, is to try to understand your own organization's culture and attitude towards bribes. You need to start to probe and identify rhetoric vs. reality gaps by asking tough and challenging questions such as:

- While the code of conduct says that we never pay any form of bribe, we realize that this is impractical in some markets. How is it done, and how is it done so that the management can either plausibly deny any knowledge of it, or that your organization can claim that it still believed it was acting within the law?
- How do the organization's own tolerance levels judge between employees being influenced through dinners, etc. by customers and suppliers, compared with the organization's own policies in respect of winning favour and influence with its own customers and other third parties?

By thinking through the above questions, you can get to know your own organization's 'appetite' and this will help you identify what you are looking for and why you are looking. Also it is important to remember that this is not always a very popular recipe with some people because it shows what people are desperately trying to hide!

The following list of documents and transactional data is not exhaustive but should help set you on the right path to discovering suspected bribery or theft disguised as bribery:

- your own organization's Code of Conduct or Ethics, and, if they exist, anti-bribery policies;
- annual reports over time (which can identify the areas of business and geography where your organization operates, as well as where the motivation for business growth may lie);
- supplier and customer master data, plus transactions;
- a copy of a trial balance (to help identify potentially loosely controlled cost accounts or commission accounts);
- transaction list (or data files) of payments which are outside of the normal payments flow (to suppliers and customers);
- lists of agents (in particular, sales agents), who have been approved and authorized to act on your organization's behalf and who could be receiving sales commissions.

Method

Table 6.3 is a selection of some of ways to find the signs of significant bribery and fake bribes. All have these have worked and it is sometimes the simplest methods that are the most successful. Typically what you will end up discovering is one transaction or a group of related transactions which will in turn open the door to a more embedded and ingrained system, which needs to be explored and unwound. It takes a long time to separate fake from real, but the most important thing is to find it so it can be looked at and it is controlled.

Table 6.3 Six methods of false bribes and how to find them

Typical manifestation(s) of paid bribes (and false bribes)	*How to detect bribes (and false bribes)*
1 Payments to front companies As emphasized in Recipe 2 in this chapter, dealings with front companies and DMCs are often the key to identifying signs of bribery	Perform a scan of payments via the accounts payable system, other payments, bank transactions, lists of known agents and receivers of commissions to identify the footprint of a company which is a pure shell (for example, typically a company in a small jurisdiction known for such companies, such as the British Virgin Islands or a front company operating from London). See Recipe 2 in this chapter.
2 The 'cash' account Sometimes it's almost too obvious to believe it is true. A review of supplier and customer master files can sometimes reveal supplier and customer names accounts called 'Cash' (or equivalent names in different languages) which have been set up for the sole purpose of making cash disbursements (or vague bank transfers).	Build up a list of key words such as 'cash' and equivalents in other languages and use them to search the supplier and customer master file names. You may be surprised how simple it is to find them and then you need to start exploring what lies behind the big transactions.
3 The other unusual accounts Following on from the 'cash account' above, other strangely named accounts in the supplier and customer master files, and the general ledger can be easy giveaways. Sometimes it is not just the name of the account but also the account number (which could be prefixed, for example, by 999 or 888, or XXX). Often these 'odd' accounts are used as a cover for the payment of bribes and other similar payments.	Something we do not do enough but maybe should do, is just sit back and read the account names (and numbers). This does sound a bit 'sad' and something we would leave to the auditors, but given the fact that experienced external auditors rarely have time to work much at this level of detail, the 'what jumps out at you as strange' is a very useful little recipe.

(Continued)

Table 6.3 (Continued)

Typical manifestation(s) of paid bribes (and false bribes)	How to detect bribes (and false bribes)
4 Odd payments outside of the regular flow Even though people can rationalize that facilitation payments (or bribes) are essential or necessary for business, nobody wants them lying around for everyone to see. Most large organizations have regular ways of making payments, through which the vast majority of payments are made. There are also a number of other ways to make payments which are less commonly used. These can include one-off bank transfers, so-called 'manual payments' and even cash. It is often in these 'odd' payment flows we can find the transactions which turn out to be bribery hiding.	Identify what are the normal ways of making payments in your organization. Then identify all the other ways payments can be made. Scrutinize these payments closely to identify regular receivers of such payments and who they are.
5 The dangling credit notes and the IOU accounts In Chapter 4, we saw how the credit note to a customer (Lazer Berman) was paid to a completely different company, in a different country. This turned out to be a bribe paid to some managers at the customer who insisted that if they did not get their 'cut', they would cancel the contract. In the example on which it is based, it turned out that our organization's salesperson was also getting a small piece of the pie, because that way the customer had a hold over them. The key indicator was that we identified a customer account that was nearly always in credit (or what we call an I OWE YOU, or 'IOU' customer account).	Identify any customer account where the balance of this account indicates that your organization always owes the customer money. Scrutinize these transactions and find where the money really goes. Similarly (although this will take a little more digging), identify credit notes which are paid out to customers rather than netted against future invoices. These could be for discounts or even damages. Identify where these payments are made and if they are different from the original customer account.
6 Commissions paid (supposedly above board) Large organizations often employ agents. Because of increasing anti-bribery legislation and regulation, there have been copious demands placed on ensuring agents are properly approved and registered. However, often in practice this can mean ensuring a sort of 'paper compliance', including formal due diligence, responding to questions such as the agent signing off on a declaration with your company's code of ethics and completing all the correct mountains of paperwork to be an agent.	Once you have identified a list of approved agents, look carefully at the invoices they send you and what work they are doing, for red flags Perform some open source research (see Chapter 8) into who the agent actually is, using whatever information you can find Quite often you will find gold exactly where everything has the semblance of being approved

One of the things that is missing from the set of recipes above is how to discover so-called 'small bribes' which could include payments to customs and other public officials, excessive entertainment of customers, etc. Sometimes the most creative schemes are used to disguise or 'legalize' bribery. For example, in one case, the country marketing manager of a commercial vehicles sales company devised a scheme to maintain customer loyalty. The customers were told that since they had purchased over a certain amount in the year, that they could be part of a lottery where the winners would receive a free trip and accommodation to a company event in an exotic location. However, the 'catch' was that every single one of the 400-plus customers won!

The ways of detecting these sorts of small bribes have to a certain extent already been covered in Recipe 1. This should be combined with careful scrutiny of sales and marketing expenses, as well as certain travel and entertaining costs.

Example 6.22 Systematic embezzlement disguised as bribery[15]

In one instance, where we followed the money paid out by an organization, it travelled from the industrial company's head office to Luxemburg to an Isle of Man company that was controlled by a member of the management team who distributed the funds to his people. However, the explanation for these payments given by the same senior manager to the board was 'unsuccessful facilitation payments to certain African leaders who in the end were either ousted or did not fully live up to their side of the deal'. These accusations were refuted widely in Ghana and Nigeria and at least one former president even went on public record to say that he had not received any bribes relating to these contracts. However, because the perceived credibility of Africa was so low when it came to preventing corruption, the African perspective was largely ignored in the West.

How to present the results ('serving suggestion')

There is no best way to present the results of what you find, as this will depend so much on the culture and attitude in your organization, the personalities of the people you are presenting to, and, in some of the more extreme cases, if they are involved or in fact if they prefer that you did not tell them so that they could live in the comfort zone of being able to plausibly deny any knowledge.

Before even speaking to anyone, it is crucial that you weigh up all these considerations, but two hard and fast rules, which will help, are:

● Stick to the facts and what you know, without introducing any form of moral judgement or rubbing someone's nose in the dirt.
● Downplay any supposed sensationalism (in other words this is a time where 'boring is best!').

Sometimes a touch of humour can help, provided it is used carefully as in Example 6.23.

Example 6.23 Trucks or noodles?

A western company was trying to expand its business by setting up a factory in Asia. They were approached by a local consultant living near their European head office. The consultant had parents who came from the Asian city where the company wanted to establish itself. There were numerous obstacles and red tape but the consultant convinced the company that he could help them open doors, get introductions to the right people and cut through some of the unnecessary bureaucracy involved. He was so convincing that he received a sizeable monthly retainer as well as an expense account for additional expenses where required. Everyone knew it was a short cut and probably involved small-scale bribery but this factory was badly needed. It was already announced that they were going to open soon in the latest annual report.

What transpired was lots of correspondence, quite a few expenses and just a few meetings, which came to nothing, but in substance, no further progress. In the end, the company said thank you and goodbye to the consultant and decided to write off the whole affair as experience. Nothing much more would have happened until at the end of a year when the curious chief financial officer decided that it could be interesting to discover where the consultant's money really went, and a small investigation into the now bankrupt company belonging to the consultant was carried out. To everyone's surprise it was discovered that the consultant and a few friends had used the money to start a noodle-import business and were planning to build a small noodle factory in the same Asian city.

The correspondence was largely fictitious and the meetings were simply meetings with the consultant's extended family and friends in the city, so it was no wonder that they came to nothing.

Useful tips

It is worth remembering that while nobody likes having his or her nose rubbed in the dirt, at the same time (as Example 6.23 shows) management don´t like being taken for a ride or being cheated.

It is worth appreciating that codes of conduct that contain sweeping statements such as 'our organization never pays or receive bribes' are common. Probably few people, including management, believe this is a true reflection of the status quo, but feel that this is what the code of conduct simply has to say. You can often use what you find to explore and probe with management this gap between rhetoric and reality.

If your organization starts paying bribes because of the feeling that it is the only thing to do, you are probably getting involved with criminals who have bigger criminal minds than yours and you are likely to be scammed yourself in the end (as Example 6.24 demonstrates).

Example 6.24 What goes round sometimes comes around to haunt you

A West European company who wished to secure the output of a metals plant in the Former Soviet Union was required by the plant owners to pay a lump sum commission of $1.25 million into a Vanuatu bank account of a Guernsey company. The company knew that probably this was a bribe but received strict assurances in writing from the owner that the commission was to cover administration fees. Turning a blind eye, they made the transaction but needed to re-classify the costs as general sales expenses. However, due to a scam, the first instalment was paid by accident to another fraudulent company, meaning that part of the $1.25 million had to be paid twice. Later this was found to be a scam and the first company and the scam company were in fact working together.

Recipe 7 Detecting an over-developed sense of entitlement

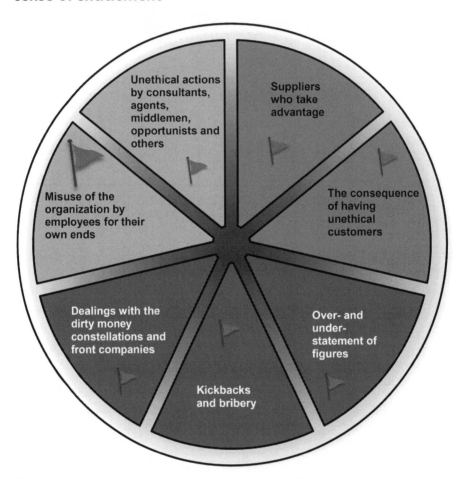

Figure 6.9 The Wheel of (mis)Fortune: focusing mainly on misuse of the organization by employees

What is an 'over-developed sense of entitlement' or 'ODSE syndrome'?

At the London–based Fraud Investigation Agency, where I worked for some years, we jokingly used this term to describe a person working inside an organization who felt they were worth more than they were being paid and who decided to do something about it ... through fraud![16] After a while, I realized that if you ask the average person working in an organization, 'would you feel your organization was being cheated if they paid you more?' few would answer 'yes'. So maybe there are many more of us with an over-developed sense of entitlement than first meets the eye, but few who would be willing to commit fraud to bridge the entitlement gap. Whatever the case, most people who do take the plunge and earn a little extra through fraud don't see it as fraud. They tend to rationalize it using excuses such as 'I am worth it' or 'I am more efficient any way'.

While an over-developed sense of entitlement can theoretically apply to everybody, the people in the organization who are most at risk often tend to be the upper management – exactly those people whom we believe have reached the dizzy heights. Some of these people still feel that, in spite of what they are paid, they deserve more (see Chapter 3 and the rhetorical question: 'What do people with lots of money typically want most?'). Other high-risk groups include those other people who simply feel that they deserve more and are not being respected enough, and people who enjoy committing fraud for the challenge of it or some personal need, or people who for one reason or another have been tempted by some outside party but wish they could find a way out. There are also so-called 'accidental fraudsters', people who commit fraud without fully or partly realizing it. Finally there is one rather rare category also worthy of mention, whom I call the 'corporate psychopath', the top dog who has absolutely no moral qualms about committing fraud, either for his benefit or for the company's benefit. He or she just believes it is the way of the world to win at all costs.

Example 6.25 The corporate psychopath shows his true colours

During a fraud investigation into bribery, embezzlement, accounting fraud and more, all under the nose of, and later found out to be on the instructions of, a senior vice president, the same vice president was found to have purchased and charged to the company two relatively expensive items of ladies clothing at Munich airport on his way back from a senior management meeting. Coincidently, the date was 14 February (Valentine's Day). The VP lied at first that these items were work-related but after been shown the proof of what was purchased, had no qualms in admitting that the items were for two lady friends (not his wife, by the way). In spite of many similar private expenses of this nature charged to the company, he could not see what the fuss was about and was visibly angry with my colleague for broaching the subject at all. After all, he, the VP, was a huge asset to the company, he had personally turned it round from loss-making to profit in the past two years in spite of very lucrative offers from competitors, and since he had been there, he had done his best to boost employee morale and culture (it was if his ODSE was off the scale!).

When we asked him if the other 499 or so employees who reported to him had contributed to the company, and if they did so, did they not deserve similar perks, I think he saw, just in the nick of time that we were being ironic, and decided not to bluntly answer the question but call for his lawyer.

As the behaviourist Professor Dan Arielly stated in his YouTube talk 'The honest truth about dishonesty' (see Chapter 5), there are some big cheaters and many little cheaters. What Dan did not also say is that there is everything in between too. Since we know that we can detect an over-developed sense of entitlement in a large number of people, it is important to decide where to focus. So before you start to look for the people inside who are causing the most damage to your organization, it is important to ask ourselves the question: What are we looking for and why? Because the last thing we want to do is embark on a witch-hunt, infringe on people's privacy or start acting like the secret police.

Ingredients and tools

Before starting out, you should have access to the following:

- a list of employees (names, dates of birth and addresses, if you are allowed to use them but it is very important not to infringe any laws related to privacy of the individual or misuse any data related to the individual);
- organization charts and authorization limits pertaining to employees and management (i.e. who has the most authority in terms of value of deals they can accept or approve);
- the dates when people started to work in your organization;
- access to free public company databases;
- expense reports but it is very important to select employees systematically or completely randomly but use no judgement in creating a sample;
- a list of suppliers' and customers' names.

Method

The method described below is an example only and not complete in any way but illustrates the type of systematic approach which can be taken in order to identify the key persons possessing the ODSE syndrome. To show that recipes can be described differently, this particularly recipe has been described like a quasi-algorithm but written out more in full sentences.

Begin:

Examine a SAMPLE A of employees of Company XYZ defined as:

All employees who have the authority to approve transactions over a value of 'n' (where 'n' = a set approval limit), OR

All employees over a certain grade, OR

All employees

For each employee who is part of the defined sample:

Identify using name, unique personal number, date of birth, or similar:

All external companies that they appear to have an active role in (Company 1, Company 2, Company 3, etc.)

For each company identified:

IF: The date the employee joined the company was AFTER the date of commencing employment with Company XYZ, THEN: Review if purpose of Company 1 is compatible or conflicts with Company, and

IF deemed not compatible, THEN mark for further review

REPEAT for each company identified allocating an indicator based on a weighted factor based on a proportion of 'p' for each employee

REPEAT the process for each employee in the sample

THEN: FOR each employee in SAMPLE A: IDENTIFY and allocate a weighted factor 'q1', 'q2', etc. based on the size of each indicator:

Diverse and unspecified posts over a certain defined amount (q1), OR

Large and repetitive round number expense posts (q2)

Other posts (q3) (to be defined as incongruent with normal behaviour in your own organization, for example, trips to Hawaii when your organization has no operations or activities in Hawaii)

SUM q1+q2+q3 + p for each employee

SORT AND RANK and EXAMINE.

You can read more about recipes to detect fraud fast together with examples in Chapter 7.

Example 6.26 Sometimes the story behind it and what comes out of it are more important than the fraud itself

A senior manager, who did not live in London, had flown into expensive conferences in London with colleagues mainly because he wanted to watch Arsenal play football at home, but he did not attend much of the conference, arriving late and leaving early. He had actually 'attended' a course which he had applied to but which was cancelled at the last minute, simply because he had promised his wife that she could join him on the trip. (Unusually he did not tell his wife that the course was cancelled, as she would probably think he was a fraudster.) Finally, he was on the board of two companies, which he had not declared to his employers and was receiving director's fees for meetings he attended when he said he was elsewhere doing his regular job. This did lead to dismissal but the senior manager was so ashamed of his own behaviour and wanted a clean start in life that he insisted on paying back every single penny that he had cost the company as well as the costs of lost working time, and the costs of the investigation itself. He even wrote an article on the company's website explaining how he got into this mess and how much he learnt from it, praising the company's top management for the way they handled it.

Example 6.27 Detecting an ODSE can lead to other things

An across-the-board search of active roles in companies highlighted one very senior salesperson, Mr R, who had recently started a property company which rented out industrial buildings. This company called 'Rybe Ltd' turned out to be renting buildings to Mr R's employer, which itself was questionable. One thing led to another and it was identified that Mr R also was in league with a number of suppliers. The final icing on the cake was that Mr R also was running a sales cartel together with competitors that artificially kept prices high. The resulting court case against Mr R took place over a year later by which time Mr R was a much-reduced person in terms of his health. His defence lawyer, pointing to a frail-looking Mr R in court, suggested to the judge that other colleagues of Mr R were jealous of his success at the time and that his client was the victim of a witch hunt.

Thankfully this was not the case. Mr R's ODSE syndrome had been discovered through some systematic tests to discover fraud, which could be demonstrated in court, to the satisfaction of the judge, and even Mr R's own lawyer.

How to present the results ('serving suggestion')

When presenting results of this sort of recipe to find fraud, as far as possible examples should be anonymized, so as not to lead to any unnecessary or undue suspicion of individuals. One should present the facts plainly and once again (like Recipe 6) in a rather 'boring' and non-sensational manner. Also no element of judgement should be used and it's important not to jump to conclusions. Sometimes a relationship diagram showing people and their connections could be used.

Useful tips

- It's all too easy to become a Rottweiler when looking at your own colleagues. Remember we are all human and we can make mistakes or succumb to external pressures. Your colleagues should not be seen as 'easy meat', unless you are dealing with a corporate psychopath or a real power player on the inside.
- Similarly, too much emphasis can be placed on digging into expense reports, which can be a very time-consuming task. Over-reviewing expense reports can lead to focusing on just the 'little cheaters' and accidental fraudsters because they are often the easiest to find. What we are looking to identify here is something a more substantial than taxi receipts and expense frauds. At the same time, people who pad their expenses have a high propensity to cheat on other things, as demonstrated by the case of Mr 'coffee and cake', the consultant Andy Stevens, in Example 6.19.

At all times consider how you may wish to deal with what you find (see Chapter 9).

Recipes to avoid

Before starting to use the recipes, it is worth providing an explanation as to why at least two types of 'recipes' commonly believed to be associated with finding fraud are not included in this book.

The first relates to ensuring as a fraud detective that you can fully defend your approach and methodology both legally, ethically and morally, meaning that you can have a clear conscience that there has been no infringement of an individual's basic rights or right to data privacy. The second recipe to avoid relates to testing internal controls for the sake of it, but not specifically looking for fraud.

 Steer clear of infringing people's rights in respect of personal data

One of the most common 'tests' which I have come across has been data-matching between supplier, customer, external partner and other data against employee's home addresses, telephone numbers, email addresses, etc. It is natural that an employer will need to have on file personal details pertaining to an employee for the purposes of contact in an emergency, to pay salaries, etc. An employer may also have, with the employee's permission, of course, similar details for the employee's next of kin. Data protection legislation varies across the world and of course there are exceptions. But as a general rule, personal data is held for a purpose and should not be misused, i.e. not used for a purpose that was not intended.

The typical data-matching test recommended by data-analytics companies purporting to be fraud experts often include matching employee's personal details against the details of suppliers, customers and other third parties. This might seem like a good idea until you consider the legal, ethical and even moral implications of using somebody's data that was provided in good faith for a different purpose. Even if you do not subscribe to the ethical or moral views, tighter data protection legislation and the cost of bad publicity, not to mention legal costs, have made this sort of simplistic test rather obsolete today.

In certain cases, there may be good reason, or just cause to use personal data in an investigation, subject to sound legal advice, but as a general thumb it is advisable to leave personal data out of the running. From experience, there are often other, more legal, ethical and moral ways to identify the same frauds, if they are significant.

Don't waste time on OCD

A missing signature on a piece of paper or a missing tick in a box is not usually a red flag of fraud. In today's OCD (obsessive-compliance disorder) world, ticks in boxes and signatures on pieces of paper to confirm we have read documents that we have not read, are rather meaningless.

As described in Chapter 2, we live in the age of small print, disclaimers, and ticks in boxes. The meaning behind a signature, which is often electronic, holds little value other than in legal battles. This is because we are expected to read a lot of stuff which we do not read. In the past, there was a family of fraud detection recipes which I like to call 'look for where the box has not been ticked', which might have identified so-called 'abusers of the system' but today these have a very diminished value because in effect a person who signs without reading what they are signing or ticks a box without studying what is behind the hyperlink, is in effect also an abuser of the system.

Some examples of fraud detection tests which may have worked in the past but today are rather ineffectual at finding fraud include:

- Where people undertake many transactions on the same day to avoid authorization limits (note this can be fraud, but it can also be so many other things). In particular, sometimes people will deliberately ensure that what they do is above their authorization limit so other people have to sign off (and take the blame). Tests on authorization limits throw up too many false positives today (i.e. things that may look unusual but are in fact quite normal).
- Incompatible access right to IT system to indicate that IT systems are compromised, and fraud is likely. With today's IT systems, access rights are so complex that they are bound to be compromised or incompatible. Anyway, a determined hacker can break through almost any normal corporate or organizational system anyway.
- Looking for the absence of documents which are supposedly meant to legitimize transactions (such as purchase orders, contracts, etc.) but were never read.

These tests may still have *some* value in that they will ensure that internal controls are working and are still as such needed, but they are not fraud tests.

Example 6.28 When a criminal signs to say they will comply with the code of ethics, it probably has little value

A large European freight company 'T Ltd' relied heavily on subcontractors. Twelve transport companies were awarded contracts across one
country. The country manager insisted that before each contract was
awarded that the owners of each company attended a meeting with the
management of T Ltd to discuss and finally sign T Ltd's code of ethics.
All twelve transport companies attended meetings and eleven of them
signed at the end of the meetings. Only one owner refused to sign. He
was told that his contract would not be renewed unless he complied
with the code of conduct. After a few weeks deliberation he also signed.
Two years later the police as part of a national action, arrested the owners
of the eleven companies and charged them with being members of an
organized crime syndicate.

Example 6.29 Putting faith in a pointless procedure

A major supplier of services was found to be grossly overcharging and
bribing employees. The head of the department using this supplier was
asked why she had not noticed anything wrong before. She said she
had been comforted by the fact that every one of the two hundred
or so invoices she had seen had had a purchase order, so she felt that
someone else must have been controlling the costs to ensure that they
were properly approved. When the purchase orders were examined,
they were found to have been put into the system between two to ten
days after the invoice was received and were in effect a replica of the
invoice and were created by the same people who received the invoice
using an authority level delegated to them. The head of the department
realized straight away that her department, by following a required procedure (i.e. every invoice should have a purchase order), were following a 'pointless procedure' creating the semblance of order and control
but in fact were creating a massive loophole which was exploited by
the supplier.

Notes

1 The methodology, invented by Nigel Iyer, Veronica Morino and John Wallhoff at Hibis is described in more detail on www.fraudacademy.hibis.com.

2 See www.chathamhouse.org/publications/papers/view/198133

3 Something that looks strange for a number of reasons but in the end is OK.

4 I say 'erroneously' as it often tends to imply that the person doing the purchasing is the initiator, whereas more often than not, the supplier is the instigator, many times where no one on the inside is wittingly involved.

5 How many trailing zeroes you decide to choose will depend on the currency and also the size of your operation.

6 The author of this book often has to brainstorm with himself as many people say they do not have a clue what he is talking about.

7 Published by Gower (now Routledge) in 1979 and has since been followed by a string of very practical, informative and sometimes rather eclectic books on fraud, corruption and bad lies in business from the Comer school of thought.

8 I think this was the moment when I realized that my conscience would never allow me to work for a big, multidisciplinary firm as an external auditor and I decided to move on soon afterwards.

9 Laws, regulations and just general bureaucracy have imposed a number of checks and controls (some of them effective) to prevent companies becoming suppliers. However, not always the same stringent controls are applied to new customers so occasionally the route into the company as a supplier can be as a customer.

10 Andy Stevens was in fact playing on both sides of the table. It came out in the end that he had taken the management for hire position partly because he needed the cash and partly because if he managed to bring in his previous and failing company Quodos as a client, he was promised a large bonus, as well as an increase in the value of his shareholding in Quodos. The coffee and cake were in fact irrelevant but were in some way his 'banana skin', the tell-tale signs that Andy was just a bit too greedy for his own good.

11 This example is illustrated in more detail in the 'The Fraud Detectives' story at the end of this book.

12 In this case, the so-called consultant was a lawyer who, when interviewed, protested that this was possible because (1) they had been working so hard; and (2) they were legally entitled to bill 15 minutes of time even if the work done was for a 30-second phone call. The client was apparently such a 'pain' that they kept calling and in this way the hours mounted up, so that on that particular day, there were in fact 27.75 hours. The ancient Egyptians, who are believed to be credited with the origins of the 24-hour day, might have cause to disagree.

13 Caution needs to be exercised at all times when looking into people's web-footprint and social media profiles. In particular, there should be no breach of privacy legislation.

14 While the 'Direct Marketing' department was referred to as 'DM', only a few people, including the head of Internal Audit, saw the irony that DM could also stand for 'dirty money'.

15 Taken from *The Continuing Imperialism of Free Trade* (Higgins, Morino and Iyer 2018).

16 This also can be explained through the 'Theory of Anomie', which was simplified for me once by Mike Comer as follows: Mr X has reached his glass ceiling at his employment and knows he will be paid no more. But he thinks he is capable of so much more and can reach the dizzy heights if only he was not blocked. So what does he do? Either Mr X throws his energies into some obscure passion and becomes champion tiddlywinks player in his village, president of the local 'river-wideners' club or, if he is feeling rather adventurous, sets his sights on becoming local champion at Haggis Hurling (presuming that Mr X is not a resident of Scotland where the delightful Haggis roams at large in the mountains of the Cairngorms, attracting large numbers of premier-league hurlers). Or, instead, Mr X takes it out on his job and turns to fraud to get the self-satisfaction he so desperately craves. He starts small but succeeds and becomes so good at it that he is both laughing quietly to himself at his colleagues and laughing all the way to the bank.

Chapter 7

How to follow the money and find fraud fast

Sometimes it is the people who no one can imagine anything of, who do the things no one can imagine.

(Alan Turing)[1]

A hot-air balloon is hovering above a field. The sole occupant of the balloon, obviously lost, calls down to a solitary man whom she sees walking on a path below: 'Hey there! Could you please tell me where I am?' The man on the ground glances up, thinks for just a second and replies: 'You are in a hot-air balloon, about, I would say, 32 or 33 metres above a field.' The balloonist cannot help laughing as she responds: 'Many thanks. I am guessing you are a chartered accountant.' The man is shocked. 'I am! How could you tell?' And the reply from the balloon is: 'Well, your information is very accurate and thorough, but completely useless to me . . . at the moment!'[2]

Follow the money, focus on fraud and let your fantasy fly

One of the most common defeatist arguments about not being able to discover fraud early which I have heard is: 'If armies of external auditors, highly trained lawyers, accountants and regulators cannot find fraud early, then what hope do I, a normal person, have?' On the other hand, the minds of accountants, auditors, lawyers and other fraud specialists might be 'too highly trained' to be able to spot the obvious. Cynics may go further in stating that if a problem is shown to be quite simple, then who would need the specialists? The recipes in the previous chapters are all tried and tested. Simple as they may seem, they consistently churn our good results. And as you hopefully have seen in the recipes and examples in Chapters 1, 4, 5 and 6, they are easy to follow and use.

This chapter is about how to let fantasy fly while simultaneously applying a sense of structure by:

- exploring what is meant by the phrase 'follow the money', how it lies at the heart of fraud detection and why a certain level of structure and methods is required to keep focused on fraud and 'stay on target', and at the same time allow more time for reflection and creative thinking;
- overcoming the 'defeatist attitude' that finding fraud is not possible, that there are too many false alarms, that it is not possible to get proof, etc.

What does 'follow the money' mean in practice?

The flow of money is one of the most reliable sources of information. And it is not just what is there but also what is NOT there which gives away that something is wrong. Like the very simple examples in Chapter 1, compact money flows are the best give-away. They are reliable and they can be analysed and evaluated in a consistent manner.

Often the flow of money is all you need. Extending our cooking analogy, a little further, the quality of the meal does not necessarily triple because there are three times more types of ingredients and cooking utensils available. Sometimes over-extending your reach can lead to more chances of failure.

'Follow the money' is a popular catch-phrase which came into being soon after the Watergate scandal,[3] and has been used since in investigative journalism, political debate and, to an extent, in popular culture. Often it means scrutinizing the money flows to see where the trail starts or leads (in the case of Watergate, that the money used to pay the company which was involved in bugging the opposition's confidential discussions in the Watergate building in Washington, DC, was suspected of originating in the White House). In the context of this book, follow the money is used as a mantra to ensure that the fraud detective pays attention to where the money goes and where it comes from and does not get side-tracked or distracted by too much spurious information. For example:

- If you were trying to identify people and parties whom your organization really should not be paying, then don't beat around the bush looking at authorization routines, lack of purchase orders, or compliance with procedures. Just zoom in on the heart of the matter and find some front companies or DMCs or organizations you really should not be paying money to and start asking yourself why.
- If you want to find those customers who are getting too good a deal, go straight to the heart of the matter and examine the deals where large credit notes are paid back to customers and see where they are paid to. You will be wasting your time looking to see if they are approved or not at the right level, as most certainly someone will have signed off on them (whether they knew what they were signing or not!).

Because money flows, where they start, where they end and the points which they pass through, are relatively consistent and uniform data, they also lend themselves to algorithms which are described later in this chapter.

A fraud detective's tale, combining rigor, method, fantasy, intuition, following the money and the magic of structured recipes[4]

Cast and background

An urban rail company in a major European capital city called Urban Rail.
Lionel Axeman was the overall Managing Director.
Benjamin Holter was the principal internal advisor on preventing fraud.
Peter and Harry are two foremen, responsible for maintenance and construction at their respective site-offices.

The fuse is lit

The trigger was an anonymous, hand-written letter containing a minor allegation:

TO MR LIONEL AXEMAN
1 JANUARY 1997

I HAVE NO 'AXE' TO GRIND MYSELF BUT HAVE BEEN
FOLLOWING MATTERS CLOSELY AND WISH TO BRING
TO YOUR ATTENTION THAT HARRY DAVIDSON AND
PETER JAMES, RESPECTIVE FOREMEN AT ALTON
AND LILSLAND INTERCHANGE STATIONS, HAVE
TOGETHER BEEN OPERATING A COMPANY WHICH
THEY REFER TO AS 'WBW' WHICH THEY USE TO DO
AND INVOICE WORK ON THE SIDE, USING COMPANY
EQUIPMENT, VEHICLES AND I BELIEVE ALSO SUP-
PLIES. YOU SHOULD LOOK INTO IT.

The call . . . and decision time

Benjamin, who had just been on a fraud awareness course,
took advice on how to deal with this letter. Very quickly
it became clear that there was some truth in the WBW-
allegation. Careful investigative desktop research showed
that Harry and Peter, who each had been employed for
over 10 years, had in fact, 18 months ago, registered a
partnership in the National Companies Register called
'WBW – What Will Be Will Be'. However, as it was just a
small company, the reporting and disclosure requirements
placed on it were very limited and other than that the
company purpose included 'providing assistance to signal
engineers, etc.', there was very little information to go on.

But it was unclear why Harry and Peter hadn't done
anything to hide it. Maybe the answer to this question lay
in the atmosphere of the organization. According to Lionel
and Benjamin, for years, there had been concerns that
from top to bottom in the company people had little businesses on the side. But apart from rumours, there was little
concrete to go on. There was also a feeling that Urban Rail
was at the beck and call of some of the powerful suppliers
and contractors whom they depended upon, especially in
the areas of signalling and maintenance. But once again,
nothing tangible surfaced.

So, the question was: should Urban Rail act on the
information provided, and confront Harry and Peter

immediately? Or should they bring out the investigative sledgehammer and throw a lot of resources, including surveillance, interviews with others and more, to try to find out the whole truth? Or was there another way . . . a more discreet and reflective way to assess the organization culture and find out what else could be going on?

The initial investigation and what it showed

In this case, the more reflective approach was adopted which led to some very interesting results. It was first proven from statements (backed up by an invoice from WBW to one of their customers) that, among other things, WBW was in fact used as a 'vehicle' for suppliers and others to steal equipment and re-charge internal work to Urban Rail back to Urban Rail. All the evidence pointed to a group of powerful suppliers which called the shots, not Harry or Peter.

An 'electrostatic detection device' (or ESDA machine) was used to analyse the original handwritten anonymous letter. An ESDA machine uses a combination of electrostatic charges and graphite power (or 'magic dust') to detect indentations on the page. which may have been made by a letter on a pad several pages above (but one which had been ripped off and thrown away). ESDA's magic dust brought to light the indentations of a whole new letter seemingly written on the pages above the whistleblower letter. It described gross malpractice and bribery related to the enormous signalling and maintenance controls and collusion between some of Urban Rail's senior engineers, who were way above Harry and Peter's pay grade, and two large contractors. The secret letter, which had all the ingredients of a conspiracy theory, even mentioned the murder of a senior engineer (who had died on site in what was concluded to be an accident a year previously).

Even at this stage it could have been easy to conclude that this was an open and shut case. Dismissing Harry and Peter would have been easy and that would have been that. The 'secret' letter, at best, was just adding oil to the fire of conspiracy theories with little concrete proof whatsoever. But

Lionel and Benjamin were fed up with increasing smoke without any fire and said they wanted either proof or were going to dispel all rumours. So, instead, a discreet but rigorous 'follow the money' approach was adopted.

What transpired from the 'follow the money' approach

Throughout Chapters 5 and 6 we examined recipes which have been used to solve the problem of 'how to find the frauds which we know are present'. These recipes are just step-by-step methods which can also be applied to data. A step-by-step method such as this, often using data, with a finite goal and end, is commonly called 'an algorithm', which is also one of the most important building blocks of a computer program.[5] By applying tried and tested fraud-finding recipes (sometimes known as algorithms) to the main financial inflows and outflows of Urban Rail (in a similar way to how an ESDA machine throws graphite dust at a charged sheet of paper), the following new cases were brought to light:

1   A scrap metal dealer had a lucrative contract to buy surplus material in huge quantities at either a very low cost, or sometimes was even paid to take materials away at no cost. Further in-depth examination showed that the materials being removed were of very high value and were resold on the open market, some at a very high profit, and some were even sold back, at this high profit to Urban Rail.

2   One supplier had sold an electrical device of some sort over 30 times for a value of around €5000 each. The company that sold the device appears, by the sequence of invoice numbers it issued, to have no other customer than Urban Rail, and the so-called 'factory' where the device was made turned out to be a terraced house in a middle-class suburb. The device itself, shown in Figure 7.1, which was supposed to be some form of 'optimizer', consisted of a rubber-clad electronics box with red and blue wires coming out of either side. Apparently, the device itself had never worked, according to one of the engineers whom we interviewed, and he said

he was rather curious what was so special about it. We persuaded him to take a hacksaw to the rubber block which he did hesitatingly but then laughed when he saw that the block was made completely of solid rubber, like an ice-hockey puck. There were no expensive electrical components in it at all.

3   Because of purchasing far too much equipment and parts, often from suppliers where there was a personal relationship between some of Urban Rail's own employees and suppliers, inventories in the accounts were grossly overvalued.

4   One of the senior engineers, who was involved in purchasing the rubber block, as well as working with the scrap metal merchant, was found to have falsified most of his higher-level engineering qualifications.

5   By examining the large money flows to the signalling companies, it became clear that costs were spiralling out of control. However, each time a significant contract payment was made, a very small payment was made to what appeared to be a small foundation for signal enthusiasts and engineers. Just a little more digging into this company showed that this so-called 'charity' turned out to be a special interest lobby group made up of an elite group of signal engineers from around the country who were promoting the interests of just ONE supplier . . . in this case, the same supplier where gross overcharging appeared to have taken place and also the same supplier which was named in the anonymous letter.

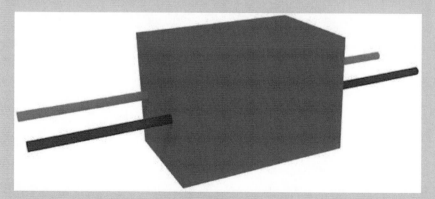

Figure 7.1 An electrical device for dummies

To their credit, Axeman and Holter used the insights given by cases 1-4 above and the anonymous letter to act against the frauds that were being committed and to address the root causes to stop them happening again in the future. However, it was harder to convince the board to initiate a more in-depth investigation into the award of a major signalling contract, which affected not just Urban Rail but also the National Rail network in the country. The evidence was only circumstantial and at the time it was hard to believe that a major European company with a pristine reputation, at the time, would bribe its way to getting a gold-plated implementation and maintenance contract with the local and national rail authorities in another country. With hindsight, it is easy to criticize the decision not to investigate at the time and the effects of a poor signal contract are still felt throughout the rail network, 20 years on.

The experiences described here demonstrate that by applying simple algorithms to the financial inflows and outflows, fraud can be discovered early without having to resort to heavy-handed, expensive and intrusive techniques. Ideally, if the algorithms had been run more regularly, then there would have been no need for the whistleblower letter either. There is no hocus-pocus to algorithms either. It is just about looking at money flows through a different 'lens', forcing what appears to be just lines of boring transactions to 'reveal their secrets'. But without creative thinking, fantasy and an unshakeable belief that fraud happens, even the most accomplished operator of the algorithms is likely to find nothing!

Example of the best money flows to follow to catch commercial fraud and corruption

In the context of fraud and corruption, money flows can be likened to the daily life-blood of an organization. Some of the most important money flows in typical organization are shown in Figure 7.2.

Two of the four quadrants represent the typical and anticipated money flows, i.e. payments to suppliers and receipts from customers. The other two quadrants represent the more unusual money flows, that are difficult to

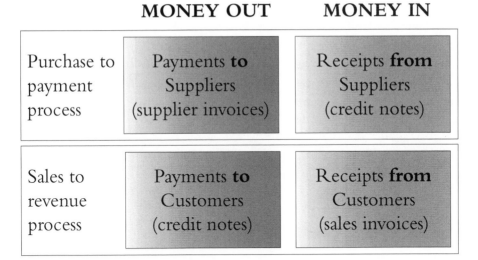

	MONEY OUT	**MONEY IN**
Purchase to payment process	Payments **to** Suppliers (supplier invoices)	Receipts **from** Suppliers (credit notes)
Sales to revenue process	Payments **to** Customers (credit notes)	Receipts **from** Customers (sales invoices)

Figure 7.2 Money out/money in matrix

anticipate, namely, when suppliers pay back money for whatever reason, and when you have to pay, or compensate a customer.

The magic of recipes applied to the money in and money out

These recipes can also be described as simple but powerful 'algorithms'. There is no need to be scared or put off by the word algorithm as an algorithm is 'A process to be followed in problem-solving operations'.[6]

For example, Alan Turing, whom some refer to as 'the father of algorithms', built a machine and programs to crack the German Enigma code, and was working with very small amounts of actual data. His machines had less computing power than the machines today, but he understood that if you ran enough tests, enough times, you would eventually 'hit the targets' that you believed were there to be hit. In other words, using computers is not about turning humans into dummies, but letting the machines do the repetitive and time-consuming work so that we, the humans, have more time to think.[7]

Because money flows are well defined and compact, they lend themselves well to structured recipes that can be run against the data. When looking for fraud and using follow the money recipes to help you, it is important to restrict how much data you have. Often just a few key fields are enough. The recipes in Chapter 6 were simply methods to combine and examine information and data intelligently, making sure that we were examining the 'right' data. Because information and most data are stored electronically, by using the right data and the appropriate algorithms, we are starting to build computer programs which help us pinpoint likely fraud and corruption rather fast. In other words, rather like Turing's machines, the program will run and run until it meets certain criteria and abruptly STOPS at the point it believes it has found your needle in a haystack.

Follow the money recipes to pinpoint patterns indicative of fraud[8] could be used to root out, for example:

- Suppliers which due to their invoicing patterns just seem to have one customer (i.e. you!) over a long period of time, where no credit notes indicate a lack of any questioning of the invoices.
- Customer invoicing where there is also a high volume, or value of credit notes, indicating that some form of preferential treatment may be given to customers in the form of discounts, settlement of complaints, or maybe because, to artificially inflate sales in an accounting period, the sales invoice was produced early, never sent but subsequently credited and then re-issued (and sent) in a later period.
- Where the flow of supplier invoices is 'interrupted' by a very occasional large, round sum credit note, indicating that possibly there was some form of dispute, normally settled by negotiation, and more often than not in the supplier's favour.
- Where a customer has more than one account, one for the regular invoice flows and one for discounts or even kickbacks to the customer, which are paid into another account.
- A customer where the balance to pay is regularly in the customer's favour, indicating that in fact the customer is, to all intents and purposes, behaving as a supplier.

They need not be more complex than this but of course the only limit is your own fantasy. By combining and fine-tuning algorithms such as these, much more advanced and sophisticated combinations can be developed to identify and pinpoint the frauds which we expect to see. But the fundamental principles remain:

- Always expect that fraud is present (if you don't, you will rarely find it, other than by accident).
- Do not overcomplicate things by using too much data.
- The follow the money recipes will only take you so far. The results must be reviewed within the context of your organization and never underestimate your own fantasy and powers of deduction.

Of course, financial flows to and from suppliers and customers are not the only key money flows in an organization. Other similar flows which are very important to capture could include payments and receipts which are outside of the normal flow (sometimes referred to as 'manual payments and receipts') and could include loans and loan repayments, payments to authorities, taxes, sales and purchases of major assets or property, bank transfers, etc. These can be included in the money flows to analyse in a similar way to the above major flows.

Payments to employees such as payroll and personal expense reimbursements are also money flows but should be treated with caution because data–protection legislation, combined with internal rules, may prohibit certain types of analysis to be done. For example, in many instances, matching of employee's home addresses against supplier and customer master data would be impermissible. Similarly, if an organization were to do an analysis of expenditure reimbursements, a systematic and 'fair' way would have to be found. Payroll in many countries is one of the best-controlled areas already being checked in detail by at least one other external authority or body.

A taste of algorithms and applying them to the money flows

Below are three simple examples of algorithms (using a series of logical statements using 'IF', 'AND' and 'OR' expressions).

Example 7.1 Finding the customer who is getting too good a deal

IF:

A customer is a significant customer in terms of how much is invoiced to them

OR: is a significant customer in terms of how many times it is invoiced

OR: there are both significant volumes of transactions

AND: significant amounts involved

AND: there are a significant number of credit notes within the transaction streams

OR: credit notes of a significant size are issued to the customer but to a different account

OR: these significant credit notes are paid out to a different bank account

OR: there are significant volumes of credit notes
    AND: the value of credit notes is high

THEN: there is a high likelihood that in some way the customer relationship is tainted by fraud, corruption or other forms of malpractice.

Example 7.2 Singling out the suppliers that are taking advantage

IF:

A supplier is a significant supplier in terms of how much they invoice to your organization is invoiced to them
    OR: is a significant supplier in terms of how many times it is invoiced
        OR: there are both significant volumes of transactions
            AND: significant amounts involved
AND: the invoice number provided by the supplier is relatively sequential
    OR: the invoice number provided by the supplier is random in some form and does not follow a pattern
    OR: the invoice number provided by the supplier contains spurious words or expressions
    OR: there is a high propensity of invoices for large, rounded sums

THEN: there is a high likelihood that in some way the supplier relationship is tainted by fraud, corruption or other forms of malpractice.

Example 7.3 Pinpointing possible dirty money

IF:

The supplier
OR: customer address field
OR: country code contains one of around a hundred keywords, such as CAYMAN, GUERNSEY, PANAMA, BVI, etc.
    OR: the bank account code does not match the recipient/payer country of domicile

AND: it is not within a region such as the EU
AND: significant value is involved

THEN: There is a likelihood that a DMC is involved

The above algorithms are simple by nature and are just illustrative of the type of code which can be created to help pinpoint fraud. It goes without saying that, for a computer, words like 'relatively sequential', 'large' and 'round', 'significant', etc. need to be well defined. These are just examples. It's not rocket science, it's about combining key data, smart programming and the capacity of the human brain to make deductions.

There are many more intricate structured follow the money recipes (or algorithms) that can be used. A collection of my top twenty algorithms based on the recipes in this book can be found on the publications pages of The Fraud Academy (www.fraudacademy.hibis.com). These include algorithms with names such as 'the supplier with a licence to print money', 'the customer we are bending over backwards to help' and 'the consultant or employee with an over-developed sense of entitlement', and many more, plus a report to show what sort of results these algorithms gave in reality.

The future: will 'AI' help?

There is a lot of talk about 'Artificial Intelligence', but the idea has been around for at least five decades. The basic principle is that, provided there are enough success stories of frauds that have been found using the sort of structured approach outlined in this chapter, then the possibility exists to feed these results into a purpose-built Artificial Intelligence (AI) shell which will then start to draw inferences (i.e. learn) how it is done and in time improve on the human methods. There has been a lot of talk about 'neural networks' and 'big data' but when it comes to basic corporate fraud, so far these systems have met with limited success. Possibly why the attuned fraud detective is still better than a machine can be compared to why humans are still better at making a good cup of tea,[9] compared to a machine. The answer lies in that 'cybernetic moment' and how we use computers as a tool as well as the 'fuzzy logic' we humans are so good at, compared to the much more precise machines.

In the future, as money flows become even more electronically controlled than they are today and crypto-currencies may become the norm, with every single detail of money flows recorded in a so-called 'blockchain', the world will be facing a whole set of new challenges, but basically the mechanics of fraud and corruption will remain the same.

Alan Turing's constant question, as portrayed in the 2014 film, *The Imitation Game*, was 'Can a machine think?' If Turing had been alive today, and was asked to crack the fraud problem, maybe he would have said. 'Are *humans* thinking?'

So, while AI may stand for Artificial Intelligence and while it can be said with some certainty that Artificial Intelligence will be helping us spot fraud sooner rather than later, probably a different sort of 'AI' is needed right now. An 'AI' where the 'A' stands for Atmosphere and the 'I' stands for Incentives.

If someone is going to stand a chance of finding fraud early in their organizations, then they need an atmosphere, which is conducive to do so, and some form of incentive to speak out and identify the ticking time bombs. And we need to carry on believing that we humans have the ability and power to think and imagine way beyond today's machines.

Notes

1 Alan Turing was the man who invented a machine to help crack the German Enigma code and help shorten the Second World War. Turing is also popularly known as a father of modern algorithms. He was the inspiration behind the work to design the MU 1, one of the world's first ever computers at what later became the University of Manchester Computer Science Department, where I studied between 1982 and 1985. Curiously while many of my senior professors were Alan Turing's students and followers, and, with hindsight, you could feel his presence and influence everywhere, the name Turing was never mentioned. But many years later, after Alan Turing was officially 'pardoned for homosexuality', the 1970s' Computer Science building where I studied was renovated and renamed 'The Alan Turing Building'.

2 My father told me this story when I was about 10 years old. In spite of this veiled parental warning, unable at that age to grasp all the nuances of the tale of the balloonist, I still became a chartered accountant. In 2018, 30 years after qualifying as a chartered accountant, I worked up the courage to tender my resignation to the Institute of Chartered Accountants in England and Wales. What I really wanted to say in my resignation letter was that I was waiting for some time after the death of my parents, who were so proud when I qualified in 1988, and that for years the auditing profession had disappointed me by not being able to be more successful at discovering fraud, in-spite of it not being difficult. However, I decided to keep a low profile and in my resignation letter I drew on the inspiration of the immortal words of Groucho Marx. 'Please accept my resignation. I don't want to belong to any club that will accept me as a member.' Funnily enough, I still have not officially left, as I was contacted by the then Chief Executive of the Institute, Michael Izza, who persuaded me that I should not leave but try to help re-energize the profession instead. So

at the time of publication of the book I probably should quote the words of another famous Michael (this time the fictional Michael Corleone from the film *The Godfather*). 'Just when I thought I was *out, they pull me back in.*'

3 Watergate was the political scandal in the USA in the early 1970s which led to the resignation of then US president Richard Nixon.

4 This story is true, but names have been changed as the case was never resolved and the consequences of the fraud can still be felt in the country.

5 Niklaus Wirth describes programming as the art of constructing algorithms in a systematic manner in his (1976) book, *Algorithms + Data Structures = Programs.*

6 OED definition: 'Algorithm: A process or set of rules to be followed in calculations or other problem-solving operations, especially by a computer.'

7 If you are looking for inspiration for algorithms you can find it in unusual places. For example, Rudyard Kipling's famous poem 'If', which starts: '**If** you can keep your head when all about you are losing theirs **and** blaming it on you, **If** you can trust yourself when all men doubt you . . . ' and ends on the note 'Yours is the Earth **and** everything that's in it, **And** – which is more – you'll be a Man, my son!', is basically an algorithm for self-fulfilment (of sorts).

8 You will find the patterns by 'joining the dots and looking backwards and you will find fraud'. Based on Steve Job's remark, presumably about his own controversial personal life: 'You can only connect the dots in your life by looking back – not forward. Connect the dots and find what you love.'

9 I still believe that in the western world at least, or at least in England or India, most people believe machine-made tea is inferior to the lovingly made human variant. In Douglas Adams' original and first book in his trilogy *The Hitchhiker's Guide to the Galaxy*, the spaceship's computer is thrown into total confusion so much by the question 'why can't you make a decent cup of tea?' that it ceases to process anything else. The program was never completed because the computer was re-booted to focus on stopping the spaceship crashing (maybe a more urgent task), so we can only speculate that the answer would be something like 'humans are just better at playing the lead role in certain matters', which I believe also includes spotting fraud (with machines helping us).

Part III:

DON'T PANIC

There is always a way to resolve things!

Chapter 8

What to do when you think you may have found fraud

People will believe anything if it is whispered through a crack in the door or down a muffled telephone line.

(Michael J. Comer)[1]

By now you should be feeling more confident, that as soon as we switch on that little fraud detective that is inside each and every one of us, we will find red flags of fraud and corruption. After all, there is a lot to find! But what we need is a recipe telling us how to progress our findings, sort out which ones are significant so as not to follow false leads and act in a way which does not cause disruption or alarm.

In Shakespeare's tragic play, *Hamlet*, after discovering numerous indications that his father was probably murdered by his father's brother, the hero found himself questioning the whole meaning of his life,[2] went on a quest for irrefutable evidence and, as a result, ended up dithering as to what action he should take next. While I am not claiming that finding red flag of frauds is as dramatic as this, there are some parallels in the sense that it is often quite difficult to know what to do next as we will never be 100 per cent sure.

Let's revisit the example of Green Brothers (and Recipe 1 in Chapter 6) and the example invoice where numerous red flags were spotted (see Figure 6.2). Before we even start to do research, the first thing we need to do is briefly summarize the most important things which we see just based on this document. From what we can see from invoice number GB 15, the company Green Brothers Ltd has issued an invoice in December 2015 where part of the 'urgent repair' work referred to is completed in January 2016, i.e. after the invoice date. The works seems to be done in a hurry and it is not clear which company is doing the work, i.e. Green Brothers Ltd or the company named at the bottom of the invoice 'AS Rohelised Vennad (OOO)'. From the email and telephone number provided, it appears that this company might be of Latvian, and not UK, origin but this is not clear from the invoice itself as, for example, one company could be trading 'on behalf of the other'. Lastly, the charge of £70,000 for plaster does appear to be a bit arbitrary (given that plaster would typically be charged for by weight).

The next step is to try and find out in a short time as much information as we can about Green Brothers Ltd, how it has 'behaved' in relation to our organization, who and what Green Brothers Ltd is, and what connections they have to other external companies, people and organizations. Even now, the objective is not to perform an extensive investigation but just to identify enough information to be able to decide whether this is a significant finding or not, whether further action needs to be taken and what this further action might be. The idea is to use a combination of internal research (looking at internal systems) and external open source research, primarily using the internet as an initial source. This is a technique we have named 'investigative desktop research' or IDR. As an illustration what was done in this case was the following:

1   By looking into the accounts payable systems, it was discovered that Green Brothers Ltd has invoiced our organization for over £1 million in the past two years. Additionally, we found invoices for a company called 'AS Rohelised Vennad' in the region of €100,000. The invoices were for similar types of activities but in some cases the addresses and contact details on the invoices were different. In one particular case the company had submitted an invoice for a compensation claim (against our organization).

2   Internet searching identified that Green Brothers Ltd was registered in the UK in January 2015, by a Mr Peter W. Cooper and a Ms Kathy Gardner.

There are strong indications (from social media sites and other websites) that both Mr Cooper and Ms Gardner are in contact with a Mr Michael Dalton, who himself has been acting as a consultant for My Organisation Ltd and working closely with Mr Rob Kearns, who in most cases has been the ultimate approver and requisitioner of the services from both Green Brothers and AS Rohelised Vennad.

3   UK Companies House information provides very limited information about Green Brothers Ltd. However, the registered company's purpose appears to be 'Advise relating to energy efficiency' but does not mention construction or repairs specifically. It also appears that the company has regularly missed its filing deadlines and is under warning to be struck off as a company.

The third and final step could be to summarize all the information we have found so far. Examples like the one above, or any of the examples in the book so far, nearly always require further exploration. There are of course many ways possible fraud can be found, through the recipes in Chapters 4, 5 and 6 or by someone speaking up about something concrete at a think like a thief workshop, as well as using 'follow the money'-type algorithms described in Chapter 7. And, of course we should include the more traditional ways of discovering fraud – by accident, or because of a whistleblower or an investigative journalist.

Whatever the starting point, we need an effective methodology to be able to clarify what we have found, so that more informed decisions as to what to do next can be taken, even if we are never going to be able to collect all the evidence. This will also help ensure an efficient and effective resolution, which in most cases, can avoid a long and expensive traditional investigation.

The seven basic types of fraud introduced in Part 1 can help us understand what kind of frauds we could be possibly looking at. However, this needs to be combined with smart *investigative desktop research*, which will provide you with more concrete information as to what really lies behind the red flags.

Investigative desktop research (IDR) in a nutshell[3]

The fundamental premise of IDR is that you have a healthy curiosity but are working from the confines of a desktop with access to primarily internal information from your organization's own systems, and external public source information, much of which can be easily accessed through the internet. While you can allow yourself a lot of freedom to think creatively and laterally, you need to stick to a few rules such as:

- Do not cause disruption. This will mean not asking people about your findings, which could cause alarm.
- Do not breach privacy. While it may be tempting to start looking into people's emails or personal records, at this stage, do not even think of doing this.
- Do not leave a footprint or change information. Use 'read-only' access when trawling internal information systems and financial systems. If going on the internet and looking at public information, make sure that you are NOT already signed in as a user to a particular website or social media platform. A very common mistake, for example, is that you are automatically signed in to LinkedIn when you come across a person's LinkedIn profile in the public domain, but by going into that profile you are actually leaving a trail that it is you who are looking (which could be construed later as 'internet stalking').
- Work with your own self-imposed time-constraint. Typically, and especially if you are doing IDR after a fraud detection review using the recipes and algorithms, there will be a lot of potential fraud to discover. You need to use your time wisely and even use a timer or stopwatch if needed. The 'time box principle' as it is sometime called, will ensure that you find information quickly, keep focused and do not go off on a tangent.
- While this might feel unnecessary, you need to keep a record of what you have done at all times. This can be simply noting down the time you did something, the systems you accessed and what was found, and in the case of public internet sites, the web address where you obtained the information, as information can easily disappear. It can also be useful to keep open a text document where you can cut and paste in information. The main thing is to be able to retrace your steps.

To perform basic IDR, you just need access to internal information systems, read-only access to financial data and transactions, and unrestricted access to the internet. Tables 8.1 and 8.2 list the most common sources of internal and external information.

Table 8.1 Important internal sources of information used in IDR

Source	Examples of what you can find in these systems
Accounts Payable Systems	Information about all suppliers and the money flows to and from them
Accounts Receivable Systems	Information about all customers and the money flows from and to them
Internal Payments and Receipts systems (if the organization operates its own internal 'bank')	Details of where money comes from and where is goes. This can be extremely valuable if the organization has its own systems rather than outsourcing this to a bank or other provider of these services. which is typical with smaller organizations
Financial statements and management accounts	Summary and detailed financial information as well as qualitative and quantitative summaries about performance, sometimes at a divisional or unit level
Purchase and Contract Systems	Information about what has been purchased and when, which frame agreements and contracts exist and quite often downloadable versions of the contracts themselves
Sales and customer information systems	Details of customers, their relationships, sales order, future potential orders, information on what was sold, possible disputes and resolutions as well as information about prospective sales
Employee database	Employee information, such as start date, positions held, email address, mobile telephone number, prior jobs, education, etc. However, this information needs to be used with care and with due respect for all laws and regulations governing the use of personal data

Table 8.2 Typical external sources of information used in IDR

Source	Examples of what you can find
Google searches or similar	Today search engines (of which Google is arguably the most popular) can take you into a vast domain of information about an organization, including what others have written about them, where they have been involved, who is associated with them, what they physically look like and where they are situated, maps, and media articles. Google is a good starting point but remember if you wish to look for information in a particular country the LOCAL language version of Google is usually much better.

(Continued)

Table 8.2 (Continued)

Source	Examples of what you can find
The organization's own website	What an organization says about itself is often very interesting, especially when you compare this to what others say about it. Also, what an organization omits to say about itself is also pertinent.
Company registries in individual countries	All countries have their own online register of companies and organizations and today most of these registries are online. Basic searches today tend to be free[1] giving information about organizations, when they were registered, who owns them, who the main officers are and often some financial information.
Telephone directories	When telephone directories are accessed through the internet today, they tend to cover the world. There are numerous providers, but the real benefit is that you are able to find information on the organization you are looking for, their address and telephone number and who else could be sharing the same address and/or telephone number
Media searches online	A lot of media articles can be found using search engines, such as Google. However, more and more newspapers and journals are putting some information behind pay walls. In many cases though, initial searches are free.
Property registers	Like corporate and company registers, many countries today have property registers where initial searches are free
Credit databases	Credit databases, while not always reliable or up to date, are available and can provide interesting and useful information such as credit rating and more importantly reasons as to why poor ratings were provided
Tax authorities	Often tax authorities can publish information, including warning lists
Courts and law reports	Similar to tax authorities, courts do publish many cases, and summary information is often publicly available in law reports
Educational institutions	Often an educational institution has a vast website with their own search engines allowing you to search, for example, past and current students and staff, partnership agreements and more
Social media profiles	Typical social media profiles are public but do heed the warning above about not accidentally connecting or leaving your own footprint

Note: [1] The organizations tend to want you to use their sites, and often more specialized information costs money. Hence, they tend to make the initial searches free, so that you get used to using the site's services.

Your primary external IDR tool will be the internet, though sometimes a making phone call (preferably from an untraceable number) to an authority or service provider can be very useful. When using the internet, different languages in themselves should not be a hindrance, given the availability of free online translation tools. However, it is very important to always proceed cautiously. Your primary internal IDR tool will be the company's own systems. internal IDR, and, to an extent, external IDR will help you to get to know your own organization. When performing IDR, even in a short time-window, it is quite common and useful to flip back and forwards between external and internal IDR as you bring together (or synthesize) lots of diverse pieces of information from internal, external, what you know and remember and try to succinctly condense it, remembering that some information is more solid than others.

The five key things to consider and look for both internally and externally when performing IDR are 'who', 'what', 'where', 'when' and 'what else stands out?' and are summarized below:

1   *Who* is behind the organization (ownership, structure, history, for example, change in ownership or names, partnerships, names of employees or directors). This includes searching for the name of the reference person on an invoice associated with the supplier name. This includes also whether they have a website, how they portray themselves (also in other places, not just their own page) and who owns the web domain. The 'who' also applies to 'who' in our organization appears to have the strongest connections with the organization we are checking up on. One should be very careful here to just register names, departments, etc., but not jump to conclusions because the names on paper may not be the most important or real person, as they could be just lower-level people in our organization who are doing their job.

2   *What* they are doing (i.e., main activity), officially and unofficially. What are they registered as doing in corporate registers?, how do they profile themselves on the net and social media (which can be different from what they officially say they are doing)?, what are they doing according to the information which is available in our own records (if any)?, and does it appear to match or differ? Also, it is important to see if they have changed that over the years (for example, from 'gardening' to 'infrastructure' or 'maintenance'). It is good to get a feeling for the size of the organization, for example, if the total turnover or other financial figures are available

and compare how this matches up with their engagement with our organization. For example, are they dependent (either as a supplier, customer, consultant or partner) in some way or are they financially tied to your organization?

3   *When.* This is different from looking back into the history of former ownerships and structures or change of purpose. We want to know when they were established and for how long they have been in business. This can be found both in corporate registers but also in potential visibility on the net (such as being mentioned in projects or events). 'When' also applies to how the organization interacts with your organization, as a customer, supplier, agent, partner, etc.

4   *Where.* We want to know where they are located physically. How far is it from where they deliver the service?, what does the landscape look like?, what else is around there?, does it make sense to have a company in that location?, how far it is from the border with other countries? Also, do they have different addresses, like a head office and warehouses?, is the registered address different from the address we have on file, or the address we find on their webpage or other internet pages? This includes finding out whether they are operating from a front address and, if so, what else is registered at that address. Similarly, the 'where' also applies to where in your organization the external company is connected and operating.

5   *What else stands out* from an internal or external perspective. It could be that you find them sponsoring one event, or that they have been mentioned in the local press, or that they have been involved in some scandal or court case, or that they are listed in some customers' or competitor's lists. Usually searches with the supplier name together with words like 'scam, fraud, court case, and verdict' can help (in this case, in Estonian, Russian, Latvian, German, use Google translate to find the best word to search for).

Useful tips

- Beware of false information and news. This often quite easy to spot as it will stand out against a mass of information which points in another direction.
- The landscape of IDR is constantly evolving. Externally, there are constantly new sources.
- Try to apply the simple rule of thumb that free online information is often the best today, even if some people will say that free information has little

value. It is not the information itself which is valuable, but how you use it. When somebody wants you to pay for something, there is always a reason.

- Where possible, try to access a primary source of information. For example, a number of government-controlled company registers are usually more accurate than a service provider which brings together information from several registers in one place because there is often a small loss of quality of information in the aggregation process.

- When documenting your findings, beware and record the date pertaining to information and pictures. Information on the internet can also be very old or out of date (for example, a picture of a street or a building may look completely different from what it looks like today).

- Always summarize and download relevant documents which you find. They could be considered as 'evidence' at a later stage.

- Take time to stop and think, even if it is just for a few minutes and review what you have before making your next move.

The quest for irrefutable evidence is a bit like looking for the pot of gold at the end of a rainbow – it's a virtual impossibility. So, you need to know where to stop and how to conclude. Finally, just be aware that IDR challenges the domain of investigators and specialists who would like to sell you this information as a service or a database subscription.

Example of how to apply IDR

Example 8.1 F&C Holdings (see Figure 4.1)

- *Who?* A Google search of F&C Ltd and F&C Holdings showed that the company was registered in Road Town, Tortola, in the British Virgin Islands but very little other information about the company was readily available. The company directors and secretaries provided in the UK and BVI appear to be involved in over one hundred other companies, indicating that these are 'front persons' of some sort. However, the contact person when the UK company was registered is given as a Mr James Murray. No website appears to exist for either company name and there are no relevant internet hits on the company itself. Internally the company appears to be linked to Britmax's international business development department headed by Joe Northfield.

- *What?* The UK Companies House shows that F&C Ltd has been registered as a small company with few details provided other than a purpose to say, 'Consulting Activities'. The company purpose registered on the open page of the British Virgin Islands companies register is 'Advisory Services'. A review of the four invoices issued to Britmax include 'Marketing Support' and 'Sales Commissions'. The total invoiced from F&C to Britmax is $1,230,401 and all invoices, bar the sales commission invoice, are for a round sum fee. Basic contracts exist for all but one of the invoices. However, these contracts are just a ratification that the service will be provided and give no additional details as to what the service actually is. The name James Murray (Lusaka) appears as the contact person at F&C in connection with the contract for West Africa sales commissions.

- *When?* The company F&C was registered in the UK in January 20XX and in the British Virgin Islands, three months prior to that. An internal trawl of supplier and customer master files in Britmax revealed that a company called Altinox Ltd has been both a customer and supplier in the past and operated from the same address in London with a similar British Virgin Islands holding company for 5 years previously, but Altinox has had no activity with Britmax since F&C started to invoice. A search on Altinox indicates that they were named as defendants in a court case in Spain, three years previously where bribery and racketeering were suspected. A James Murray is mentioned in the Altinox court case as being one of the key people involved in Altinox.

- *Where?* F&C's address in London, according to telephone directories and current map searches, indicates that the company has no physical presence there. Similarly, the address in the British Virgin Islands strongly appears to be an accommodation address. Internet searches on James Murray reveal that the James Murray involved with Altinox, the James Murray appearing as a contact person for F&C and a James Murray residing and working in Lusaka, Zambia, could be one and the same person.

- *X?* James Murray is a relatively common name. However, initial searches indicate that a James E. Murray was named as a middleman and intermediary in connection with a sanctions-breaking deal some years ago. A James Murray and Joe Northfield of Britmax are mentioned together, with a photograph, in a French trade exhibition online magazine two years ago. It is common knowledge internally that Britmax have been trying, somewhat unsuccessfully, to develop the market for their services in West Africa and rumours have circulated in the past about the use of intermediaries and the payment of commission.

Consider as possible bribery of customers and/or embezzlement of funds. Collate all information gathered so far and analyse.

What to do next

Once you have completed an initial IDR review under strict time constraints, such as the one above, it is important to take a step back and consider 'what we have achieved so far'. When summarizing what you have found, write down all the unanswered questions you may have, possible theories as to what could be happening, and, if you had more time, what you would do next. It might be useful to test out your theories in confidence with a colleague whom you can trust. Remember, at this stage you do not need to be certain of anything or have irrefutable evidence, as your goal now is to present what you have found in a balanced and, as we will see in Chapter 9, a best-case/worst-case scenario manner.

Very occasionally you might decide to do a little more digging because the indicators and example are of such a serious or critical nature that spending a few hours more is warranted. In this case, the term 'drains up'[4] comes to mind where you use a little more time examining and collecting information, still without causing disruption, from every possible IDR source you can think of.

Normally, however, the most important thing to do is to summarize, concisely the information you have found in a format which allows you to see at a glance what the key issues are related to each example.

Other complementary forms to describe each example include the 'short story' form, which can be accompanied by a simple relationship diagram, when appropriate.

Finally, a note of caution. Even when you have unearthed what you think is the most obvious and compelling example of fraud and corruption, do not expect that others are going to believe you.

Example 8.2 Theft of the entire business (or 'Reiderstvo')

Using the type of algorithms described in Chapter 7, significant payments meant for a business advisor living and working in Russia are made to a company in Liechtenstein. Internal and external IDR identified a lot more:

- There was no visible footprint of the Liechtenstein company or trace of who owned the numbered bank account in Switzerland into which the money was paid.
- Linked to the sales business which the advisor was helping develop were sales of the company's product to a company in Cyprus which was in fact a law office. The actual shipping documents linked to these sales showed that the goods were being delivered to the Ukraine to a whole variety of companies which were not in any way known to be customers of our company. The largest of these companies had a name which was very similar to our own organization, was using a logo which was almost identical to our own logo. However, no one had ever heard of this company before.

There had also been numerous complaints about quality from the Cyprus company, which resulted in a series of substantial refunds being paid back to this company. The findings were set against a backdrop that the new business venture was in fact loss-making, and senior management, together with their Russian business advisor, were meeting to consider closing down the business. They had a 'man on the ground', an ex-patriot, who was from head office, handling the situation and while he reported back that the closure was unfortunate, the problems encountered were due to changes in local market conditions and laws, plus the continued activities of local crime gangs at ports and terminals which impeded clean business.

   The red flags identified were not enough at the time to convince management to act as they believed they already had the situation under control and asking more questions would undermine the complete trust they had in their own person and their Russian business advisor.

In this case, which turned out to be a very serious 'Reiderstvo' or asset-grabbing type fraud mentioned in Chapter 2, in order to steal the whole business involving also the business advisor and the ex-pat manager (see Chapter 7), the fundamental reason why senior management could not recognize this when presented with the red flags was that they could not imagine the worst-case scenario and did not really *want* to see fraud and corruption in their organization. This tends to push them in the direction of making every effort not to see it for what it is. Add to this the possible shame and embarrassment they would have felt, this led them instead to treat the enthusiastic fraud detective whom they themselves had asked to look for examples like this as a 'bringer of bad news who must be disproved at all costs unless they could come up with irrefutable evidence'.

Sometimes you may think that you have all the information and arguments on your side but people higher up still do not want to listen to you! The reasons for this and how to turn bad news into good are covered in Chapter 9.

Notes

1 With the express permission of Michael J. Comer, author of *Corporate Fraud* (1977) and numerous other books on fraud, deception at work, bad lies in business etc. *Corporate Fraud* is arguably one of the first books of its kind. 'Mike' (as he is generally known) is also famous for his often-used quote 'Shit happens . . . and so does fraud'. In spite of the use of terse language, this phrase does in fact ring true. There is a lot of fraud and corruption around, and rather than be scared of it, we should accept that it happens.

2 For example, when Hamlet says '2B or not 2B . . . that is the question' we are left wondering if Hamlet is deciding whether he should do something about it. Or if he just is deciding if he can accept to sit in the middle seat on his flight from his native Copenhagen to London.

3 The term IDR can be best summed up by my colleague and experienced investigator, Veronica Morino, from whose work and writings a part of this chapter is drawn. Veronica also recognized many years ago that to be able to look forward, organizations need to look back (i.e. 'without a history, you do not have much of a future'). With the continuing trend towards highly integrated internal systems and the constant explosion of open source information, IDR became possible. The drawback was that now there was too much information available. So, a structured approach is needed to identify, analyse and correlate information in order to make sense of it. And this requires practice and focus.

4 'Drains up' is an American expression meaning to sort out a problem, based on clearing a drain by sticking a rod up it. 'To establish in detail what has occurred, typically after the failure of a process and/or system.to lift the drain cover up and explore what has been flushed down and try and rescue it. We had a real problem with this customer when we delivered their goods, and they are really annoyed. the best thing to do is have a 'drains up' on what went wrong with the delivery and then tell the customer what we are going to do to fix it.' See www.urbandictionary.com/define. php?term=drains%20up. Not necessary each and every time but it can be useful to think: what can we flush out?

Chapter 9

Resolving fraud and corruption and restoring normality with minimal panic and maximum humanity

An eye for an eye will make the whole world blind.

(Mahatma Gandhi)

Introduction

Over the past two decades new laws, regulations and systems have been set in place to make it easier for people to speak up or blow the whistle on fraud and corruption. The systems that have been put in place may even work, but just for one minute we need to consider whether in fact this is actually right. It feels as if we have to come to rely more and more on whistleblowers or external sources to find fraud and corruption, so much so that it almost has become the norm. Maybe this has been a knee-jerk reaction to the fact that oversight by regulators, supervisors and auditors, and, possibly, management do not find fraud and corruption, but what about all those people working in organizations who see red flags and want to and are able to do something about it in a constructive and systematic manner?

It's possible that in society that we have gone too far in relying on whistleblowers, whether this be some poor frustrated employee who decides to speak up and stick their neck out, an investigative journalist, or someone else like a supplier, customer or business partner. On every fraud case, one feels there has to be a whistleblower (or it would not be a case!).

Many organizations have spent a lot of money on their whistleblowing channels, with multi-language systems and trained people working in call centres. But it seems that we are missing the obvious. A whistleblower channel should really be the last port of call – the channel of last resort. Ideally, we should never need it as we should be systematically finding fraud before it finds us, for ourselves. In this chapter we will take a look at why not waiting for the whistleblower works, and, more importantly, how fraud and corruption, if found early, can be resolved with the minimum of fuss and bother.

Example 9.1 'Reiderstvo': six months on

In Chapter 8, we described Example 8.1 where through early detection techniques we discovered payments to an advisor/consultant in a DMC, a customer which seemed like a front company, which had started to cause payment problems, and rumours about a managing director who maybe was not as loyal to his employers as he made out to be.

In this case, after the facts were reported to senior management, they chose to park them – in other words, do nothing for now. They based their decision on the fact that the red flags and evidence uncovered in a short time, were not irrefutable, that there could be a logical explanation for everything, and also that they felt sure about the managing director as he was 'one of them'.

Six months later, management received a long email, with attachments (in the local language) from a former finance manager, who accused the managing director of serious fraud, including colluding with the advisor to set up a shadow company which had already started to take over the assets, customers and revenue streams of the company. In some ways, the person's story (which turned out to be true after it was investigated) was too preposterous at the time to believe. Management decided, since the former finance manager came from a culture and country, which, according to the Corruption Perception Index, was 'corrupt', to confront the managing director and ask him what was going on. He gave plausible explanations, including that the finance manager was probably involved with a local organized crime gang.

But a few months later the financial problems of the company got worse, the head office management went back to an astute internal auditor (who had originally discovered the red flags) and asked them for advice. Internal audit did some preliminary research into the red flags they had raised earlier and gave a short presentation to management which confirmed what had happened. The finance director, when seeing the DMC invoice and how clear a red flag it was now, asked the question 'Which idiot approved that invoice?' to which one of his colleagues replied, 'You did.'[1]

Once tempers had calmed down, and after a short, but effective, investigation, it was clear that the former finance manager was telling the truth, that the advisor was in fact a sophisticated criminal with a long history of assisting in similar 'take-over' or 'Reiderstvo' schemes, a shadow company had now been established and in fact the assets and customers had all been transferred. In other words, the subsidiary which we thought we owned was no longer ours and all we were left with were debts. The managing director was in fact officially dismissed, but most important of all, steps were taken to save the parts of the business that could be saved and learn the lessons so that similar events did not happen in the future – probably the most profitable part of the whole exercise.

The head of the company even wrote a letter of apology to the whistleblower, thanked him for his efforts and offered to compensate him by helping him set up a clean business partner company (something he wanted to do).

Example 9.1 illustrates that the earlier you find the red flags and sort them out, the less painful and drawn out the investigation and normalization process will be. It's very similar to discovering cancer – the earlier one finds it, the less painful it is to treat. But whatever the case and however late the fraud and corruption is discovered, it is possible to resolve it and gain from the process (as in the case above, there WAS a win).

Some of the greatest obstacles to recognizing and dealing with red flags early and effectively can be summarized as:

1   The age-old denial that fraud and corruption happens – especially to us, which, of course, is wishful thinking.

2   The belief that before accepting that it happens, one needs 'irrefutable evidence'. While we know deep down that getting this is virtually impossible or extremely time-consuming so that we never find it, it provides a plausible reason to deny that there is a problem.

3   Senior management find potential good news much easier to stomach rather than possible bad news, which causes their advisors and underlings to behave in what could be described as a 'yes-man' fashion. A well-known behaviourist account professor called Daniel Kahneman talks about how people have a much greater aversion to losses rather than equivalent gains. And my mentor, Martin Samociuk, would often say that there was no good or bad news – but just 'news' (except when he inadvertently found out that his client and the organized criminal consortium he was investigating were one and the same – this *was* bad news).

4   Examples and cases when presented can seem so complex or preposterous, often because they are not presented well enough, that management simply do not understand them, and if they, who are highly experienced and qualified, cannot understand them, then they 'cannot' be true, and it is easier to 'hope for the best'. In one such instance, someone in the management team pointed out that because there was no whistleblower, the case could lack credibility! Alternatively, the example might be so sensitive or painful that management do not want to accept it.

5   Conversely, once management are in fact convinced that there is a major problem, there can be a tendency to over-react by initiating a massive investigation, bringing in armies of external professionals and almost organizing a vendetta against the people whom they believe have let them down. Or it could be a way to show strong leadership and meet public and internal expectations. History shows that often such investigations which become campaigns are often costly, fail in their objectives, are harmful to everybody, and the only people who 'win' are the lawyers and professional advisors – and the other fraudsters, whoever they may be.

6   Because investigations are often tiring experiences, when they are finally over, it is tempting to think that because we have dealt with one issue in such depth, we can now relax as our fraud problems are over.

Surmounting these obstacles, what I term as the 'management block', which are in fact normal human reactions, can often be the aspiring fraud detective's greatest challenge. If management are unable to recognize fraud and corruption happens to them too and that there are very effective ways to discover it early and sort things out with the minimum of fuss, the process of large investigations and getting irrefutable evidence will simply wear you out. because going down the path of more and more evidence will wear everyone out.

But in recognizing the obstacles above also lies the clue to dealing with fraud and corruption effectively. There are no magic answers or silver bullets, but different strategies work better in different situations. One such strategy lies in stopping portraying fraud and corruption as a bad thing but giving it a positive news aspect. For example, spotting it early will save money in the future, maybe even recover losses, you will learn important lessons and help make the whole organization financially and culturally more robust in the future. It's all about getting management to see everything as a 'gain' for them and the organization and be convinced that, by finding everything early and dealing with it, they will be, and will be seen as, leading-edge management who also adopt the maxim, 'there is only one thing worse than finding fraud – and that is not finding it'. The irony of finding lots of fraud (even if you evidence it in the form described in Chapter 8), is that the more you find, the less likely that people high up will believe you.

Turning perceived bad news into good news and positive opportunities

If we are truly going to be able do something about fraud and corruption, one of the first things that needs to be done is to focus on all benefits which can be achieved from finding it early, resolving it efficiently and putting into practice the lessons learnt. To do this requires a much stronger focus on opportunities rather than problems and a willingness to explore and use methods which realize these opportunities. Negative emotions, such as the desire for revenge and retribution or the need to find someone to blame, need to be avoided as much as possible as these often obstruct clear and positive thinking.

When presenting the facts of examples which have been found, you need to present them clearly, concisely, and in as positive a light as possible, focusing on all the opportunities that discovering fraud early presents in terms of money saved, larger problems avoided and also valuable relationships that can be restored to normality or even improved. So rather than divide an organization, which is common when fraud and corruption is discovered, we should be using fraud and corruption to bind the different functions in the organization even more tightly together. A variety of approaches exist to choose from, including investigation, and these are described later in this chapter.

First, when presenting the examples, it is important not to overwhelm management. Often it can be better to present your findings in an understated manner, allowing management themselves to ask questions and make judgement calls. One example which can work well is the 'best case – worst case'[2] method (Example 9.2).

Example 9.2 Management presentation based on a limited Fraud Detection Review

The summary of seven examples is based on a Fraud Detection review of the XXXX division which was conducted jointly by Group Compliance, Financial Control and Internal Audit. The review was limited in scope, so the examples described in Table 9.1 (which were the subject of detailed examination) are representative of 42 similar potential examples which were identified in the review.

Table 9.1 Possible best- and worst-case scenarios

Key facts*	Possible 'best' and 'worst' case scenarios (worst cases in italics)
The supplier EnRich88 Ltd is highly dependent on our organization. The company has been dormant for six months but has continued to invoice for consultancy services in that time. Ultimate owners of EnRich88 are not officially registered. Total invoicing in past 12 months = €2.4 million	Genuine consultancy and administrative errors where we overlooked organizational changes at EnRich88 Ltd *Undocumented services provided, which includes overcharging and possibly collusion with insiders.*
The company Artemiza Shipping Inc has invoiced for shipping. The company is an intermediary company where mark-ups applied to the underlying cost average at 18%. Artemiza was registered on 31.10.20XX, has one registered employee, a person who officially left our organization on 09.11.20XX. Total purchases in last 12 months amounted = €1.1 million	An arrangement which has been approved in order to increase the efficiency of the procurement of bona-fide shipping services *An ex-employee who used contacts within our organization to furnish themselves with a lucrative contract after resigning, by masquerading as a shipping agent, buying transportation services from well-known companies and applying a heavy mark-up.*
Flamantora S.A. is both a supplier and customer of diverse raw materials. The company is registered in Switzerland but has no employees registered or no base-of-operations. There is no visible record of where materials originate from on the documentation provided. Initial public record searches show that some of the persons behind Flamantora S.A. have criminal connections.	Flamantora SA is a reputable trader of raw materials, allegations are unfounded and there is no cause for concern related to purchases from or sales to, this organization. *Purchase of 'stolen goods' or goods of questionable origin from a front-company. Risk that some of the same goods purchased from Flamantora SA are sold back to Flamantora SA at a significant loss.*

Key facts*	Possible 'best' and 'worst' case scenarios (worst cases in italics)
Eleganta Ltd is registered as a provider of financial services. The company has invoiced our organization once each month for a total of €351,076 in the past 18 months. Eleganta Ltd is registered in the UK. The directors of the company are lawyers operating from London and Panama. Description on invoices of work provided include 'Consultancy Fees', 'Sales Commission on XX contract', 'Fees'.	A long-term, transparent advisory relationship where all payments can be fully substantiated *A non-transparent relationship where it is not clear how money paid to Eleganta is accounted for and who the ultimate recipients are. Frauds could include bribery, theft (via invoicing for fictitious services), reverse-laundering and tax evasion.*
Johnson Inc has been a major customer for the past nine years. Analysis of transactions show that on all sales, an average of 28% is returned to the customer in the form of credit notes. So far around one-third of these credit notes (a sum amounting to €180,134 in the past 12 months) has been paid out to a company called 'John UAB' in Lithuania which according to Johnson Inc's financial statements and other enquiries do not relate to Johnson Inc. In addition, express transport costs (€12,482) related to sales to Johnson Inc, were charged to 'general marketing expenses'.	An accounting error, which when rectified will demonstrate that Johnson Inc has been a consistently profitable customer over the past years and all credit notes paid were transparent and properly accounted for *An illicit and systematic kickback arrangement has been in operation for a number of years. In addition, costs relating to sales to Johnson Inc have been suppressed in order to give the impression that the relationship with this customer is more profitable than it actually is.*
Substantial (€12 million in past year) sales to a company called Haian Ltd, based in Singapore, were made. Product shipments were made, on the other hand, to China. Initial analysis indicates that profit margins on sales to Haian Ltd are very low (around 2% when all costs are considered). According to public record, Haian Ltd is not registered as a purchasing agent for Chinese manufacturers.	An official and fully transparent relationship with the nominated representatives of a genuine Chinese manufacturer and customer *A middleman which purchases on behalf of manufacturing companies, but does not take physical possession of the goods but takes a large profit for doing almost nothing. Risk that our own employees may be involved.*
Sales to EAB Systems AB were accounted for in 20XX but these sales actually took place the following year. A sales invoice was registered on 23.12.20XX to EAB System for €300,000 but credited on 04.01.20XY. A new invoice for the same services but for €311,385 was issued on 07.02.20XY	A genuine error, but one that resulted in sales being accidentally overstated in 20XX by €311,385 *Deliberate manipulation of overstatement of sales figures by invoicing and crediting a customer which in reality was not involved.*

Note: * A summary report of all the relevant underlying facts is available for review. In addition, a detailed presentation has been created. The seven examples selected are not exhaustive but are believed to be representative of the 42 similar and potential examples identified. Before any further action is taken, we suggest that the existing facts behind each example are reviewed and a decision taken by management, in each case, to either ignore, explore further, or take some mitigating action now based on the information already provided.

Constructive approaches to resolving fraud and corruption

Let's say that 'doing nothing' is not a smart option. What then are the different possibilities open to us? Here are seven different things we can do, to consider the options available, appreciating that fraud and corruption, once it is discovered early, can be dealt with in a more forward-thinking manner.

1 Damage limitation: cutting your losses (stop dealing with wrong people and stop paying them as of now!).
2 Identify quick and easy ways of getting money back where you can.
3 Understand not just what went wrong but also *why* it went wrong. Trace the root causes and rectify them.
4 Use the examples of what you found (anonymized of course so as to never unnecessarily 'shame' people) to spread the word through learning and training.
5 Where you need to do investigations, ensure that they are effective and well managed.
6 Ensure that where sanctions are applied that they are proportional to the misdemeanour.
7 Tap into the power of restorative justice (see Example 9.3).

The first six suggestions above should be obvious and intuitive to most of us. The seventh requires a little more consideration and reflection.

Restorative justice applied to fraud and corruption

The best form of investigation is where the perpetrators or at least some of them cooperate. But restorative justice means doing things right and all sides win something.

Example 9.3 Truth and reconciliation two decades on

A few years ago, in Johannesburg, South Africa, I held a short session for around 2,500 people on how pro-active investigation, coupled with a liberal dose of understanding and forgiveness, motivates people to speak up, thereby tackling the epidemic problem of fraud and waste in social uplift programmes. Just before I spoke, the Minister of Trade, Bob Davies, read a short speech where he reiterated the policy of 'zero tolerance', saying that his government would show 'no mercy' when it came to cases of suspected corruption and fraud. I met Bob briefly afterwards and he seemed like a very pleasant chap, but I was left shocked and wondering whether Mr Davies's speech-writer had ever witnessed the success of Nelson Mandela's Truth and Reconciliation Committee and one of the most famous examples ever of restorative justice in our times. (And imagine the reaction of Bob's children if he came home one day and announced that from now on he would show no mercy and absolutely zero tolerance to any misdemeanours and wrongdoings in his own family.)

Avoiding a blame culture

Fraud and corruption is all around us. Surely if we are so heavy-handed with the few 'sinners' that we catch, won't the large majority who did not get caught breathe a huge sigh of relief and just try even harder to stay hidden? And what does our no mercy, intolerant stance, say to the people who are caught? Won't they feel hard done by, unlucky or in most cases bitter?

Whether it's a new scapegoat the media has in its sights, or some more fallout from the 'Panama Papers', I feel that we are becoming an intolerant, dispassionate society where there is less and less room for people to stand up and admit they are wrong. Even though we know that there are hundreds of examples out there, we carry on pointing the finger at scapegoats, because it is safe to do that.

Example 9.4 When the past catches up

The CEO of a bank was under pressure because it was discovered through a leak called the 'Panama Papers', that his company has been dealing with customers who have accounts and shell companies in one or more of the dirty money centres.

With the help of his PR and legal advisors, he managed to defend himself admirably in the media, both accepting full responsibility for not having done more and for not being more aware, but at the same time raising the understandable issue: 'How could I possibly know everything that goes on in a company as large as this?' Had this same CEO forgotten that many years ago – albeit in a former life and in a much more junior position – he was rather involved and instrumental in sending money to so-called dirty money centres? The purpose of the money was defined as 'finder's fees', 'commissions' and facilitation payments which he now knows have been the subject of media investigations into bribery and corruption involving a number of countries. Of course, he was only carrying out the orders of his superiors – and he never took any money for himself, but with hindsight, he feels that he behaved rather naïvely at the time.

The question remains: What should he do now? If he genuinely wants to lie flat and 'bare all', he feels he must talk openly about his past experiences. But, on the other hand, today's intolerant society would crucify him, and a scandal-hungry media would have a field day. So, he does as many of us do and hopes that the past stays hidden. In an ideal world, our CEO would be able to 'come clean' and admit his mistakes even more fully, earning respect for this action, and encouraging other executives who feel trapped by similar circumstances to also step forward and talk about their past experiences and what we can all learn from them. But to get closer to this ideal world we all need to invoke those human traits in us called forgiveness and compassion and turn the zero tolerance down (for a while at least).

As the epigraph states, 'An eye for an eye will make the whole world blind.' When it comes to how much corruption and fraud is costing the world today, I believe that we are blind already. The word 'truth' (or veritas) is used a lot in the legal world and 'reconciliation' also describes an accounting tool used to show that money matches!

Surely, we want societies where people are allowed to tell the *truth*, societies where people are encouraged to own up to their mistakes, so that we can *reconcile* the money to where it should really have gone? For this to happen, we need to think afresh. We need new ways to deal with fraud and corruption. Ways that actually work.

Where do we go from here?

Fresh ideas need fertile soil, in which to germinate and this implies a new mind-set. The starting point should, in my view, be based on a recognition that fraud and corruption amounts to an unnecessary cost which, if we thought collectively (rather than individually), we would all prefer to avoid. In other words, finding fraud early needs to be seen as 'good news' rather than a shock. But this also means that we need to all work together and avoid playing the 'blame game'.

We should want fewer whistleblowers rather than more because we have a reinvigorated belief that, by working together, people can detect fraud and corruption early and deal with it calmly, efficiently and (unfortunately for the media) in a rather unspectacular way.

And let us stop relying on others like the police, the media, regulators, external auditors (or the whistleblower who incidentally may never turn up) to find fraud. Even if we don't know it as yet, the tools and techniques to find fraud before it finds you are available to us all. As we enter a new and more democratic age, today *everyone* can find fraud and corruption, remembering that at the same time it pays to show as much forgiveness and compassion as we can.

Notes

1 In Chapter 6 (Example 6.3) a similar incident occurred in a different case when a managing director asked the question 'which idiot signed off on these?' only to find out it was he himself. It is my experience that most of the time senior executives are a long way from being idiots. More so, they are very intelligent and capable people who have simply too many things to do, and too many things to approve so that they are forced to blindly rely on others to scrutinize things before they sign them.
2 Thanks to Arto Tenhula, head of Internal Audit at the international paper company UPM, for giving me this idea.

Chapter 10

Good news for management

The mind is like a parachute, it works best when it is open.

(Dalai Lama)[1]

Being a fraud detective is usually fun but it can be no fun at all if management prefer it to stay hidden. But fraud is, in fact, just a waste of resources and it is in management´s interest to incentivize its own people to spot fraud early.

Re-writing the narrative about fraud and corruption in a positive way

With predictable regularity over the year, something that has been seen as a waste product is suddenly recognized as valuable and useful. Examples include aluminium which can be almost 100 per cent recycled, gas from offshore oil-fields, which was simply burnt off in the early days, and re-cycled paper (for which there is a huge demand today). So, building on our litter analogy in Chapter 1, where we compared fraud and corruption to litter, there is a lot of it around, all that waste from fraud and corruption could be treated as an unnecessary cost. Once we are able to recognize it exists, we are able to see it, and by sorting it out, we will be able to reclaim lost profits, or at least 'make money by stopping losing it'.

> If a smiling junior financial controller approaches the chief executive saying, 'Hey, Marjorie, I just wanted to spread the good news that we have found lots of fraud', Marjorie will probably find it hard to understand why her controller used the phrase 'good news'. But if Marjorie thought about it for a while, she would realize that what the controller is actually telling her is that 'we have found ways of saving money and protecting the organization better in the future and we may even be able to recover some of that money that we have lost'. Furthermore, Marjorie should be smiling too because her own people have diligently discovered it, rather than it being found by someone else. This probably means that it has been discovered early too.

The 'fantastic that we found it' attitude is a radical departure from the 'shock and horror' often associated with discovering fraud and corruption, possibly for the reason that so rarely it is discovered early. A common enemy binds us together more than ever, the feeling that we are all doing something useful together fosters teamwork, and the thought of saving money so that it can be used for more useful activities than wasting it on fraud and corruption should give plenty of food for thought.

'Less blame, less shame': better together

Every time fraud and corruption is discovered, the hunt for someone to blame starts and people ask the question, 'Where were the auditors?' Maybe 50 years ago when organizations were rather less complicated, and an audit entailed a meticulous going-over with a fine toothcomb, there was a much better chance that fraud would be found by auditors. But we should remember that today it is not even the responsibility of external auditors to discover the kind of frauds described in this book, or at least the auditors would argue strongly that it is not their job, given their limited scope and budgets. But despite all of this, even today many chief executives of companies, when interviewed, would say that if there was major fraud, they would have expected the external auditors to have found it and they take comfort in an external audit report. It's time to move on and face up to the fact that the best people to find fraud early are people working in the organization, working together as a team, with the support and involvement of the senior management.

Similarly, it's time to shed the stigma of being defrauded. Of course, if you were cheated by someone, it is embarrassing, but at the same time, since it happens so often, if everyone conceals that it has happened to them, nobody will learn, and no action will be taken. Like all bad things that are swept under the carpet for years, the result of them being revealed can cause an explosion and overly strong reactions with a call for 'heads to roll', the singling out of scapegoats and a loss of trust and focus.

Example 10.1 Concrete proof

A chief financial officer (CFO) uncovered a corrupt relationship whereby a senior purchasing manager had received a shipment of concrete at his home address from a supplier who had won a tender for a construction project for the company. The concrete was used to build a new driveway. However, on being informed, the CEO decided to take no further action because the supplier had a long-established relationship and had successfully delivered on a number of projects. There was no suggestion of a corrupt relationship involving the CEO. The CFO was unhappy with the decision and notified the Chairman who agreed that not taking any action would set entirely the wrong tone throughout the organization. After a showdown with the CEO, the Chairman obtained the backing of the majority shareholder to overrule the CEO. The supplier relationship was terminated, and this information was made public, both within the organization and across the industry. The Chairman reasoned that setting the correct tone would act as a deterrent for any future improper relationships. However, it took a determined effort to repair the relationship between the Chairman, the CEO and the CFO.

Ensure that the rules are working in your favour

It's easy to point to all the new rules and regulations which are supposed to help prevent and detect fraud and corruption, saying that if every box is ticked, then we have done our best. Alternatively, one could describe the mountain of rules and regulations as 'necessary bureaucracy' which has to be overcome, rather like Figure 10.1. Instead, the clue is to use the rules and regulations as a platform for action, simplify them as much as possible and get them to work in your favour.

Figure 10.1 The challenge of too many rules and regulations

Empower the organization to have a healthy curiosity

Simply put, management should encourage everyone in the organization to have a healthy sense of curiosity and take up issues that they feel are unusual, rather than presume that someone else, or some complex system, will spot them. For example, compare and contrast the effectiveness as well as the positive social message of 'neighbourhood watch schemes' where communities get together to prevent and help each other detect and fend off burglary to expensive security walls, gates, cameras and electronic surveillance systems. Combine healthy curiosity with a 'follow the money' approach and we will find fraud fast.

By encouraging the whole organization to participate in detecting fraud early, we are in a similar way creating a 'Fraud Watch' community inside the organization, which is better attuned and more able to respond to any kind of attack on the organization.

Make fraud and corruption training enjoyable and fun!

To be able to empower the whole organization to find fraud early, some training is required but it is important that this training recognizes that people are in fact very good at spotting fraud and corruption as long as they are encouraged and asked to do so. Training programmes in fraud and corruption should be anything but boring and should contain key messages such as:

- Can you spot the red flags! (Yes, we can!)
- We are protecting the innocent rather than just 'going after the bad guys'.
- There is a common enemy out there (which is *generally* not in the room).
- We will fight and find fraud together.
- Let's try to out-think the criminals and see what methods we can come up with by thinking like a thief or putting a dishonest person in our shoes.

In my experience, the most effective fraud and corruption training should neither consist of 'reading of the rules' or 'putting the fear of God into the employees'. It is OK to list a few types of common fraud, including the typical 'seven basic commercial frauds' and also talk about new trends, whatever they may be, such as 'Phishing', 'CEO fraud', 'Ransomware' or whatever the new buzzword is, as this helps build context. But always remember that most new frauds are variations on an old theme. Phishing is just people looking for information, CEO fraud is impersonation, and ransomware is blackmail. So, remember to focus on the fraud and corruption which is most relevant and real to the organization and also recognize that, if asked the right questions, the people inside the organization, whom you are teaching, probably can tell you way more about which big frauds could take place than you could tell them!

Training is a collective activity and as the head of the Swedish Financial Police once said when he just realized he had fallen over what later turned out to be Sweden's largest financial fraud[2] at the time, 'When you give away knowledge to a receptive audience, you often get ten times the knowledge back.'

And, finally, it is always worth focusing, at least to start with, on how the multitude of external parties could commit fraud, rather than an insider. Focusing on insiders to start with in ANY training session can cause participants to feel unnecessarily guilty (similar to 'white coat effect' where your blood pressure is higher when it is taken in a medical setting than it is when taken at home).

Resolution not retribution

We need to re-think the idea that finding more fraud means more investigations, as that is often a huge barrier to anyone wanting to even look! Long-drawn-out investigations often mean high costs, a large chance of failure, reputational damage and lengthy and painful litigation.

Example 10.2 Gandhi's first case[3]

Few people are aware of this but before he became Mahatma Gandhi, one of Mohandas K. Gandhi's first ever cases as a lawyer was a fraud case, in South Africa. It involved two family members who were fighting over money, both believing that they were totally in the right and willing to fight an endless legal battle to win. Gandhi, recognizing that the case was going to destroy a family, managed to bring both sides together and examine the facts calmly. In the end, both he and the warring opponents recognized that it was pride and not money in fact that was the main issue at stake and Gandhi was able, by acting in the interests of both parties, to engineer a resolution where both parties were happy and reconciled to each other.

Unlike today where zero tolerance is the mantra and investigation is the norm, if management are going to allow people to find and deal with and resolve fraud and corruption, alternative, but equally ethical, resolution strategies need to be explored. These can include 'damage limitation', 'reconciliation', 'stop the loss and cut out the key players', 'win back the money' and many more.

Investigations and litigation should be the option of last resort and most definitely not thinly disguised vendettas or acts of retribution. Even investigations, when they are undertaken, can be done quickly and effectively.

Robustness and resilience

Returning to the narrative surrounding fraud and corruption, it is crucial that every single person in and around an organization, from the owners and the supervisory board to the lowest-level employee, is encouraged to think in terms of the robustness of the organization. How can we make the organization resistant to fraud and corruption and resilient when it inevitably happens?

In addition, the less people, or departments are thought of as 'fraud specialists' or internal or external 'experts', the better, because in effect this alienates them, creates silos which prohibit communication, and prevents the whole organization from having the feeling of being galvanized as fraud detectives.

Maybe the Finance Director (or 'FD' as they are often known) should suggest that 'FD' could also stand for 'fraud detective' from time to time . . .

Notes

1 Tenzin Gyatso (aka the Dalai Lama), whom I had the complete and unexpected pleasure of meeting in February 2015, at an international conference on corruption and fraud. He was asked by a student which person in the world he would have most liked to meet and he answered without hesitation, 'Gandhi.'

2 The Trustor Case, in 1997, where I and a colleague, Matthew Gilham, accidentally spotted in the financial papers of a cash-rich company, that Trustor, a company on the Swedish Stock Exchange, had probably been secretly 'hijacked' by criminals who were planning to transfer the hundreds of millions of dollars to their own Cayman Islands bank account. This was swiftly reported to the Swedish Financial Police.

3 From the biography of Mohandas Karamchand Gandhi, *Gandhi the Man*, by Eknath Easwaran. The book was originally published in the United States in 1973 by Nilgiri Press and since has been published widely and was an important inspiration for Richard Attenborough's film *Gandhi* (1982).

The fraud detectives
A true case in point

Preface

The events related here are based on a true story involving a close friend of mine whom I helped pro bono, when she found herself in between a rock and a hard place as a reluctant whistleblower. For both of us, the journey was an educational, and, in the end, deeply moving experience and I believe that the lessons learnt as well as the precedent in court have been used both in teaching and also to inspire others in a similar position.

In this story, names have been changed partly to protect the identities of the people and companies involved but primarily so as not to take attention away from what is in fact a very common, but rarely told story. The case itself is in fact on public record but I believe has thankfully attracted little media attention as it has been resolved to the satisfaction of almost all the parties involved.

This story presents fraud and corruption from the different perspectives. Legal issues aside, this story illustrates that fraud and corruption, and not least who is to blame, are not a black and white issue. We find ourselves making decisions when the facts are blurred, or grey at best. The events of the story itself took place between 2011 and 2013 and involve Britmax Engineering, part of a large UK-based group with operations in a number of countries.

This has been the only time I have represented someone in court as their lawyer, something I had to apply to the courts to do, as I am not a lawyer. I wish to thank *all* of the characters involved, and Judge Simon A of the Central London Employment Tribunal, who in his first ruling recognized how important it was to stand up for and support a person who was willing to stick their neck out for the company, even though they themselves were unlikely to benefit personally, and in the second court session, masterfully convinced all parties to draw on the powers of restorative justice.

The law may be a deterrent to fraud and corruption but it does not stop it. What stops fraud and corruption is people from all sides working together against a common enemy. But at the end of the day we need to determine what is the right path for each of us to take, balancing our own perceptions of right and wrong with the risks that taking action may entail.

In this story, in some way, some of the characters are a kind of fraud detective because detecting fraud is not only about investigating other people's behaviour, it's also about investigating one's own conduct too. The key for all of us is whether we can sense and spot when something 'appears' wrong and then have the maturity to be able take the next step and explore it in more depth (rather than ignore it). It is said that one day Artificial Intelligence will also become the best fraud detective. This may be true but today I think if we use our intelligence, we as humans are still far ahead of the less compassionate machines.

It was one of the most satisfying pieces of professional work I have undertaken. It is my humble pleasure to share it with you.

Introduction

Sanjay Sharma's story

I won't be doing this again!

Imperialist hypocrites! Once more, my generosity is thrown back in my face. What is it with these arrogant corporations? Now that I have my severance pay, I am certainly going to take a break and regain my health.

Breaking into the Indian market was never going to be easy for Britmax Engineering, but the cards were in our favour. And my family had all the connections you would need, especially with B.J. Mehta on our side. I feel I have let B.J. and Dad down. The imperialists always have to have it their way and when it goes wrong, they just parade that slanderous map of the world, which puts India near the top of corrupt countries. They can talk! They only invented all these anti-bribery laws so that they can take advantage of the loopholes! According to them, even being seen having dinner with someone could be called bribery but all the money they were pouring into developing so-called relationships was fine. How do you think they built the pyramids, the Taj Mahal or even America without a bit of bribery to oil the machinery of progress?

These cowards are too scared to carry out their threats and that includes my former boss, Joe Northfield.

The one person I do feel a bit of sympathy for is their internal auditor, Daniella Evans. She is plodding but she was just trying to do her job, thankless though it was. I only met her twice. The first time she was very polite and the second time she lost the place with me completely. The irony is that they got rid of Daniella too because, like me, she knew far too much. She had a meaningless job anyway, checking that everyone ticked all the right boxes and not looking too hard below the surface. Then when her hand was finally forced, because some stubborn employee with an over-developed conscience wanted to turn on the company, Daniela is, all of a sudden, expected to be an ace fraud investigator.

I hope she enjoys her new job – I think it is some sort of charity job running an end-of-life care home or something. I really hope I won't be visiting one of those places myself soon because I'm going to enjoy my new life, far away from the world of Britmax.

Joe Northfield's story

In the old days when you wanted to develop a business, you just got the job done and turned a blind eye to all those trivial things. Now, with all these new rules you can't even enjoy a quiet glass of wine with a client before someone shouts 'BRIBERY'. Instead you need to be stealthy and find the loopholes and exploit them – which, ironically, is lawyers' work. I should have listened to my head but instead, I followed my heart when Sanjay said, 'Joe, you've got to stop worrying, I'll take care of things.' Maybe in another time and another place, we could have pulled it off.

Bringing in Anthea was probably the best and worst business decision I have made. Our company's culture of insisting on profits in the first year is unrealistic. I should have realized this, but I was blinded by Sanjay's big numbers and optimism so that I overlooked him cutting corners. As for Anthea, she might not have been commercially minded, and she definitely did not realize what she was getting into at the start, but when she did, she had the guts to point out that what we were doing was never going to work. I probably have her to thank for my ass not being hauled over the coals. The biggest lesson I have learnt is to pay more attention to the actual money we spend rather than believe in other people's fairy tales.

Daniella Evans' story

I think this will be my last job, but as the new finance director of the Sunset Care Home, I am already putting the lessons I have learnt this past year into practice. And so far, this has been the most satisfying and humbling job so far. It's a hands-on job, making people's last moments count. Yesterday my day included motivating the fundraising team, playing the clarinet, badly, of course, at the residents concert, chatting with an upbeat but terminally ill Mrs. Jenkinson about how to cut the crap and follow your dreams, and organising the menus for gourmet night where we have persuaded a local 'celebrity' chef to attend. Every day I spend here feels like I am doing something worthwhile and meaningful, which is so much more than my last job.

It's a stark contrast to business-classing it around the world of the Britmax Corporation, convincing myself that I was important, or as some macho corporate types would describe it, 'kicking ass'. We always talked about teamwork, but in reality, it was everyone for themselves.

I have found very few frauds in my life . . . and then almost always small ones with a bit of help from a whistleblower. Then one day Anthea drops a nebulous case into my lap. Bribery, hands in the till, greed, false accounting. You name it, it was there. We had a chance to clear things up but got nowhere because the company feared killing a business – scared of rocking the boat. I probably should have stayed and fought, for Anthea's sake at least – she was the one who stuck her neck out. But I am not sure if I ever would have got this management's support. They wanted people like me to tell them that everything is OK. Not to point out what's wrong and trace it to their flaws. But I could have stood up to them more, and even if rubbing their noses in it got me fired, it would have been more satisfying than being their fall girl.

The last time I spoke to Anthea, she said, 'Why did you not find all of this with your army of a hundred auditors? Why did it have to be me who did all the work?'

1

A year ago

Joe Northfield's story

I studied civil engineering, but my heart tells me I'm a builder of businesses. Even so, what annoys me most is all the corporate bullshit and show. Let's take our annual B.I.R.D conference, this year it was held in Dubai. Bird . . . yeah . . . it's supposed to stand for Britmax International Regional Development, but this year we had these internal marketing specialists in from a company called 'FRESH'. There were paper birds flying all over the conference hall. 'Seek out and Soar' that was this year's motto. It can get *very* tiring. I have this fancy title too. Director, International Business Development, but the truth is I am a glorified salesman.

The important thing this year on the International Business Development agenda is India and we really need this break. Especially after the last foray into Africa. So much money spent schmoozing politicians and generals and we ended up with nothing to show for it. But since I picked that one up from my predecessor, he's the one who got the blame – and early retirement.

In the morning, I had a meeting with our irritatingly cheerful internal auditor, Daniella Evans. She's doing something she calls a fraud risk assessment of my department. I told her, I don't have time for this but she said everybody in Britmax goes through it. It's just form filling, if you ask me, as if I don't have enough of that already. She says fraud and corruption is part of every business area, so it must be part of mine too. Well, *of course*, it is. How else can we give people better cities, wider roads, cleaner environments with all the bureaucracy and red tape around?

Last time I was Delhi Airport, the officer in the starched white shirt told me that something was wrong with my visa – it wasn't – but it was 'fixed' for 50 dollars. According to Daniella's definition, that's corruption. I just call it life. In her book, I should have taken the next plane home and tossed the important meeting we'd planned. So, I didn't say anything to her, why should I? Instead she was happy that I could demonstrate that everyone in our department has signed the Britmax Code of Ethics. She can find that out for herself if anyone bothered to read it. I certainly didn't.

My philosophy is to employ people who don't need their nappies changing all the time. People who take tough decisions and live by them. Like Sanjay who looks after our India operations. We are partnering with his father's company and they know how to open doors. But to keep the Britmax flag flying, I have put in one of my own people as local managing director. I hired Anthea last month and she is moving out there soon. Sanjay said he wanted a local who could cope with the culture, which was exactly what I did not want. Let's see how Anthea Graham does. She's worked in Asia and the Middle East before, she's got an MBA and seems pretty no-nonsense. It could be good to have an older person to keep Sanjay's feet on the ground.

Daniella's story

Five and a half years into this job, still hardly anybody knows what my department does. We changed the name from Internal Audit two years because it was, well, let's put it frankly, a bit of a dull name, and people thought we only existed to point out everyone else's faults.

I never wanted to be an accountant or auditor, but after I finished my English degree at Kings College in London, I felt at a loose end and after some cajoling from my Big Eight Accountancy Firm father, I sort of fell into it.

The new department name, Group Risk and Assurance, has a much better ring to it than Internal Audit. They told me once, 'If there are any big frauds in Britmax, we are counting on you to find them, Daniella.' We have a fraud hotline, which Group Legal oversees, but my team gets involved in the investigations. There are some minor cases coming through there, frauds like expense fraud, but most of the reports we receive are too vague or are personal grievances against a colleague.

But the big ones must be happening because, according to the newspapers, they are happening in other companies. Maybe we just don't look hard enough?

We still do internal audits of the company, of course, but we almost never find any fraud ourselves. I went on this fraud masterclass recently run by a supposedly seasoned fraud investigator called Max Smythe. It was rather entertaining but Max gave the impression that finding fraud was easy, just follow the money. Those techniques are nice in theory but very hard to put into practice in a politically sensitive organization.

Today, I had a meeting with Joe Northfield, who runs the International Division, and met his right-hand man in India, Sanjay Sharma. Sanjay seems a bit young but very driven with impressive credentials, and, according to Joe, he gets the job done and India is growing. While it's been hard to pin Joe down and get his time, he seemed to like the idea of a fraud risk assessment workshop with his department. Sanjay even gave me some tips about how lobbyists in China work.

2

Sanjay's story

Joe is pretty insensitive at times. Today, in front of my India team, he waved a map of the world which showed all the corrupt countries in red or orange. Because this one was printed in *The Economist*, in Joe's mind, it was gospel. He laughed about India being dark orange. Maybe it's his way of deflecting attention from that Africa fiasco I heard he was drawn into. From what I hear, he had a lucky escape.

But who am I? I was hired by Joe, not because of my family's connections but because of my engineering and sales track record. India's crying out for urban development and shiny new infrastructure, like the Delhi Metro which I worked on. What stops the progress is the bureaucrats, so sometimes you need to short-cut the endless red tape. But play the game honestly and just do what is needed, whether it be a white lie on a CV or an occasional payment to expediate the processes and you will go far. Sometimes you need to cross the line if you want to take part in the race.

If not, the entire world would just grind to a halt, like an engine without lubrication. This Anthea whom they sent out as the local managing director – she's clever but she really does not know India. A solid engineer, mind you, and very professional at client meetings. She has no idea how the business world works, though. But

I think we will get on. She seems to respect me, despite her being 15 years older than me.

Anthea Graham's story

As a civil engineer, people assume that my career has been constructing buildings, bridges, roads and car parks. I was a car park specialist once upon a time, but today's civil engineer is a team player. In the old days, architects grabbed all the glory but now we collaborate more than ever before. I have worked with development planning, infrastructure and transport projects, new business parks, shopping malls in India and even the biggest snow-dome in the world – in Dubai – of course. And it feels good too most of the time, contributing to development all over the world.

There's just one snag. The recent market crashes left me out of a job. I returned to London after our stint in Dubai. My other half, Ron, is chilled about it. Our kids are at university and he has always told me to follow my dreams when I can. As a respected academic, he can just glide into a research or teaching post.

This short break has given me some time to look in the mirror. I like challenges and when I retire, I want to look back and say, 'Hey, I did something I was proud of, I helped someone – I made a difference.' But getting a new job was not as easy as I thought. My experience is in my favour, but my age is not. After four months of hunting, persistence has paid off. One of my juniors from an old job kindly put me in touch with Joe Northfield, the International Director of Britmax Engineering. Joe's looking for someone to head up his new venture in India.

When we met, Joe told me that he had the final say on the Managing Director role. Joe wants it to be someone from over here, with international experience. But I had to meet Sanjay, Joe's business development director, because Joe needed to be sure that we would get on. Sanjay's from Delhi, he lives in Abu Dhabi, but shuttles between India and the UK. Apparently, his wife, who is Greek, prefers living in the Middle East to London or India. He's 35, a sort of whizz-kid, he was one of the lead engineers on the Delhi Metro project, which went in on time and on budget and is a bit of a marvel, considering India's reputation. His father runs a transportation engineering company in India, they have contacts in government and Sanjay is finishing his PhD at Imperial College London.

When we met, he talked non-stop for two hours. At the end of the interview, if you could call it that, he said he liked me even if I wasn't Indian . . . whatever that was supposed to mean. He would let me get on with my part of the job while he brought in the business.

On the train home, I rang Ron, of course, to tell him the good news. He said that he would try to join me as soon as he could get a Visiting Professorship post sorted out. I also called some friends who were very happy on my behalf, one friend from university, Max Smythe. Max studied computer science and management but today he thinks he is some sort of maverick fraud investigator. Maybe I half-expected it but Max was not wildly excited about my new job. He told me to be careful as there were no free lunches. He's a funny guy and a good friend too but I couldn't help thinking he was being over-sceptical – or jealous – or both.

Daniella's story

I am wondering if Joe really was interested in my fraud risk assessment. He makes all the right noises but is very hard to pin down. He's very enthusiastic about his India venture and gives his protégé, that Sanjay character, a free rein. I think my department and I should take a closer look at what is going on there soon.

What I have found out is that they are setting up the new operation in Delhi far away from our large international accounting centre which has been in Mumbai for years. But the good news is that they have hired an experienced managing director from over here to run their operations. I've not met Anthea Graham, but I am pleased that they hired her. This company is far too male-dominated as it is. But I fear she could be walking into a trap with Joe and this Sanjay, pulling the strings in India. After Joe's loss-making venture into Africa, he is desperate to make this one in India work. I am planning a trip to review procedures at our head office in Mumbai, so I think I will stop over in Delhi on the way over.

Joe's story

Today, my whole day was wasted sitting in pointless meetings. Let's face it. fraud and corruption has been around for centuries and we're never going to wipe it out. All this paperwork, policies and compliance, which I don't claim to fully understand either, is just window dressing at best. And if I have more time-wasting meetings like this, the real business will grind to a halt.

Our latest financial statements just came out. For once I read the external auditors' report. It's rather dry and long, but they mention corruption and fraud and risks a lot. If they couldn't find anything bad, then we must be doing something right.

3

Daniella's story

Anthea emailed me saying she's looking forward to seeing me in Delhi when I make my next visit. That's good, but I will need to push my trip back a bit, so I can finish some paperwork for the external auditors who are doing a mandatory review of another company we have just bought.

I nipped out to the nearby deli at lunch time, and the faded poster which said, 'If you're tired of London, you're tired of life!' made me think it should be the other way around. Most of what my team and I do is a huge paper exercise to check that all the so-called 'internal controls' are in place. But we rarely look behind when people tick a box, or sign something, we can't be sure that they have really read or understood what they are signing. We hardly ever dig into the details or follow the money. I am beginning to think that if there were any big, unwelcome surprises, I would get the blame for not spotting things earlier.

I am looking forward to Delhi. I have not been there before, and it would be good to squeeze in a visit to the Taj Mahal. I need the inspiration.

Anthea's story

Apart from Sanjay's shenanigans, Delhi is fabulous. It intoxicates and overpowers the senses. I wish I was here for pleasure like those English people in that film, *The Best Exotic Marigold Hotel*, which, like every other British-Indian film right now, seems to star the actor, Dev Patel. Ron desperately wants to come out and see me, but I've told him to wait a bit as work is not everything it promised to be.

But I digress. I'm starting to suspect that this job is a double-edged sword and I should probably have seen this coming. In one-way, Sanjay reminds me of Dev Patel's over-optimistic, anything-is-possible character in the Marigold Hotel. He's full of promises and expounds them with panache but there is not much behind them. It all seems to hinge around his father, and his father's friends who know some people in high places. That is what worries me. Last week we put in a development proposal for the Bombay, sorry, Mumbai, Formula One circuit, and I was in Ahmedabad to discuss a new robot-park (that's a car park run by robots). And next week, it's a pod-rail system in Bangalore and something in Singapore possibly. These are all feasibility studies and I think it's very unlikely that these schemes will ever happen. They are so-called 'signature projects' – which usually have the backing of a politician, so they can make a name for themselves. Also, I think Sanjay is rather selective with the truth, especially where I am concerned. Call me methodical but the list of red flags I've been keeping is growing and I don't know what to do. Here are some specifics:

1   We are paying rent to Sanjay's father's company 'Sun Jivan PVT' for our share of the offices. The offices are OK, but I did some comparisons and the rent per square metre rental is about three times the market rate in that district.
2   This is probably just a white lie and we did not get the Kolkata metro extension contract anyway, but Sanjay put down on his CV he had three years of tunnelling experience. I asked him if he had ever been in a tunnel, let alone design one, and he gave me an odd dirty look.

3 'B.J.', or Mr B.J. Mehta is a rotund friend of Mr Sharma, Sanjay's father. He drops into the office a few times a week and I found out that we pay him a retainer of about $2,000 a month as a door opener. He does generate lots of leads, but I also discovered that he also will get 3 per cent of every contract which we win. And it's 3 per cent of the sum first talked about, once the client has said 'yes' in principle, not the final sum which can be a lot lower after contract negotiations. That's a lot of money and at this point no one knows where it is paid, probably somewhere offshore.

4 I'm hiring people every day to cope with the workload, but we are not allowed to bill many of our clients yet, because the final contract negotiations have not been completed . . . Sanjay, as usual, tells me it's just India and everything is going to be fine. I wonder if we are going to be able to bill anyone at all in the end.

5 My driver overslept a few days ago and picked me up half an hour late. On the way into work he told me that he had been out very late after one of Sanjay's and B.J.'s corporate entertaining sprees. He even dropped a hint that they had been delivering bags of money at certain ministerial residences but would not say where or what money when I tried to press him.

6 I am sure that some of our subcontractors and consultants are overcharging us. I have seen some of the bills although I must rely on my staff for the ones which are mostly in Hindi.

7 This one seems petty but the other day Sanjay blew over £2,500 of the company's money for champagne and extras at a swanky millionaire's club in London on clients. It seems that Joe absorbed the bill into one of his business development accounts, so I didn't have to sign off on it.

When I have raised these things with Sanjay, he either says, 'You Scots worry too much', or goes off on tangents or even makes me feel it's my fault by saying, 'You're the boss, you need to sort it out', which I find rather offensive. It seems as if our finely balanced relationship only functions when I don't second-guess him and let him get on with the deals and clients and I get on with . . . to be honest, I don't know what my position is any more. We just keep accumulating hours which we can't bill because the contracts are not completed. The finance people in London have already hinted to me that they are getting nervous about the cash drain, as they call it.

Sanjay tends to throw a tantrum when he wants to make a point. He did that when I questioned the repair and maintenance people who seem to invoice us for whatever they feel like because they are friends of the family, and he also completely lost the place when I took up the permanent presence issue again. This one is quite ridiculous. It's obvious that Britmax has a permanent presence in India, but Sanjay keeps insisting that if we say that it is only temporary, that way Britmax pays a lot less tax. So, for a while I played along, lying to the authorities, and when I finally threatened to put my foot down, Sanjay sends off an email to everyone higher up, including Joe, with a list of matters where I am being obstructive, slow, and pedantic. He even said that I was incapable of doing something as simple as opening a local bank account.

In my apartment on Sunday, I started to feel a bit low, so I Skyped my old friend Max and told him my sob story which I am sure Ron is tired of hearing. Max was decent enough not to do the whole 'I told you so' routine, but I am sure I saw he was grinning. He said I am already complicit and could be arrested for bribery and thrown in an Indian jail, I told him he was overacting. I was just having a bad day and just needed to let off steam. He got rather angry and said I was naïve and foolish, and I only managed to placate him by agreeing to meet a good friend of his called Derek Armani in London when I am next back in the UK. I have heard of Derek – he's one of Max's schoolfriends, who did rather well in business. Apparently, he has a lot to do with India too. Once, Derek had to help someone who was in a similar position to me get of jail. It all sounds a bit extreme to me.

After the call, I felt a little knot in my stomach. Could it really be as bad as Max says? He's trained to see the worst side of things but this time he really seemed worried about me. He told me to keep notes and email things to him on a regular basis from a private email. I agreed to do it but it all sounds very cloak and dagger and a bit unnecessary.

Sanjay's story

After just a couple of months, Anthea is annoying me a lot. Everything was OK to start with, but these days she reminds me of my Indian family – my mother, my aunt and my sister all at the same time. She keeps lists of everything and then takes up all her issues in company meetings in her super-structured way. She has no idea of how things work here and approaches everything as if it's a problem to be solved. It's driving me nuts and I think Joe is having second thoughts about his decision to bring her in.

Derek Armani's story

Bloody Max. He can't get through to his friend Anthea so I have to do his dirty work. But I love the café I have picked to meet her. Alice's Teacup is the newly opened London branch of a weird and whimsical chain of New York teashops which I tend to visit when I work in Manhattan.

She's so polite, far too polite, and almost a bit too straight-laced, but we both agree that Max is impetuous, paranoid and irritatingly self-absorbed. For someone of her age and experience, Anthea seems pretty new to the tough world of international business. On the café wall is a picture of the March Hare and the Mad Hatter stuffing the dormouse into the teapot. I draw Anthea's' attention to this and tell her bluntly that this is what Sanjay and Joe are going to do to her if she is not careful. I also told her about my friend. Like Anthea, my friend was a puppet ex-pat managing director. And he saw the same signals of corruption, but the Indian police did their job, and arrested my friend, since he was the managing director, and put him in a local prison. Instead of helping him out, his own company in the UK cooperated with the Indian authorities as if it was his fault! My business partner in India pulled a few strings and we managed to get his passport back and bring him home. I think this story started to wake her up. I had a picture of him looking terrible when I met him at Manchester Airport and since I had the picture on my phone I showed it to Anthea. That shook her.

'Anthea listen to me. There was a good reason Max wanted me to take the time to see you in person. From what you've told me, the same thing is going to happen to you. You've stupidly signed the papers that say you are the managing director and Sanjay runs rings around you. Joe's not going to take the fall for this one. My advice is get out now and save me the trouble of fishing you out of the teapot.'

I think she gets it but I have the feeling that the Alice in Wonderland references went right over her head. As a kid she was probably too busy reading the adventures of 'Captain Carpark', the multi-storey hero. I told her bluntly to cut her losses and quit.

She said she could not thank me enough for this, but I have a sneaky feeling that she is not going to give up the fight yet. I can see why Max likes her – she's gutsy. She had an interesting choice of tea though. I recommended a calming and detoxifying Pai Mu Tan, but she insisted on one called Sicilian Vespers.

Joe's story

I just got a call from Anthea. She seemed very agitated and was babbling something about bribes, Sanjay's expenses and the Indian tax authorities. I remember she said something two months ago about some of this at the board meeting in London, but I thought it was all cleared up now. This worries me. Anthea was delighted with the job when she started.

She also said she had received an email from Daniella Evans, who was going to swing by our Delhi office and see her when she visits Mumbai. I said it was fine by me but make sure not to alarm Daniella with these rumours, and to underline how much code of conduct training and anti-bribery training we have done in India already. And she should not start accusing Sanjay of anything she can't prove, and certainly not to Daniella. This is a divisional matter, which is my responsibility.

After she called, I rang Sanjay straight away. He said Anthea is doing an excellent job on the technical side, but he repeated his request that we really need a local managing director who did not get the Indian authorities' backs up. He would say that, because I insisted on hiring Anthea and not one of his people. He also tried to put my mind at rest that there were no bribes as such, whatever that means, and he promised to lay off the entertaining. He avoids talking about B.J. I met the guy once. Sanjay brought him along to the B.I.R.D. conference in Dubai. Meeting him once was enough for me.

Looking at last month's sales projections, I hope Sanjay does not cut down completely on the wining and dining, as we need some new customers. I think I am going to set up a conference call with Anthea and Sanjay. It's time to bang their two heads together and tell them to quit squabbling.

The use of the 'b'-word is an uncomfortable reminder of the African fiasco I got dragged into. Some years back, when we were trying to build up Africa, we got ourselves into this situation with a huge project in Ghana. We were asked to pay some money to a consultancy company, called Gamma Capital Ltd, based in Bermuda, who was lobbying and brokering the deal. Our lawyers said it looked OK, if I thought it was OK, but it was my signature on the payment itself for $600,000 to Gamma Capital. Looking back now, I am not so sure it was such a great idea. We never got a good deal in Ghana and I have absolutely no idea what happened to the money. I know that there was also some fuss in the African press about bribery involving us, but the news died down and never made it to the UK. Even the former president of Ghana was accused of receiving money, something he vehemently denied. My suspicion is that in this case the consultants took us for a ride, but we were never able to prove anything. Still, I feel bad about it and was reminded about it again when Anthea called. I am a bit more comfortable in India because Sanjay is under my control – I hope.

4

Anthea's story

Three months ago, when Daniella made her whistle-stop trip to Delhi, she probably asked me three times in the space of a short meeting if there were any problems or anything I was worried about and wanted to talk about with her in confidence. Each time I told her no, since I was comfortable with Joe, and I did not know Daniella. We were polite with each other and both in a hurry, but I am not so sure now if I shouldn't have been more open.

I am sick and tired of Joe and the other Britmax directors asking 'is everything OK?' when I am sure they know it's not. And I have tried to tell Joe in the most constructive way, but if he can sense any bad news on the horizon, he blocks it out. On top of that, all the London big bosses keep doing boring anti-bribery presentations for me and my staff. And I have been thinking about that conversation in the Alice in Wonderland café with Derek Armani. He's probably right. A lot of stuff is going on underneath my nose which I am not seeing. And by not speaking up, it makes me feel that I am also involved. The problem is that the minute you raise a problem or throw a spanner in the works, you personally get transformed into the problem.

Ron was out here for a couple of weeks to attend a conference on applied ethics in Delhi. He enjoyed the conference but said that I am living the real thing.

Sanjay's story

Yesterday there was a big family party. Wonderful food! And is often the case at family parties, when the bhangra-dancing starts, Papaji (that's Dad) ushers me and Rohan, my brother, into his study for a talk. B.J. was there too. He attends most of our family functions. All three of them said I need to keep a close eye on Anthea. None of them like her.

It seems that while I have been out winning business with B.J., Rohan tells me that Anthea has been moaning to him and dad, questioning my expenses, and everything I am doing. It's out of order and ungrateful, considering all we have done for Britmax and her. Rohan, like the typical hothead that he is, wants to teach Anthea a lesson, but B.J. and Dad just told us to keep our cool and inform London, which means Joe. He told me that I need to grow up and send Mrs Thatcher – that's what he calls Anthea – home.

Anthea's story

Daniela's second visit was different. I had given her a call after my meeting with Derek Armani and said we should talk as I had to be rather sparing with the truth the last time I met her. She suggested that we could meet at a weekend in Mumbai which was perfect for me as I am beginning to feel a little uncomfortable in Delhi. Daniella sorted out my flight and hotel too. I've been to Mumbai many times but first we had lunch at the Taj Hotel near the Gateway of India and then I took her for a bit of alternative sightseeing to the Haji Ali mosque and Crawford Market. She said she had only seen the office and hotels before and I could sense she was a bit out of her comfort zone. She was clutching her bag and looking behind her all the time, but it was fun and good to get to know her a bit more. She said that it was best that no one knew we were meeting.

Over dinner and then with a glass of wine in her room, I told her everything as Max had instructed me to do. Daniella was very understanding – she did not judge me or blame me for saying anything earlier. Then, like co-conspirators, we made a plan. Daniella assured me that she would do her best to sort things out. What worries me most is that Daniella will give up or get overruled. I've put my neck on the line now.

And Sanjay keeps doing new deals and abruptly tells me to get on with it. He produces nice-looking draft contracts, but Indian law seemingly does not allow us to bill the customer until the final contract comes through. So, we just keep accumulating hours which we cannot bill yet. Daniella was really concerned about that one.

I took the early morning flight to Delhi on Monday to find Sanjay already there deep in conversation with his brother Rohan, who runs their traffic modelling company, Sanjeevan, with their father. They looked busy when I walked past the boardroom, but Sanjay came after me and asked me to join them. Rohan shook my hand and I noticed that his knuckles were badly cut and bruised. I think he wanted me to stare at his hand, which I did. He said that last night he was in a nightclub and some loudmouth had called him a cheat and a liar and tried to punch him. Rohan hit him with a glass which broke in his hand, hence the cuts.

To top it all, Joe still ignores me, even more than before. It's as if the conversations we had never took place.

Daniella's story

This was quite an eventful trip. I did not get to see much of India again, but that meeting with Anthea over the weekend was interesting. After Anthea returned to Delhi, I bought that well-known book called *Shantaram*. It captures the sights and smells of some of the places she took me around in Mumbai. Anthea's quite fearless compared to me. I have just zoomed passed page 137 when the main character, an escaped Australian convict, is given the name Shantaram by some honest villagers he is staying with. He wonders if they gave him the name, which means 'man of peace' because they see in him a better person than he does, or if they want him to be a better person than he is.

Intuition is an odd thing. So is premonition. You can push them away, but they still gnaw at you. I should have trusted my original intuition about Joe's fledgling operation in India. Anthea pre-empted me. I could have course been angry at Anthea for not coming to me much earlier but I would have done exactly the same if I had been in her shoes. But by keeping silent for so long, she could be accused of being involved as well.

Anthea and I get on well. I realize now what she is up against and our culture of paper compliance, empty rhetoric and denial in the face of facts does not help. She said that she was not fully forthcoming with me the first time I went, as she had to be loyal to Joe and she did not know me or know if she could trust me. She had never been in this situation before and thought she must be imagining things. But it's all water under the bridge. We're on the same team now.

Jet Airways upgraded me on the way back to London which is great because I am dead tired. I can't stop thinking about Joe and how I succumbed to his flattery. Anthea told me that Joe and many of the others she met quite openly refer to audit and compliance as 'a load of bollocks'. It's rude and uncouth and certainly out of line but I am wondering if they have a point. After my third glass of wine and while I was doodling the words **C**ompliance, **R**isk analysis, **A**udits and **P**olicies on my Jet Airways serviette, I noticed that it spelt 'C.R.A.P.' The lady sitting next to me started laughing and it turns out she was the UK finance director of an international Danish toy manufacturer. She'd been on holiday to Goa but work had persuaded her to fly home early for some meeting. She told me that my serviette sums up her job too and she even made a replica on her own serviette to present it at the next finance conference, as the Danish CFO, and Danes in general apparently, have a wicked sense of humour.

Leaning back in my chair with the eye-shade on at 45,000 feet over central Asia, my brain is filled with questions and doubt. Why don't *we* pick up what Anthea has seen? We could if we wanted to. We have access to most of the money flows and documents today from London. Am I just an overpaid tool of management who jumps when they say jump and only looks in the directions they want me to look? Maybe I should stop looking for the perfect world and notice a few cracks and instead just look at it for what it is. Vulnerable and exploitable? *Hamlet* was my favourite play at school. I am having a 'Hamlet' moment when I know what to do but keep on looking for more and more evidence to confirm my suspicions, so I can delay doing anything about them. Why do the external auditors never find anything? And how much do I care?

With these mostly unanswered questions swirling around in my mind, I dozed off.

5

Daniella's story

Dreams on night flights can be quite lucid though I am not sure how much of this one was a dream. A couple of hot towels later and I am refreshed. What worries me most is not what Anthea knows but what she does not know. The more complicated things get, I fear the less that management are going to want to believe me. Their natural defences kick in, making them ask for more and more evidence so that when I cannot produce enough, they can tell themselves that they did not have enough to prove anything either way. I remember that is the way the African case went. I am branded as the bringer of bad news. Anthea does not understand the intricate politics and sensitivity of all this. And she's not aware of the history of our company's fiasco in Africa. I took over the tail end of that investigation from my predecessor. He told me he had seen transactions in Bermuda, the Cayman Islands, front companies in London and what looked like very dirty money. But each time he raised a concern, management would say things like 'Well, we have a signed contract with them', or 'We did the due diligence on these partners and there were no red flags', or whatever they could plausibly deny so that they could push away any criticism aimed at them. On the other hand, when management do get excited about something, they tend to over-react, like when the cleaners were stealing bathroom supplies.

Looking out, I can see we are flying over the Alps. Anthea believes B.J. has an account in Switzerland which is where he banks his 'commissions'. She was at a house party at Sanjay's once and she said B.J. was showing pictures of him in Switzerland. It didn't seem to her like he was there for the skiing.

But we have no real proof yet. I need to soften my message to management and try to find a way to turn it into good news . . . somehow. I made some notes on another napkin, not the 'C.R.A.P' one of course, which I am keeping for myself.

India Britmax Engineering – notes on flight home

1   Evidence of increasing costs in our operation.
2   Mythical accounting: Booked sales are overstated and estimates of future revenues are too ambitious. It is likely we will need to write off large customers' debts. We could be making big losses soon.
3   Inappropriate business partner in Sanjeevan Pvt.
4   An ongoing legal dispute with the Indian government and tax authorities. Been going on for some time and we were not informed. Large fines looming and they could even shut us down.
5   Signs of large facilitation payments and agency fees (bribes?) which could be breaching the UK Bribery Act.
6   Britmax's ex-pat managing director out of her depth and desperately needs more support.
7   Numerous other small discrepancies (if we dig more, who knows what we could find – <u>definitely don't write this!</u>)

Joe's story

Am I nervous? Perhaps. These days Sanjay asks me to sign absolutely everything. It feels like he's passing the buck, and I don't quite know what the buck is. Yesterday he wanted me to approve yet another payment to B.J. It was quite a hefty one, but Sanjay sent me the signed contract with BJ . . . or as emphasized, I had signed with B.J. I'm only doing it because we are in fact winning some business, but it concerns me that a lot of the business we win is not going to be profitable for us. To add oil to the fire, our 'infernal' auditor, Daniella, has insisted on having an urgent meeting with me about the situation. The last thing I need is her breathing down my neck. I told Sanjay once again to make sure everything was clean out there.

Anthea's story

It's now over two months since Daniella visited and I'm getting cold feet. All I've had from her was one call and a few text messages. She told me she cannot say too much to me for my own protection, but I've gathered that Daniella and her colleague, an investigator called Chris, have been doing some background checks and looking into Sanjay's behaviour. I just don't understand why people like Daniella with the resources she has at her disposal, don't do more. One thing is having the case gift-wrapped like the one I have given her, but why has she not done more to discover these sorts of things before people like me stumble across them? It's me who ends up sticking my neck out. I am sure Sanjay has guessed I am on to something. He knows – he can probably tell from my sheepish demeanour and how I try to avoid eye contact whenever he is around. I am guessing he has said something to Joe who has totally cut me out.

On that note, I found out just now, I don't even report to Joe any more. He has put this guy in between us called Ian Buchanan, whom I have never met, but judging by his daily communiqués, he's clueless about what we are doing over here. He has not even offered to come and see me, instead he prefers to speak on MSM messenger and after some insistence he has promised me a Skype meeting one day soon – lucky me! Most of what Ian asks for are financial figures, cash flow forecasts, cost calculations and updates on weekly sales. He must be some sort of accountant. What I do know from the few times I interact with Sanjay is that he talks about rising costs and that my expat salary and package are a huge part of that. If that was not a subtle enough hint that he wants to see my back, I don't know.

What's keeps me sane is Ron and Max. Max drove down to meet with Ron and discuss my situation. I think they had a good night at the pub, as Ron said Max ended up staying over in the spare room. But they did also talk about me and how they were going to help me out of my little fix. I am glad Ron and Max get on.

Sanjay's story

Idiots! I came to London despite everything else that is happening in my life, believing I was having an important sit-down meeting with Joe and Ian. But Joe calls in sick and Ian is nowhere to be seen. Instead I am ambushed by this Daniella Evans lady who proceeds to read me the Riot Act. I met Daniella only once before and she was very charming. Now she's spitting venom, accusing me personally of bribing our customers, pulling the wool over management's eyes and bringing her company's name into disrepute. Britmax happens to be my company too, Daniella!

It's a total and utter insult to someone who has only tried to do the best for the company from the get-go. I've got my doubts now about Joe and I don't believe he really is sick. My guess is that he and this company need a fall guy or scapegoat if their mistakes blow up in their faces.

Despite Daniella's false accusations, I can show that everything I have done was approved by Joe or Anthea in advance or was a simple clerical mistake. The only thing I could not refute, and this is stretching it, is that in my CV, I once put down that I had three years tunnelling experience. All I was doing was massaging the truth a bit to fit the customer's needs. Since I was a lead Engineer on the Delhi Metro project and some parts of metros normally do go in tunnels, the customer found it plausible. The truth is that I am claustrophobic and only worked on the over-ground sections. That's also why I must take taxis when I am in London instead of taking the Tube. And the white lie was all done to help Britmax win the deal with the company.

She went on and on about the money we are paying to B.J., again to win business. Where this lady Daniella got her fancy education from, I don't know, but she has no clue about client relations and lobbying. If it was not for people like me, she would be out of a job – and I told her that, to her face, that she is lucky that the hard work of people like B.J. and me, keep her in a salary.

I still must find out who is behind this vendetta, whether it's Joe or someone even higher, because it's clearly not her. But Daniella was rather clear about one thing. I am out.

Without really listening to my point of view, she tells me all formally that I am being suspended pending further enquiry and calls someone from security to escort me off the premises. Since I don't have any of my things in that building, I decided to just leave on my own accord and the guy did not stop me. But before I stormed out, I did remind Daniella that I know about the fiasco in Africa and those consultants and that Bermuda company they used. B.J. had told me lots about that, how he knows I have no idea. That was Joe's funeral and its people like him and the consultants who Daniella should be going after. Not us. We're the good guys. I hope Joe's shitting himself now.

I'm relaxed. They need me more than they think, in or out. What is funny, is that while I was very pissed off at being treated in this way, it was she who was the nervous one. She kept scratching her right ear and twiddling bits of her hair when she was talking to me.

And then, just after I left the building, my hands felt clammy and the pain in my chest started . . . a lot of pain.

6

Daniella's story

My interview with Sanjay did not go well. Before I sat down with him, there were a lot of discussions. The management and audit committee agreed my seven major flaw points about Joe's India operation, but they wanted me to quickly focus all my attention on Sanjay and leave Joe out of it for now. Not an optimal strategy but I was left with little choice in the matter. They must be protecting Joe because he knows too much and could bring them down too. I did still manage to have a chat with Joe in advance. He kept repeating, I think until he believed it himself, that he had delegated responsibility to Sanjay and Anthea jointly with the firm message that everything must be clean and compliant. Poor man!

Sanjay started off belligerent and carried on that way to the end of our little tête-à-tête. He insisted that the sums we were paying for sub-letting his family company's offices, which I showed him were around three times the going market rate, included so many extras and additional services that it was a bargain at the price. And when it came to B.J. and the commissions we are paying for introductions, he kept going back to our company code of conduct. In addition to him signing it and reading it regularly, he had even persuaded B.J. to sign it. So, of course, there were no bribes, according to Sanjay. And his standard reply was that Joe and the rest of the management had approved what he did every step of the way.

As for his expenses, it was the same story. Everything was approved by Joe or Anthea and he even came out with that old chestnut, 'you need to speculate to accumulate'. Everybody tells white lies on their CVs and anyway he only put down tunnelling experience because no one had it and he was the closest thing.

I caught him out on a private trip to the USA which he admitted he 'accidentally' put through the company. He added that on that private trip he visited an Environmental Building Fair in Chicago for the company. I could detect the heavy sarcasm when he took out his wallet and threw it on the table saying, 'If you feel that none of that trip was business expenditure, of course, I will pay you back. How much do you want?'

He told me I should have come to him earlier if I felt that something was wrong rather than sneaking up on him like I was doing now.

One thing was odd. He hardly spoke about Anthea. But he did seem to know a lot about our African venture in the past, more than me in fact and implied that what I was accusing him of, even if it were true, was nothing compared to what Joe had got himself into in Africa.

Despite all his attempts to shift the blame, I felt I had enough to suspend him on full pay, pending further investigations, as this is what the management had instructed me to do. I could see how bitter he was inside, and I was not feeling particularly comfortable either. After just over two hours I ended the interview and, yes, it sounds rather dramatic, but it wasn't, I called someone from HR and as per our normal procedure he escorted Sanjay out of the building.

After he left, I just sat there in the interview room staring at the wall, thinking what I could have done better. I should have used more time to prepare. And rather than bombarding him with facts which he naturally interpreted as accusations, I should have tried to find out more about what he thinks and what was going on. We could have done more research into his company, his background and not least the movements of B.J. And we should have included Joe in on this and looked deeper into the accounting transactions which both Sanjay and Joe approved. But the real thing that gnaws away at me is that we *could* have found all this out earlier – if we had wanted to look.

All this could be lessons for the future, but it was now too late to turn the clock back. I have a niggling feeling that Sanjay was blackmailing Britmax over Africa.

Anthea's story

Not good news. I got the message that I am being called back permanently from Delhi to London. I rang Daniela who said there was nothing she could do but we'd talk about it when I got back. But I want to go back. I miss home.

On the flight, I'm thinking, if I had not spoken up, none of this would have happened. I would not have adventured down the rabbit hole into Fraud-land, and I would be none the wiser. Probably I would have cast aside my suspicions and still be running the Indian operation. Even if that was as Sanjay's or Joe's puppet, at least I would not have realized that. Britmax Engineering in India is almost an empty shell now. Most of the employees have gone, including Sanjay. The chief accountant is nominally in charge now.

I heard rumours that after being interviewed by Daniella, Sanjay checked into London's St Thomas's hospital with a heart complaint and had a pacemaker fitted. If he wasn't on our medical scheme, he would have sent the bill to Joe. Daniella must have been rough on him, though. I need to silence the voice in my head saying that the jumped-up little shit deserves it. I am sure he will bounce back and threaten to sue Britmax and Daniella for intimidation.

While I am sitting around the London office doing very little, I get an official email from HR that a meeting is planned tomorrow in London with them, me and Buchanan. Ian Buchanan recently de-friended me on LinkedIn, which I thought was rather unnecessary. And I am pretty sure what this meeting is about.

7

Joe's story

Big mess. They've sacked Sanjay and my Indian operation has crumbled almost overnight. Clearly it was not profitable despite what Sanjay and Anthea were telling me. What's good is that Daniella was forced to take a severance package, probably because of her inept way of handling things with Sanjay. It worries me that nobody has told me whether they think I had a role in this mess.

An engine will not work without oil and it's the same with business. You need to lubricate the machine, like it or not. So rather than accepting the realities of business life, we keep working against one another instead of pulling together as a team. I feel sorry though that Sanjay had to take most of the rap for it. I liked his company.

Daniella's story

I feel bad that Anthea was pushed out, but at least, unlike me, she's not connected to what happened to Sanjay after our chat. I found out that hours after he checked into St Thomas' hospital, he was diagnosed with a heart condition and had a pacemaker fitted. I am sure he already had the problem, but the timing couldn't have been worse. I am out of the loop, thankfully, and Britmax have offered him a severance package because they know that if he hires a lawyer, that lawyer is going to have a lot of fun. I think Sanjay knows that the package is his best option.

Maybe it's a blessing in disguise but they have offered me a package too. My guess is they believe I know too much. It's one year's salary with a non-disclosure agreement attached. In other words, I must keep my mouth shut and cannot help Anthea if she decides to fight her dismissal.

I gave Anthea a call to say I am sorry which I think was the proper thing to do. She was gracious enough, I'm sure she thought I was wet, and suppose I am. But I think I can do something useful in my next job and maybe everything I have done so far will help Anthea and Britmax in the long run. My parting advice to Anthea was to walk away but I think she might not. She got a much worse deal than either Sanjay or me, a month's severance pay and a CV with a hole in it.

8

18 months later

Anthea's story

What an experience. Not just a poisoned chalice but more like fair-ground ride through a meat-grinder. I am glad to say that I have a new job in London and much more time with Ron, the kids and my friends.

Time is a great healer and, with distance, I can admit to myself that the experience, while not pleasant, was eye-opening and educational. Here's an abridged version of what happened after I left.

I was moved back to London where monkey-boy Buchanan told me immediately that they did not have a position for me there, so they were letting me go. Since I had two months' notice and one month's severance pay, job hunting became the priority as Ron's professor salary is a bit thin still.

I did get an offer, the job I am in now, just after I left but the process of employing me took longer than I thought and it was subject to references from former employers. I knew that even if I tried to take Britmax to court for unfair dismissal, which it was, they were either going to mess up my reference or give me a bad one. No new employer likes a whiner. And Buchanan was stupid enough to say to me the one and only time I met him, that as long as I did not cause any trouble, I would get a glowing reference from Britmax. So, I played their game and I got the job.

But I still felt hard done by, especially since I was unemployed for two months and this job, although exciting, is at a considerably lower salary. All I had ever done was speak up to try to save the company and its reputation. So, four months after I left, and now safe in my new position I filed an unfair dismissal claim with the courts in London, Max ended up representing me, which is funny as he has a reputation for disliking lawyers.

The courts told me that normally the maximum time window in the UK to make an unfair dismissals claim was three months after you leave, and it was very unlikely that Britmax would agree to a late submission, whatever my reasons or circumstances. But I decided to try, and, as expected, Britmax opposed it. However, the appointed judge convened a short hearing with both parties present to review the facts before deciding.

On the day of the hearing, the head of HR at Britmax turned up in court, represented by a partner from a fancy law firm, and I arrived with Max and one of Max's old investigator friends, called Allan, who was supporting from the otherwise empty visitors' gallery. Once the judge had gone through the preliminaries, Britmax's lawyer, called Glynn, spent what seemed like ages reviewing all the legal precedent as to why a late submission must not be accepted, meticulously reviewing all the exceptions such as 'the fax machine in the courts ran out of ink', and other extraneous circumstances.

Max, who was meant to be defending me, responded that he completely agreed with Glynn and that under normal circumstances the judge should not waste any of his valuable time and throw the case out. We just asked for 20 minutes of the judge's time to review the facts.

The honourable judge agreed to listen and then Max, as per our plan, put me on the stand and I calmly explained to the judge what had happened. After that, I was subjected to a barrage of cross-examination by Glynn, which went on for some time, a bit of rebuttal from Max and quite a few probing, but intelligent questions from the judge.

Then around mid-afternoon the judge announced he was going to record a verdict. He spoke for around half an hour into his recording device, and in the middle of it, he said something none of us will forget. While this had never been done, he was convinced by the serious nature of the evidence and my situation. He said that I was left with no alternative but to file my claim late if I wanted to get a reference from the company and a new job. He ruled that there would be a full trial in a few months which both sides would need to prepare for.

When he finished, the rather shocked Glynn and the Britmax HR person marched out of the courtroom without even acknowledging us. I was too surprised to be pleased so Allan took us out for a calming and well-deserved drink. That was also the evening Max's daughter told him that she was going to become a lawyer.

The next few months there was an arduous process where both sides swapped papers (something called 'disclosure') and there were some telephone conferences between my team, Glynn and the judge.

A few weeks before the date of the trial, Glynn called Max asking him if we would like to enter mediation. This took place in the courts with the same judge in the position of mediator but this time it was done around a table much more informally. Our side asked for a basic salary differential and a written letter of apology which I could use to back up my biography if needed in future. In the end money was not Britmax's problem. It was the official letter that was the sticking point. We held firm and late in the day the new Chief Executive of Britmax Engineering made a trip down to the courts, overruled his own lawyer and agreed to it. He was quite decent and even thanked me personally for helping the company.

So happy endings all round . . . almost. I've not seen or spoken to Daniella and I don't know if I will, but I hope she's content in her new job. I have no hard feelings. If I'd been offered the sort of 'keep your mouth shut' severance package she got, I probably would have taken it too.

There's a lot to learn from this kind of baptism by fire and it makes me wonder why we don't cover the realities of corruption and fraud in MBAs or management training. But I hope sharing these experiences with others can one day be an inspiration to others like me who get caught in the same mess and decide to stick their necks out.

But I know the real solution is not to have more whistleblowers like me. The real solution is when we see fraud and corruption for what it really is, a threat which undermines everything we do and causes us to tear each other apart.

Daniella's story

My closing thoughts? I jotted them down in case I want to pass them on to any would-be chief financial officers, risk managers, heads of internal audit, compliance, my successor or whoever in fact cares!

- Lots of people could spot fraud. We need to stop thinking how perfect we are compared to everyone else and start to recognize how others would cheat us.
- Everybody should be trained to spot fraud, especially the management.
- Work as a team – mostly the real enemy is not in the room.
- Understand the mindset and methods of the criminals.
- Encourage open dialogue without retribution (sometimes a form of 'restorative justice' works best).
- Don't take any comfort in the external audit report when it comes to fraud!
- Avoid long-drawn-out and painful investigations. Look for viable solutions and move on. But remember to still follow the money and find things early.

I learnt lots, but what I realized most was that no one will succeed doing anything about fraud until the management are on board and want to see it. Fraud and corruption is everywhere, and we should not be scared of it. And in fact it's everybody's job to be a fraud detective. It's not the hallowed turf of a select few.

Postscript

Derek Armani's story

Good on you, Anthea. You had the staying power to see this one through to the end. But you still need to be pragmatic when it comes to corruption. Just careful. Sometimes you need to do the wrong thing to get the right thing done, but this time they were doing the wrong thing to get the wrong thing done.

'Fraud detectives' – nah, I still don't agree with my mate Max and his 'anyone can cook or find fraud' line. He's quite a good cook himself and I'm not a bad one either but not everyone can be a great fraud detective – you have to have a bit of passion for that because, more often than not, you will find yourself banging your head against a wall that hits you back.

Max Smythe's story

It's always easier to advise from the touchline while others are in the game. But this time I really felt I could help Anthea win back her self-respect and her case against Britmax. I'm glad it worked out in the end, for Britmax too, because they avoided a complete meltdown in their international operations. Anthea's back on her feet and Ron has thanked me several times too.

And just to clear up any possible misunderstandings. I don't despise lawyers at all. Just corrupt lawyers.

Sanjay's story

Just in case you are wondering about me, I'm doing fine. Last week I read an article in the *Guardian* online which called the United Kingdom the 'Capital of Corruption'. The article was rather dull but I found the title funny. I heard that Joe was given the push and is with a smaller firm today, probably spouting the same 'make things look clean' bullshit and doing what he does best, i.e. look after Joe. I was naïve enough to consider him a friend and introduce him to my family and people like B.J. It's taken me a while to get over him stabbing me in the back. The pacemaker is ticking along well and this chilled new job in the Australian sun is just what I need.

References

Booker, C. (2004) *The Seven Basic Plots*. London: Continuum.2

Comer, M. (1979) *Corporate Fraud*. London: Gower.

De Bono, E. (2009) *Lateral Thinking*. London: Penguin.

Higgins, M., Morino, V. and Iyer, N. (2018) 'Imperialism, dirty money centres and the financial elite', in *The Continuing Imperialism of Free Trade*. London: Routledge.

Kvalnes. O. (2015) *Moral Reasoning at Work*. Basingstoke: Palgrave Macmillan.

Kvalnes, O. (2017) *Fallibility at Work: Rethinking Excellence and Error in Organizations*. Basingstoke: Palgrave Macmillan.

Tickner, P. (2010) *How to be a Successful Frauditor*. Chichester: Wiley.

Wirth, N. (1976) *Algorithms + Data Structures = Programs*. Upper Saddle River, NJ: Prentice Hall.

Index

References to illustrations are in **bold**.

AI (Artificial Intelligence), and fraud detection 163–4
algorithms: collections of 163; definition 165n6; examples 161–3; 'Follow the money' 160
Arielly, Dan, on dishonesty 68, 142
asset grabbing *see* Reiderstvo

Barings Bank 111
bid waiver, case study 32
Billion Dollar Bubble, Equity Funding Corporation 110
blame culture, avoidance of 191, 193, 195–6
Booker, Christopher, *The Seven Basic Plots* 17
box-ticking 9; case study 33
bribery 20, **109**; ambiguity of term 132; case studies 133, 138–9, **139**; 'cash' accounts 135; commissions 136; creative 137; credit notes 136; deniability 134; detection methods 135–6 (table); embezzlement as 137; fake bribes 132; IOUs 136; odd accounts 135; odd payments 136; organizational attitude to 133–4; presentation of results 137–8; rationalization of 132; small bribes 137; tolerance of 134; Wheel of (mis)Fortune **131**

Camus, Albert 33
case studies: bid waiver 32; box-ticking 33; bribery 133, 138–9, **139**; corporate psychopath 141–2; corrupt relationship 196; customer-related fraud 122–3; Dirty

Money Constellations 107–8, 133, 191–2; financial risk 86; 'Follow the money' 126–7, 137, 153–8; fraud and corruption 41, 67; fraud detection 34, 36, 91; fraud detectives 201–40; front companies 31; Gandhi's first law case 199; Harold Shipman 70–1; hidden warehouse 116; hotel expenses fraud 117; IDR 170–1, 177–9; invoice fraud 94, 100–2, 126–7; leasing fraud 121; ODSE 141–2, 144–5; pointless procedures 148; presentation of evidence of fraud and corruption 188–9; red flags 100–1, 121, 121–3, 125, 170; Reiderstvo (asset grabbing) 93, 180, 181, 184–5; thinking like a thief 65, 80; truth and reconciliation 190–1
chartered accountant, personal narrative 164n2
Comer, Michael J. 66; *Corporate Fraud* 99, 181n1
commissions, bribery 136
company, theft of 22
consultants 126
'cooking the books' 20
corporate psychopath, case study 141–2
corruption *see* fraud and corruption
Corruption Perception Index 35
cost of fraud and corruption 22, 28, 27, 76
credit notes: bribery 136; excessive 160, 161–2
Cressey, Donald 28
customer-related fraud 19, **118**, 160; case studies 122–3; presentation of 122–3; red flags 119–23

dirty money *see* DMCs
dishonesty, Arielly on 68, 142
DMCs (Dirty Money Constellations) 19, 21, 60;
 case studies 107–8, 133, 191–2; countries 104;
 definition 104–5; identification of 162–3;
 payments to 135; red flags 106–7; unethical
 uses of 105; Wheel of (mis)Fortune **103**, **109**,
 118; *see also* front companies
'drains up' action 179, 182n4

embezzlement, bribery as 137
employees, misuse of the organization 19, **140**
Enron Corporation, figure frauds 109–10
entitlement *see* ODSE
Equity Funding Corporation of America: *Billion
 Dollar Bubble* 110; figure frauds 109
expenses, falsified 112
external agents 126; red flags 128–30; Wheel of
 (mis)Fortune **125**
external auditors 34

false costs 114
false figure frauds 20, 112; altering discrepancies
 113; detection of 112–16; Enron Corporation
 109–10; Equity Funding Corporation of
 America 109; false costs 114; false names
 114–15; and healthy curiosity 111–12; hidden
 warehouse 116; hotel expenses 117; inflated
 accounts 114; manifestations of 112–16;
 personal account 110–11; presentation of
 117; sales commissions 114; special accounts/
 codes 113; stock manipulations 116;
 unexplained adjustments 115; Wheel of
 (mis)Fortune **109**, **118**
false names 114–15
'Follow the money' 11, 72, 93; algorithms 160;
 case studies 126–7, 137, 153–8; meaning
 152–3; *see also* money flows
fraud *see* customer-related fraud; figure frauds;
 fraud and corruption
fraud and corruption: advice about 238;
 awareness raising 37–8, 38, 68, 73–4; case
 studies 41, 67; conditions for 16, 30–1;
 costs of 27–8, 74; defences against 37–40;
 definition 15, 26; examples 39–40, 91–2;
 expectation of 160; historical 15–16, 24n2;
 and human nature 76; ignoring of 40–1, 67;
 identification 8–10, 23; looking out for 7–8;
 motivation for 75; opportunities for 74–5;
 organizational profile 81, 84–7; personal
 examples 6–7; personal memoir of xvn1;
 pervasiveness 9, 17, 26–7, 66, 87n1; positive
 attitude to 194–6, 197–8; punishment as
 deterrent 37; rationalization for 16, 69–70,

141; recognition of 68–9; resolution of
 190; and restorative justice 25n10, 190–2;
 risk analysis 67; risk assessment menu 64;
 scenarios 4–6, 22; and technology 17, 30;
 and thinking like a thief 38; traditional
 defences against 32–7; who does it? 74;
 see also unethical behaviour
fraud detection: and AI 163–4; case study 34, 36,
 91; post-workshop action 83; pre-emptive
 action 72; presentation of evidence 99–103
 (table); recipes 10–11, 72–83, 89–148; record
 keeping 172; things to avoid 146–7
fraud detectives: case study 201–40; definition
 3; encouragement of 39; goal 39; ingredients
 and tools 72–3, 81–2; methods 73–6, 82–3;
 motivation 8; requirements xiv, 239; *see also*
 thinking like a thief (TLAT)
Fraud Risk Factor, calculation 86
front companies 19, 31; case study 31; payments
 to 135; *see also* DMCs

Gandhi, Mahatma, first law case 199

healthy curiosity xii, 6, 8, 38, 39, 43, 61–2; and
 figure frauds 111–12; promotion of 197
honesty test 29

Iceland, financial collapse (2008) 66, 87n3
IDR (Investigative Desktop Research) 23,
 154; case studies 170–1, 177–9; external
 information sources 173–4 (table) 175;
 internal information sources 173 (table) 175;
 key considerations 175–6; next steps 179;
 rules to follow 172; tips 176–7
Institute of Internal Auditors 17
investigating fraud and corruption *see* resolving
 fraud and corruption
investigative desktop research (IDR) 23, 171–182
invoice fraud, case studies 94, 100–2, 126–7
IOUs, bribery 136

Jobs, Steve 17
Joly, Eva 23n1

Kahneman, Daniel 186
kickbacks 20, **118**; Wheel of (mis)Fortune **131**

lateral thinking 68, 88n5
Leeson, Nick 111

middlemen 126
Minority Report (film) 8
money flows: algorithms 159–60; examples 161;
 matrix 158, **159**; *see also* 'Follow the money'

obsessive compliance disorder, avoidance of 9, 147
ODSE (Over-Developed Sense of Entitlement)
    140–2; case studies 141–2, 144–5; detection
    of 142–5; presentation of findings 145
organization, misuse by employees 19, **140**
organizational profile, fraud and corruption 81,
    84–7
outsiders, harmful actions by 20
overpricing 21

personal data: avoidance of misuse 146, 172; and
    data protection law 146, 161
pointless procedures, case study 148
professional scepticism *see* healthy curiosity
purchasing fraud *see* suppliers who take
    advantage
pyramid scheme 21

recipes: fraud detection 10–11, 72–83, 89–148;
    use of 90
red flags 18; case studies 100–1, 121, 121–3,
    125, 170; customer-related fraud 119–21;
    detection exercises 47–60; DMCs 106–7;
    examples 214–15, 226; external agents
    128–30; obstacles to recognition of 185–7
Reiderstvo (asset grabbing) 22; case study 93,
    180, 181, 184–5
resolving fraud and corruption 183–193, 198
restorative justice, and fraud and corruption
    25n10, 190–2
risk assessment menu 64
robustness and resilience 199
rules and regulations 32–4

sales commissions, figure frauds 114
Samociuk, Martin 64, 65, 186

self-belief 10
Shipman, Harold, crimes 70–1
special accounts/codes, figure frauds 113
stock manipulations, figure frauds 116
structured creativity *see* lateral thinking
suppliers: abnormal behaviour 98;
    complacency of 97; dependency on 97;
    'litmus' tests on 98–9; Wheel of (mis)Fortune
    92, **109**; who take advantage 19, **92**, 95–103,
    109, **118**, 160, 162

technology, and fraud and corruption
    17, 30
tenacity, examples 11–12
thinking like a thief (TLAT) 38, 64–5, 68; case
    studies 65, 80; forms **81–2**; recognising fraud
    and corruption 76–81; workshop 76–81;
    see also fraud detectives
truth and reconciliation, case study 190–1
Turing, Alan 159, 164, 164n1

unethical, meaning 15
unethical behaviour **109**, **118**; by employees
    140; motivation for 28; opportunity for 29;
    rationalization for 29; reasons for 28–9

Wheel of (mis)Fortune 7, 17, **18**; bribery **131**;
    customer focus **118**; DMCs **103**, **109**, **118**;
    employees' unethical behaviour **140**; external
    agents **125**; false figure frauds **109**, **118**;
    kickbacks **131**; suppliers **92**
whistleblowing xiv, 9–10, 16, 17, 22, 31;
    avoidance of 193; reliance on 36–7, 183–4;
    sanctions against 42n6
workshop: follow-up action 83–7; 'thinking like
    a thief' (TLAT) 76–83